AMERICAN REGIONALISM

Our Economic, Cultural and Political Makeup

Timely Reports to Keep
Journalists, Scholars and the Public
Abreast of Developing Issues, Events and Trends

Editorial Research Reports
Published by Congressional Quarterly Inc.
1414 22nd Street, N.W.
Washington, D.C. 20037

81-   72577

About the Cover

The cover was designed by Art Director Richard Pottern and Staff Artist Robert O. Redding, who also executed the maps that appear in this book.

PRINTED IN THE UNITED STATES OF AMERICA
July 1980

Editor, Hoyt Gimlin
Associate Editor, Sandra Stencel
Editorial Assistants, Karen Rohan, Claire L. Tury

Production Manager, I. D. Fuller
Assistant Production Manager, Maceo Mayo

Library of Congress Cataloging in Publication Data

Congressional Quarterly, inc.
    Editorial research reports on American regionalism.

    Bibliography: p.
    Includes index.
    1. United States — Economic conditions — 1971-
2. United States — Politics and government — 1945-
3. United States — Social conditions — 1960-
4. Regionalism — United States.   I. Title.   II. Title:
American regionalism.
HC106.5.C67345 1980   973.926   80-18934
ISBN 0-87187-156-4

Contents

Contents

Foreword

Americans have been hearing for a long time that their regional distinctions are being smoothed off and flattened out by national television, fast-food franchises and lookalike downtown office buildings. Under such pervasive influences, a great cultural blandness spreads across the land. Southerners start pronouncing their "r's" and New Englanders stop putting them where they don't belong. Home-baked beans give way to tacos in Massachusetts and pot likker becomes only a memory in Georgia. The sons of Kansas wheat farmers dream the same golden dreams as California surfers. Soon, it is said, a traveler won't know if he is in Omaha or Knoxville.

Any reasonably observant person can see some signs of these prophecies being fulfilled. And yet, sectional differences remain and may prove to be more resilient than we imagine. These differences are never more evident than in a presidential election year. This year, beginning in January with the Iowa caucuses, a basically urban nation was reminded that there are places where farm life still flourishes — and where farm concerns are translated into political concerns. Then came the first primary in blustery New Hampshire, which retains its flinty Yankee character despite an inflow of industry and people from outside.

Then the primary selection process moved to the South, which has been transformed in many ways by rapid change but still holds to peculiarly southern traits. And on through the industrial East, out to the western plains and across the Rockies, it finally came to an end — geographically and politically — on the West Coast.

The nine Reports that make up this book look at the American cultural, economic and political mosaic by examining the separate regions, or in the case of California and Washington, D.C., separate pieces of regions that assume an importance or uniqueness of their own. Aside from New England, there is no agreement even among experts as to precisely what constitutes each region in the 48 contiguous states. One of this country's outstanding academic regionalists once tried to define the outer limits of the South by looking at the horse and mule population in the fringe areas. The notion that the South lagged behind the rest of the country in replacing its mules with tractors did not seem so quaint at that time. Now one might search vainly through the Mississippi Delta and the hill country of Tennessee for a farmer with a mule.

Regional mapmakers have looked to political affiliations, religious preferences and ethnic origins of the people in an attempt to determine the proper label for the exact geographic space they occupy. Walter Prescott Webb, the late historian of the American West, believed the true West began on the Texas, Oklahoma, Kansas, Nebraska and Dakota plains where the rainfall tapered off to less than 20 inches a year.

So when we at Editorial Research Reports set out to write about the regions of America, there were endless choices to be made and an endless stream of advice about what should be included or excluded — through none of it related to mules. In each Report we have attempted to explain why we think the various combinations of states have the geographic, historic, cultural, economic and political cohesion to be called a specific region. Whether or not our readers agree with the way we have redrawn the map, we believe that it is beyond argument that regionalism remains strong in the United States — and for good and proper reasons in a country of such size and diversity.

Hoyt Gimlin
Editor

Washington, D.C.
July 1980

NEW ENGLAND'S REGIONALISM AND RECOVERY

by

**William Sweet
and Hoyt Gimlin**

**Feb. 8
1980**

NEW ENGLAND'S REGIONALISM AND RECOVERY

F ROM THE DAYS of the Revolution the notion has taken hold, from time to time, that the United States is not so much "one nation, indivisible" as a federation of more or less distinct regions. Down to the Civil War, the nation's politics were dominated by a struggle between North and South over tariffs, slavery and control of the emergent West, and under those circumstances everybody took the importance of regions for granted. In 1889 Henry Adams devoted the first six chapters of his monumental *History of America during the First Administration of Thomas Jefferson* to a description of the varying social worlds of New England, the South, and the "megastates" — New York and Pennsylvania.

Thirty-six years later another influential historian, Frederick Jackson Turner, asserted in a major essay[1] on American sectionalism that "Statesmen in the future, as in the past, will achieve their leadership by voicing the interests and ideas of the section which have shaped these leaders, and they will exert their influence nationally by making combinations between sections and accommodating their policy to the needs of such an alliance." Some of Turner's assumptions and theories have not fared well among later historians. Some scholars have pointed out that regionalism, as an interpretative model for America, has been much subject to intellectual fashion and fads.[2]

Whatever regionalism's merit as an ultimate explanation may be, one thing is certain: In a presidential election year there simply is no substitute for looking at the country in terms of sections. Campaign strategies are based largely on construction of regional coalitions, and of course a candidate's travel plans must reflect optimal use of time and money in each region. While Americans may ordinarily think of themselves as divided into rich or poor, Protestant, Catholic or Jewish, white or black, Mexican American or Native American, campaigns are organized primarily by region. This goes especially for the delegate selection process, increasingly — in this age of universal primaries and caucuses — an exceedingly important aspect of campaign organization.

---

[1] "Significance of the Section in American History," first published in 1925. Turner is best known for his thesis that the frontier explains most of America's traits. For an appraisal of Turner's influence, see Richard Hofstadter's *The Progressive Historians: Turner, Beard, Parrington* (1968).
[2] See "Resurgence of Regionalism," *E.R.R.*, 1977 Vol. I, pp. 154-162.

As the focus of the presidential selection process shifts from state to state, each in turn heavily reported by press and television, America rediscovers its regional differences. In the early stages of the 1980 campaign, the coverage from Iowa preceding its Democratic and Republican caucuses on Jan. 21, viewers and readers across the nation became aware of the concerns of an essentially agricultural state, where high prices for grain or hogs tend to spell prosperity and low prices lean times. Then with the approach of New Hampshire's first-in-the-nation primary on Feb. 26, familiar New England scenes appear nightly on the network news — of snow and blustery weather, small towns with white-steepled churches and textile mills beside old waterways. These mills may be deserted or, equally likely, they may house new industries — reflecting New England's and especially New Hampshire's economic recovery *(see pp. 18-20)*.

The Nation's Most Strongly Defined Region

New England, alone among the nation's regions, has a precisely defined identity. While people may argue about what the Midwest or even the South includes today, New England consists of Connecticut, Maine, Massachusetts, New Hampshire, Rhode Island and Vermont — nothing more and nothing less. The inhabitants of this region call coffee with cream "regular" and carbonated beverages "tonic." They pronounce Bingo "Bean-O," and when they bowl they use candlepins rather than tenpins. Those who live in Boston, which most New Englanders recognize as their regional capital, eat hot dogs, beans and black bread on Saturday evening, and on Halloween they drink apple cider. Above all else New Englanders are Yankees, people whom all Americans think of — however accurately or inaccurately — as conscientious, hard-working, terse, frugal, and (like the climate) cold and inhospitable to outsiders.

Outside the United States people think of all Americans as Yankees, reflecting New England's tendency to project its own traditions, practices and beliefs onto the nation as a whole. The Puritans, who came to New England in 1620, were the first to articulate what was to become Protestant America's characteristic image of its place in the world. "For wee must consider that wee shall be as a Citty uppon a Hill, the eies of all people are uppon us," said John Winthrop, one of the Bay Colony's first and most influential leaders.

Every schoolchild learns to think of New England as the cradle of liberty, and many a tourist's visit to New England begins with a walk along Boston's Freedom Trail or a trip to the nearby villages of Lexington and Concord. Further outings are likely to be to take the visitor to the seacoast, to the historic towns of Salem, New Bedford and Nantucket, where descendants of Puri-

"My section of the country, right or wrong!"

tans built a thriving trade on whaling, slaves, sugar and rum. That trade generated the capital which, together with Yankee ingenuity and water power, provided the basis for New England's — and indeed the country's — industrial revolution.

New England's strong identity, its pronounced sense of self-interest and its leadership abilities are responsible for many of the nation's most noted achievements, and yet these same qualities also have repeatedly put the region at odds with other sections of the country. In the period of Jeffersonian democracy the New England Federalists were deeply disaffected, and during the War of 1812 and the Mexican-American War (1846) there was talk in New England of secession. Crusading New Englanders provided much of the impetus behind the Abolitionist movement, which was an assault on the South's "peculiar institution," slavery. After the Civil War, New England capitalists enjoyed — together with their allies in New York, Pennsylvania, and the industrializing Midwest — a generation of

5

political hegemony. But after the turn of the century the region's economy went into a protracted decline.

In the early 1970s, just when signs of economic revival were beginning to appear, oil prices started to jump by leaps and bounds. The repeated OPEC (Organization of Petroleum Exporting Countries) price hikes delayed the region's recovery and have put New England, once again, into conflict with the main line of national energy policy. Prices for home heating oil, on which the region is highly dependent, have doubled since President Carter took office, and Sen. Edward M. Kennedy, D-Mass., has been strongly critical of Carter's decision to decontrol domestic oil prices. After announcing his candidacy for the presidency, Kennedy repeatedly said that Carter should have won Senate approval for a satisfactory "windfall" profits tax on the oil industry before decontrolling prices. It remains to be seen whether Kennedy can win a majority of Americans to his region's position on oil prices, or in fact whether energy is an issue of such overriding regional importance as to provide him crucial primary victories in the New England states *(see p. 23)*.

Geographic Divisions; Settlement Patterns

Had Kennedy been running for president in 1680 rather than 1980, his task might have been easier. For in 1680 the Bay Colony consisted of Boston, some adjacent communities, and little else. The early settlements closely approximated the belt of high-technology, education-intensive industries that now cluster along Route 128 around Boston.

In 1694-95 and 1699-1700 the Massachusetts General Court (the colonial legislature) enumerated towns in which inhabitants were forbidden to leave on pain of dispossession or imprisonment. These towns formed an officially designated frontier line which followed, according to Turner: (1) the outskirts of settlement along the eastern coast and up the Merrimack River into New Hampshire, areas that were threatened primarily by the French and Indians from the north; (2) a ribbon of settlements stretching into the upper Connecticut Valley, which was menaced by Canadian Indians by way of Lake Champlain; (3) an "intervale" around Brookfield in mid-Massachusetts to the east of the Connecticut River; and (4) still farther to the east, an "inferior agricultural region, where the hard crystalline rocks furnished a later foundation for Shays' Rebellion. . . ."[3]

The people inhabiting these towns early developed the traits which Turner associated with frontiersmen, namely a rough-and-ready egalitarianism, contrasting with the stern and elitist

---

[3] Frederick Jackson Turner, "The First Official Frontier of the Massachusetts Bay," 1914, reprinted in his *The Frontier in American History* (1976 edition), p. 43.

New England

Lake Champlain

Burlington

VERMONT

Montpelier

Rutland

MAINE

Augusta

NEW HAMPSHIRE

Concord

Portland

Kittery

Merrimack River

Manchester

Nashua

ATLANTIC OCEAN

Lowell

Lawrence

Connecticut River

MASSACHUSETTS

Boston

Worcester

Springfield

ROUTE 128

CAPE COD

CONNECTICUT

Providence

Hartford

Middletown

Groton

RHODE ISLAND

New Haven

LONG ISLAND SOUND

MILES

0   50   100

Puritanism of the Bay settlements, and an impatience with taxation and government regulation. Daniel Shays, who led the 1786-87 rebellion against taxation and in favor of paper money, anticipated slogans that were to reappear in Jacksonian democracy, late 19th century populism, and the recent tax revolt.[4]

Human settlements continue to follow mostly in the patterns that Turner described in the earliest days. The Connecticut Valley, which in glacial times was a vast lake stretching roughly from today's Middletown, Conn., to the middle of New Hampshire and Vermont, is the region's most fertile area. Together with Maine's northernmost county, Aroostook, the home of the

[4] See "Property Tax Relief," *E.R.R.*, 1978 Vol. I, pp. 361-380.

Maine potato, the Connecticut Valley is virtually the only part of New England reasonably well suited to modern agriculture. Tobacco is cultivated in Connecticut, with the aid of migrant Latin labor, and to the north flourish Vermont's dairy farms.

In addition to agriculture, the Connecticut Valley shelters numerous liberal arts colleges (e.g. Mount Holyoke, Wesleyan, Smith and Amherst), experimental schools (Bennington, Putney, and Goddard), music festivals (Tanglewood is known nationally), and second homes for the well-to-do who are attracted by the area's natural beauty, its colonial atmosphere, cultural assets and thriving crafts industries. The rest of New England has not been able to support modern agriculture. Stone walls, small family cemeteries, and lonely chimneys are picturesque reminders of how the soil once was tilled, but modern New England produces less than 2 percent of the nation's farm income.

The Merrimack Valley, where the world's largest textile mills flourished during the 19th century in towns like Lowell and Lawrence, Mass., and Nashua and Manchester, N.H., was the part of New England hardest hit by out-migration of industry during past decades. In recent years, however, Boston's high-technology belt has expanded up the Merrimack to re-occupy industrial sites once deserted. New Hampshire's low taxes, low wages, scant unionization, and pro-business philosophy have done much to foster this redevelopment of the Merrimack. Similarly, Vermont has brought many industries into the much more remote Burlington area.

North-South and Urban-Rural Differences

In the northernmost and westernmost reaches of New England are some truly wild areas, and because of the region's protracted agricultural decline, these areas have become larger rather than smaller. In contrast to 1830, when roughly 60 percent of New England's land was cleared for cultivation, by the early 1970s over 80 percent of the region was covered with forest. These forests provide native dwellers with an important alternative to oil, and the relative merits of wood-burning stoves have become as big a topic of conversation in New England as farm prices are in the Midwest, stock prices in New York, or real estate prices in Washington, D.C.[5] In Maine, where the holdings of private timber companies are vast, loggers in the north still used lakes and rivers until recent years, when environmental legislation required overland transportation.

Turner remarked over 50 years ago that Maine's "long blood-stained frontier" — he had Indian fighting in mind — had im-

---

[5] See "New England's Return to Wood" by Colin High in *Natural History,* February 1980, pp. 14-32.

New England at a Glance

State	Pop.*	Area (sq.mi.)	Entered Union Year	Entered Union No.
Connecticut	3,116,000	5,009	1788	5
Maine	1,920,000	33,215	1820	23
Massachusetts	5,771,000	8,257	1788	6
New Hampshire	869,000	9,304	1778	9
Rhode Island	932,000	1,214	1790	13
Vermont	487,000	9,609	1791	14

*1978 estimates by the Census Bureau.

parted a "western tone" to the state's people that still endured in his day.[6] Like the early frontiersmen, who resented being taxed and regulated by citified folk while they were fighting the Indians and conquering the elements, many of New England's rural residents still resent government, are suspicious of outsiders, and have little tolerance for greenhorns. The north country is much less solidly Republican than it once was, to be sure, and in Maine especially the Democrats have made strong inroads under the leadership of Sen. Edmund S. Muskie.

In all three of the northern states an influx of professionals, retirees and back-to-the-land people — all of whom tend to be attuned to environmental concerns — has had a liberalizing impact on local politics. This has been true above all in Vermont, which passed pioneer legislation banning billboards and non-returnable bottles, and least of all in New Hampshire, still the most rock-ribbed of the New England states. New Hampshirites, reluctant to delegate authority, are governed by a 300-year-old legislature which is the third largest legislative body in the English-speaking world, after the U.S. Congress and British Parliament.[7] The state motto is "live free or die," and the state constitution explicitly affirms the right to rebellion.

In strong contrast to the sparsely populated north, the southern New England states of Connecticut, Massachusetts and Rhode Island are among the country's most densely populated and highly urbanized. Whereas the northern states are populated mainly by Yankees and French Canadians, the ethnic

[6] Frederick Jackson Turner, *The Frontier in American History, op. cit.,* p. 45. Trouble with the Indians in Maine, Connecticut and Massachusetts — and also in New York — has taken a new form in recent years. In the 1970s some tribes took legal action in attempts to regain ancestral lands. See "Indian Rights," *E.R.R.,* 1977 Vol. I, pp. 265-288.
[7] The New Hampshire House of Representatives, which once had more members (443) than Congress (435), has been limited to 400 since 1942. The New Hampshire legislature observes the 300th year of its founding on March 16, 1980.

stock in the south was radically altered by waves of immigration from Ireland and continental Europe, starting with the famines of the mid-1840s. Heavily Catholic and strongly committed to old-style urban machine politics, the Irish, Italians, Portuguese and Greeks, to name just the biggest groups, vote Democratic.

In New England as a whole, an uncharacteristically wide gulf separates rich and poor. To some extent this reflects the division between the richer urban people and the poor rural residents, many of whom live in Appalachian-like poverty. But even in the cities social classes are unusually distinct, going back perhaps to the old divisions between the Yankee Brahmins and the ethnic poor. In a study of 31 major U.S. cities made in the early 1970s, Neal Peirce reports that "Boston was found to rank second (and Hartford 13th) in terms of intensity of income inequality between poor and wealthy families."[8]

While the southern New England states vote Democratic most of the time, when the elections are over the relatively poor industrial workers and the still more impoverished unemployed squabble among themselves. Thus Massachusetts is represented not only by Kennedy, who is generally conceded to be the leader of the Democratic Party's left wing, but also by Louise Day Hicks, an outspoken foe of busing to achieve racial balance in schools, and by a governor, Edward J. King, who is a conservative Democrat.[9]

From Covenant to Melting Pot

T HE PURITANS who founded New England believed they were on an "errand into the wilderness," as described by the late scholar Perry Miller.[10] Strongly molded by John Calvin's preoccupation with the Old Testament, the Puritans believed that they had "entered into an explicit covenant with God" and that their mission was to found "a pure biblical polity" in America. Like the Hebrew people, who were confident that any deviation from the terms of the covenant would be punished with immediate manifestations of divine wrath, the Puritans felt that success in the New World would depend primarily on their faithfulness to God's will. A task of transcendent importance, accordingly, was to stamp out all signs of sin or heresy.

In the latter part of the 17th century, a pessimism came over

---

[8] Neal Peirce, *The New England States (1976),* p. 47.
[9] See Michael Barone, et al., *The Almanac of American Politics, 1980,* p. 389.
[10] *Errand into the Wilderness* (1956) is the title of one of Miller's books on Puritan life and religion which won him high praise in academia.

second generation Puritans. When the Bay Colony's assembled clergy and lay elders met in formal synod under the leadership of Increase Mather in 1692, they enumerated a shocking number of transgressions against divine law: mixed dancing, extravagance in attire, crowded taverns, a prevalence of Quakers and Anabaptists, thriving lawyers, a growing disposition to lie, and speculation in land.

Evidently rigid customs already were breaking down under the exigencies of the new society and the attractions of prosperity, but according to Miller this was not the only source of discomfort to the Puritans. They also felt a growing anxiety that they were perhaps on a "fool's errand," that the Old World — far from keeping its eyes fixed on Massachusetts in rapt attention — did not care about its fate and indeed was going a wholly separate path. They were aware that Oliver Cromwell, the leader of the Puritan revolution back in England, had decided to tolerate dissenting sects provided they were willing to fight against the Crown in his New Model Army.

In addition to the religious and moral strains detected by Miller, historians also have discerned a growing tension between rich and poor in late 17th century New England. As the more energetic and advantaged members of society consolidated their position, and as population began to press against the colonized land, the numbers of landless or near-landless began to rise and the proportion of colonists entitled to vote fell. In Dedham, Mass., for example, the term "the poor" first came into written usage in 1710, and from that time on contributions were taken up for the needy almost yearly.[11]

Hungry for land or eager to escape the enforced religious orthodoxy of the Bay Colony, settlers pressed into what became the other states of New England. Roger Williams founded Providence, R.I., in 1636. And in 1638 Connecticut, though just as orthodox as the Bay Colony, adopted the New World's first constitution, the "Fundamental Orders," which were drafted by the Rev. Thomas Hooker. From the mid-17th to the mid-18th centuries settlers migrated into southern Maine and New Hampshire and, after the fall of French Montreal to the British in 1760, into Vermont as well. New Hampshire, the only one of the northern-tier entities to be incorporated as a colony by the time of the Revolution, had its eastern and southern borders fixed in 1741. The colony's leaders had made a direct appeal to the Crown because the authorities in Massachusetts were arresting New Hampshirites for refusing to pay Bay Colony taxes. Thus began New Hampshire's career as a tax haven.

---

[11] See Kenneth Lockridge, "Land, Population, and the Evolution of New England Society: 1630-1790," *Past and Present,* No. 39, pp. 62-80.

Though the American Revolution started in New England, and though the war provided a powerful stimulus to the region's nascent shipping and manufacturing industries, New Englanders played perhaps a smaller role in the actual fighting than the colonists to the south. Certainly, the men of Philadelphia and Virginia contributed far more mightily to the framing of the Constitution, and with the advent of Jeffersonian democracy in 1800, the New England Federalists took to sulking over the course of national politics and policy.

New England in 1800; the Dawn of Change

New England in 1800, as Henry Adams described it in the opening chapters of his *History of America during the First Administration of Thomas Jefferson,* remained at best a tiny outpost of European culture. "Of the whole United States," Adams wrote, "New England claimed to be the most civilized province, yet New England was a region in which life had yet gained few charms of sense and few advantages over its rivals." Boston was a city of less than 20,000, with unlit streets and few police.

Communications with the rest of the nation were tenuous, though a "tolerable highway" connected Boston and New York, "along which, thrice a week, light stage-coaches carried passengers and the mail, in three days," Adams wrote. New Englanders still wore homespun cloth, homemade clothes, and hats made by the village hatter. "Hence came a marked air of rusticity which distinguished country from town — awkward shapes of hat, coat, and trousers, which gave to the Yankee caricature those typical traits that soon disappeared almost as completely as coats of mail and steel head-pieces."

Harvard College at this time was small and still struggling. As for Yale, Adams recounted, it was "but a reproduction of Harvard with stricter orthodoxy." The theater already had gained a firm foothold in Boston, but horse racing was forbidden throughout New England and a ban on Sunday travel was enforced. As everywhere else in the United States at this time, "every grown man took his noon toddy as a matter of course," and although "few were seen publicly drunk, many were habitually affected by liquor." The early temperance movement, according to Adams, "was said to have had its source in the scandal caused by the occasional intoxication of ministers at their regular meetings."

While the clergy was no longer quite so "minute and inquisitory" as it had been up to the Revolution, it remained the dominant force throughout New England, and in country parishes it was "autocratic." Offending parishioners would be barred from contact with their neighbors, and anybody placed under the "ban" fared badly. "Nothing," Adams said, "tended so directly to make respectability conservative, and conservatism a fetish of respectability, as this union of bench and pulpit." European deism and the tumultous events of the French Revolution represented the incarnation of evil, and after the 1800 election of Thomas Jefferson — a deist and Francophile — "the clergy and nearly all the educated and respectable citizens of New England began to extend to the national government the hatred which they bore to democracy."

New England in 1800 was a region clinging desperately to the past but on the verge of great changes. Already the Napoleonic Wars were revolutionizing New England's shipping industry, encouraging the growth of banking and maritime insurance. Hartford's first insurance company was incorporated in 1795 and its best known company, Hartford Fire Insurance Co., in 1810. Availability of capital and improving communications in turn stimulated manufacturing. In 1793 Samuel Slater founded the New World's first mechanized and water-powered textile mill at Pawtucket, R.I., initiating an economic revolution which was to sweep first the Northeast and then the country as a whole.

Rise of Unitarianism and Transcendentalism

With New England's growing prosperity and widening horizons developed a new class of intellectuals, eager to meet the emergent bourgeoisie's spiritual cravings. Dissatisfied with inherited traditions, strongly influenced by the romantic movements that were in ascendancy in contemporary Europe, and fascinated by the contrasting worlds of industry and nature, these new intellectuals gave birth to the first great age of American letters.

"Our age is retrospective. It builds the sepulchres of the fathers," Ralph Waldo Emerson said in the opening sentences of his essay *Nature.* "Why should not we also enjoy an original relation to the universe?" he continued. "Why should not we have a poetry and a philosophy of insight and not of tradition, and a religion by revelation to us, and not the history of theirs. . . . The sun shines today also. There is more wool and flax in the fields. There are new lands, new men, new thoughts. Let us demand our own works and laws and worship."

Unitarianism and Transcendentalism emerged from the intellectual ferment of this period. Clergy of a liberal bent who retreated from the Calvinist severity as then expressed in Congregational pulpits found favor with a form of religious belief that had reached New England from the European continent by way of the mother country. It came to be called, at first by its conservative foes, Unitarianism. It was based on the conception of God as one person, hence Unitarian, rather than the Trinitarian of orthodox Christianity. Aside from that theological distinction, Unitarianism is perhaps best known for its tolerance of differing religious opinions and the value it places on reason and conscience as guides to religious truth.

Together with New England's Unitarian intellectuals, notably William Ellery Channing, the so-called "transcendalist" writers — of whom the best known were Ralph Waldo Emerson and Henry David Thoreau — made major contributions to religious and social reform, educational innovation, aesthetics and ethics. Transcendentalism, a philosophic and literary movement that flourished between about 1836 and 1860, especially in Emerson and Thoreau's hometown of Concord, was a reaction against 18th century rationalism and the confining religious orthodoxy of New England Calvinism. Despite inherent contradictions from drawing on eclectic sources, "in its larger outline the belief had as . . . its fundamental base" an "indwelling of divinity" in man that made the "soul of the individual identical to the soul of the world."[12] Transcendentalism gave strong expression to self-reliance, individualism and an optimism of life.

Although viewed largely by their contemporaries as dreamers and radicals, this group of New England thinkers and writers exerted an influence that ultimately was far-reaching. Thoreau's doctrine of civil disobedience, for example, was an important inspiration not only in America's civil rights movements from the Abolitionists to Martin Luther King Jr. but also in such struggles abroad as Mohandas K. Gandhi's "passive resistance."

Other New England writers of the same era carried on the Puritan ethos by continuing to ponder the theme of man's sinfulness. Nathaniel Hawthorne, a native of Salem, Mass., wrote of people who are isolated physically or morally from their neighbors — a dark, brooding world nourishing fantasy and obsession. Herman Melville, who spent much of his life either in New England itself or in the world of New England shipping, greatly admired Hawthorne and once wrote that Hawthorne had dropped "germinous seeds" into his soul. "He expands and deepens down, the more I contemplate him," Melville wrote, "and further and further, shoots his strong New England roots into the hot soil in my southern soul."[13]

Melville wrote his greatest novel, *Moby Dick,* at Pittsfield, Mass., and set it in the world of Nantucket's whaling industry. Critical of both industry and nature, and skeptical of providence

---

[12] So described in the *Oxford Companion to American Literature* (1965, fourth edition), James D. Hart, ed.
[13] Quoted by Warner Berthoff in the introduction to *Great Short Works of Herman Melville,* Harper and Row Perennial Classic edition (1966), p. 9.

to the extent that modern critics think of the book as the first major absurdist novel, *Moby Dick* told the story of one man's driving quest for vengeance.

The fantasies and obsessions first explored by Hawthorne and Melville have haunted American literature ever since. And among the young and old people who have migrated to New England in recent years — be it to retire, do handicraft work, or just take up an ordinary job in an extraordinary setting — there are still plenty of dog-eared copies of Thoreau's *Walden* to be found. Puritanism lives on in a few remaining blue laws and in the Brahmin's bearing. But to have a book or play banned in Boston, once so dreaded, already in the 1920s was becoming the badge of success. Two centuries ago horse racing was prohibited in New England; but today, of the eight states that permit as many as three forms of gambling, five of the states are in New England.[14]

New Immigrants, Brahmins, and Yankees

By the mid-19th century Puritanism had long since given way to the Great Awakenings — revivalist movements which began in the 1740s and have strongly influenced American Protestantism to this day. Yet the descendants of New England's Puritans, despite the skepticism expressed by writers like Hawthorne and Melville, retained a lingering faith in their destiny as a chosen people. Nowhere was this faith so strong as among the region's prosperous gentry, the class which Oliver Wendell Holmes later dubbed the "Brahmin caste," whose members could be readily distinguished from the Yankee farmers, seamen, artisans and industrial workers. Although the two groups led increasingly separate lives as the 19th century wore on, they continued to respect common values, and both seemed to take it for granted that the Brahmins should speak for the community as a whole.[15]

Despite the self-assurance felt by the Brahmins at mid-century, new migrations already were threatening to erode their position. Between 1815 and 1865 some five million people came to New England from western and central Europe, the overwhelming bulk of them impoverished Irish. Unlike the other European migrants, many of whom came on their own volition in search of economic opportunity and political freedom, the Irish came for the most part because the alternative was to starve.

Systematically dispossessed at home by the British, and hard hit by the potato famines that began in 1845, the typical Irish migrants put all their meager resources into the voyages across the Atlantic. They came to Boston in large numbers simply be-

---

[14] Maine, the sixth New England state, permits only two — lotteries and horse racing. See "Gambling's New Respectability," *E.R.R.*, 1979 Vol. II, pp. 709-724.
[15] See Barbara Miller Solomon, *Ancestors and Immigrants: A Changing New England Tradition* (1972), pp. 1-3.

cause that was the terminus of the most direct shipping route from Liverpool. When they got to Boston, unlike the better-off Germans and Scandinavians, who tended to push on to the rich agricultural lands of the plains states, the Irish had no choice but to stay put.[16]

In the latter part of the 19th century the Irish were joined by new waves of immigrants — groups of French Canadians, Poles, Italians, Jews and Portuguese, and smaller numbers of Greeks, Armenians, Syrians and blacks. Like the Irish, many of these "newer races" or "New Immigrants," as they were called, had customs and beliefs sharply at variance with the dominant white-Anglo-Saxon-Protestant (WASP) culture: the new immigrants tended to be Catholic, to drink with unseemly zest, and to dislike England.

By 1920, a strong contrast had developed between the older New England of small towns, white-steepled churches, and town meeting halls, and the newer urban New England of ethnic voters and big Irish-Democratic political machines. Two-thirds of the people in Massachusetts were immigrants or children of immigrants. Rhode Island, the state founded as a haven for dissident Protestants, had become the most heavily Catholic state in the nation.

Brahmin-Yankee-New Immigrant alliances, together with the well-established tradition of gerrymandering, enabled the Republicans to dominate state-wide elections long after the Irish Democrats had taken control of the municipal governments. Whereas the Irish were overwhelmingly loyal to the Democratic Party, many of the New Immigrants were successfully courted by the Republicans.[17] In some cities an odd-even pattern developed: The most recent immigrant group would ally itself with whichever party happened to be the enemy of the next-most-recent group.

In Rhode Island, the Protestant elite neutralized the ethnic groups by placing "shocking limitations on the right to vote,"[18] and the state went Democratic for the first time only in 1928 when Alfred E. Smith — a Catholic and an opponent of Prohibition — exerted an irresistible appeal to the ethnics. In New Hampshire, where a cleverly drawn line divides the two great concentrations of ethnic voters in Nashua and Manchester into separate congressional districts, the Yankee elements have tended to be in the saddle down to the present day.

---

[16] See Oscar Handlin, *Boston's Immigrants* (1971), pp. 25-53.

[17] See J. Joseph Huthmacher, *Massachusetts, People and Politics, 1919-1933* (1959), pp. 3-16. Gerrymandering, the rearrangement of voting districts to favor the party or person in power, takes its name from a Massachusetts governor, Elbridge Gerry (1810-12). During his governorship, some districts were grotesquely arranged to aid the Jeffersonians against the Federalists.

[18] Peirce, *op. cit.*, p. 52.

Economic Decline and Comeback

THE END of World War I marked the end of a boom for New England's manufacturing and mercantile industries and the beginning of a long period of economic decline. Textile and shoe manufacturers increasingly relocated in the South, and by 1929 over half the textile spindles in the nation were in the South.[19] Employment in the textile and shoe industries dropped from well over 500,000 in the early years of this century to less than 150,000 by the early 1970s.

World War II, like World War I, gave New England's economy a badly needed boost. From the days of the Revolution, New England had been a major supplier of precision equipment in time of war. Col. Samuel Colt, together with Eli Whitney, did pioneering work in developing mass production techniques at a gun factory they started in Hartford. The Winchester rifle company was started at New Haven during the Revolution. And the Springfield Armory, now a museum, first produced guns for the U.S. military services in 1795. Shipbuilding, above all the submarine construction and repair facilities at Groton, Conn., and Kittery, Maine-Portsmouth, N.H., became a mainstay of the region's economy. But New England's universities also did highly important research and development work for the military, notably on radar, and from the end of the war to the present day the region's industries have built a wide variety of military equipment — jet engines, electronic components, and missile and space systems.

In the 1970s, however, reductions in the U.S. defense budget cut more deeply in New England than in any other part of the country. The loss of research and procurement work, together with the closing of many bases,[20] posed a threat to the regional economy. When, on top of that, energy prices began to rise sharply in late 1973, the long-term outlook for the economy seemed bleak indeed. Exceptionally dependent on energy, and more reliant on fuel oil than any other region of the country, New England seemed to many a place whose day had passed. Both the 1969-70 and 1973-75 recessions hit exceptionally hard. In May 1975, for example, New England's unemployment rate was 11.6 percent, compared to 9.2 percent nationwide; in Rhode Island it was 16.2 percent.

---

[19] Robert Goodman, *The Last Entrepreneurs* (1979), p. 126.
[20] See the Northeast-Midwest Congressonal Coalition, *The State of the Region* (1979), p. 73. Formed in 1976, the coalition of 213 U.S. representatives from 18 states, including New England, seeks to inform its members about regional implications of national policies and proposals. It operates the Northeast-Midwest Institute, a research center.

Signs of Recovery Since the Middle 1970s

Much to the surprise of the doomsayers, however, New England's economy has proved to be quite resilient since 1975. Manufacturing employment in the region has kept abreast of the nation as a whole in recent years, and there are signs of vitality in many areas. High-technology industries, many of which have located in abandoned mills around Boston, along the Merrimack into southern New Hampshire, and in Connecticut, continued to prosper.

The fishing industry has revived after years of suffering from foreign competition in New England's offshore waters. Congress in 1976 declared that national economic interests extended for 200 miles out to sea, giving U.S. fishermen priority in this economic zone. Since then, many of New England's coastal towns have refurbished their waterfronts not just as tourist attractions but as commercial centers.

A legal and public-relations battle has been fought for the past two years between competing economic interests over the Georges Banks, fertile fishing grounds 100 miles off the New England coast. The fishing industry, aided by environmentalists, has bitterly opposed the U.S. Interior Department's sale of leases to a dozen oil and gas companies for drilling rights to 660,000 underwater acres on those fishing grounds. New England governments, no less than the public, seem divided between a desire to have a source of needed oil in their own backyard and their fears of ecological and economic harm to the beaches and fishing industry.

New Hampshire, with low taxes,[21] low wages and a pro-business governmental zest for luring out-of-state businesses, is New England's current economic success story. According to Lynn E. Browne, economist for the Federal Reserve Bank of Boston, New Hampshire alone among the New England states is in the same league with the fast-growth "sunbelt" states. New England overall is keeping up with, but not outperforming, the rest of the country. Even in New Hampshire the rural areas, especially those north of Concord, the capital, have not shared — or shared fully — in the new prosperity. In 30 years, Gov. Hugh Gallen recently recounted to a visitor,[22] Berlin's population has been halved, to about 14,000 today. But he spoke approvingly of a replacement industry, a roller skate factory relocating in the town.

While rural areas and small towns account for much of the remaining economic stagnation, it extends also to urban workers

---

[21] In addition to being the only state without a sales tax or state personal income tax, New Hampshire has no corporate income tax — only a tax on profits.
[22] Interview, Jan. 24, 1980.

New England Employment

Unemployment Rates	Jobless Rates 1979 Avg.	1978 Avg.
New England Total	5.4%	5.7%
Connecticut	5.1	5.2
Maine	7.2	6.1
Massachusetts	5.5	6.1
New Hampshire	3.1	3.8
Rhode Island	6.6	6.6
Vermont	5.1	5.7
U.S. Average	5.8	6.0

Source: U.S. Bureau of Labor Statistics

	Non-agricultural Employment Oct. 1979 (add 000)	Change from 1978
New England Total	5,380.2	+2.0%
Connecticut	1,403.8	+2.7
Maine	411.7	+0.6
Massachusetts	2,584.1	+2.0
New Hampshire	384.3	+4.6
Rhode Island	399.2	−1.2
Vermont	197.1	+2.6
U.S. Total	90,151.0	+3.1

Source: Federal Reserve Bank of Boston, *Economic Indicators,* December 1979.

who lack good job skills. This is because much of the new industry is technology-based, such as required for computers and telecommunications. And although these high-technology companies are growing and expanding beyond the Route 128 arc around Boston, they nevertheless have not reached the stage where they employ thousands on a mass-production basis. "Very many firms are still new and small," Ms. Browne said, "tied to MIT [Massachusetts Institute of Technology] and Harvard. Their owners went to school here. When they expand they look to somewhere nearby in New England. But they may employ only a few dozen people."[23]

Job Creation Through Technology and Taxes

The High Technology Council, representing 89 fast-growing computer and electronics companies in Massachusetts, complains that the state's reputation for high taxes ("Taxachussetts") repels many out-of-state engineers and man-

---

[23] Interview, Jan. 23, 1980.

19

State and Local Taxes

State	As Share of Personal Income	Rank Among All States	Tax Collections Per Person
Massachusetts	15.1%	5	$1,870.71
Vermont	14.5	6	836.75
Maine	13.3	12	757.54
Rhode Island	12.5	21	848.13
Connecticut	11.6	30	940.88
New Hampshire	10.5	45	669.46

Source: Census Bureau, for the 12 months ended June 30, 1978.

agers they seek to attract. The council recently entered into a so-called "social contract" with Gov. King, promising to create 150,000 new jobs in the state by 1982 if he brings state taxes down to the average for 17 other industrial states. In a move attributed to lobbying by the Associated Industries of Massachusetts, the state legislature last year cut the state's capital gains tax by 60 percent. And the governor has limited local government spending to a 4 percent yearly increase, bringing about property tax reductions in more than half of the 351 cities and towns.

New England prospered before on technology-based industry. Textiles and shoes, in their New England beginnings, were considered high-technology industries. But textiles moved south and shoe manufacturers encountered strong foreign competition. But the memory of what happened before does not take the edge off of the region's modest economic gains in recent years. New England bankers, who only a few years ago "were quite downcast, now are upbeat," Ms. Browne said. This optimism translates into loans for new business ventures and tends to have a snowball effect. While this region shares the entire country's concerns over the threat of a recession, experts at the Boston Federal Reserve Bank have pointed out that New England is likely to suffer less than the rest of the country from drops in automobile manufacturing and housing construction.[24] Increased defense spending, as requested by President Carter, would be a boon.

Most economists would agree that New England will continue to benefit from the same assets which have enabled it to stay afloat so far: its early adjustment to problems such as high energy costs, problems that the rest of the country have yet to fully confront; its university-based research establishment, its sizable

---

[24] See Lynn E. Browne, "Monitoring the National Recession in New England," in the Boston Federal Reserve Bank's *Economic Indicators,* November 1979, pp. A3-A4.

skilled labor force, and its experience in precision manufacturing; its possession of numerous cultural assets (including attractive scenery and historic sites) which make New England a pleasant place to live and work; the ready accessibility of capital, both in the Boston banking business and the Connecticut insurance industry; and, not least, its disproportionate political influence at the national level.

New England's Political Clout

MASSACHUSETTS, since World War II, has given the country two Democratic House Speakers, John J. Mc-Cormack and Thomas P. "Tip" O'Neill, and one Republican Speaker, Joseph Martin (1946-48); one Democratic president, John F. Kennedy; and two major presidential contenders, Robert F. and Edward M. Kennedy. The eighth congressional district, which includes most of downtown Boston, is the only district in American history to have been represented successively by a U.S. president and a House speaker.[25]

In addition, New England has given the Democratic Party two of its most influential chairmen, Lawrence O'Brien, who was born in Springfield, Mass., and John Bailey, chairman of Connecticut's Democratic Party from 1946 to 1975. The major force in creating this startling record of national political achievement has been Boston's Irish political organization, working in close alliance with Bailey's machine down to the early 1970s. And the major force in the Boston organization has been the Kennedy clan.

Boston's Irish "mafia," from its earliest days, has constituted an exceptionally complicated and competitive political organization. Largely because of the city's elaborate fragmentation into small and shifting ethnic communities, no single "boss" was able to mold the Democrats into a single, well-oiled machine in the early part of the century. "Instead," J. Joseph Huthmacher wrote, "a number of leaders with ward or personal followings, men such as Martin Lomasney, John F. Fitzgerald, and James Michael Curley, vied with one another for supremacy.... [I]n the first years of the twentieth century Irish politicians were interested in local affairs, and few were widely known beyond their own bailiwicks."[26]

---

[25] Barone, *op. cit.*, p. 407.

[26] Huthmacher, *op. cit.*, p. 14.

The volatile affections of the New Immigrants greatly complicated the work of the feuding bosses, though "in some instances, under the stress of circumstances, Irish Democratic leaders accommodated the newer immigrant elements and secured their allegiances. In Boston, for example, Martin Lomasney and John F. Fitzgerald ['Honey Fitz'] found their formerly Irish wards transformed into Italian and Jewish neighborhoods as Irishmen moved to better quarters. In order to insure their own supremacy Lomasney and 'Honey Fitz' shared a minimum of rewards with their new constituents, and consequently their districts continued to return Democratic majorities."[27]

Until the late Twenties, according to Charles W. Van Devander, Boston was dominated by the Hendricks Club, "for forty years the personal political property of the 'Czar' Martin Lomasney," and the Tammany Club, "which produced the fabulous James M. 'Jim' Curley and served as his vehicle to temporary dominance of the state."[28]

The power of Boston's Irish machines began to slip badly in the Thirties and Forties with the introduction of a non-partisan system of electing the mayor, with the passing from the scene of Lomasney and Curley, and with the creation of a well-financed and well-run Republican organization capable of launching impressive Brahmin candidates like Henry Cabot Lodge and Leverett Saltonstall.

"Honey Fitz" attempted to lay claim to Lomasney's Hendricks Club but was defeated in 1943 in a bid for a seat on the city council. As for the Democratic City Committee, which was chaired by another of the major figures in Irish politics, Billy "Mother" Galvin, it had become — in Van Devander's 1944 assessment — "impotent." Van Devander foresaw in 1944 a long period of rule by the Massachusetts Republican State Committee, a machine made of "the conventional parts, but . . . highly streamlined and equipped with some interesting new gadgets that make for better control and smoother operations."

The Revival of Boston's Democratic Party

Evidently Van Devander failed to appreciate the implications of certain marital alliances in Boston's clannish politics. Joseph P. Kennedy, who had made much of his fortune in the liquor business during the Depression and who was known in the Thirties for his characteristically Irish distaste for the British, had married a daughter of "Honey Fitz." Together they spawned the remarkable group of sons who were to play a key role in re-

---

[27] *Ibid.*, p. 16.
[28] Charles W. Van Devander, *The Big Bosses* (1944), p. 118.

vitalizing Boston's Democratic organization and — still more — in projecting that organization's influence into national politics.

John F. Kennedy, who defeated Henry Cabot Lodge Jr. for a congressional seat in 1946, proceeded to steer a political course that left many of his opponents disarmed. While taking care to nourish his roots in the ethnic wards, Kennedy also cultivated his father's ties with New England's and the nation's establishment figures. Kennedy's middle-of-the-road policies proved popular not only in Massachusetts but also at the national level in the cautious atmosphere of the 1950s, and his presidential ambitions got a big boost from Connecticut's John Bailey, who circulated a memorandum in 1956 explaining why a Catholic candidate would be an asset rather than a liability for the Democratic Party. After Kennedy's election as president in 1960, he named Bailey national chairman of the party.

With the assassinations of John F. and Robert F. Kennedy, the family mantle fell on Edward M. Kennedy. Now a Senate leader who seems "to be at the center of every legislative issue,"[29] he has been re-elected every six years (1964, 1970, 1976) with overwhelming majorities since he was first elected in 1962 to fill John F. Kennedy's unexpired term. This year, to the surprise of many, Kennedy's quest for the Democratic presidential nomination encountered trouble from the outset and suffered a stunning setback in Iowa, which President Carter won 2 to 1.

New Hampshire's Primacy in the Primaries

Although New Hampshire accounts for but two of the 36 Republican primaries and 34 Democratic primaries, Feb. 26 is virtually certain to be a critical milestone in the 1980 campaigns. Political analysts regard a Kennedy victory over Carter as essential to the senator's quest for the Democratic presidential nomination, and a strong showing by Ronald Reagan as necessary to retain a national backing in the Republican race.

New Hampshire voters, even though hardly representative of the national electorate, have built up a remarkable record of influencing key campaigns. In 1928 Alfred E. Smith and Herbert Hoover won the primaries, and in 1932 Franklin D. Roosevelt defeated Smith. A Truman slate won in 1948, and Dwight D. Eisenhower beat Robert A. Taft in 1952, the first year the primary grabbed the nation's political spotlight. That same year, Estes Kefauver established himself as a serious Democratic contender. Eugene McCarthy's unexpectedly strong showing in 1968 contributed mightily to Lyndon B. Johnson's decision not to run for re-election. A strong New Hampshire showing turned Mc-

---

[29] So described by Barone, *op. cit.*, p. 392.

Govern into a front-runner in 1972 and Jimmy Carter into a national candidate in 1976.[30]

The Vermont and Massachusetts presidential primaries will come on March 4. Connecticut's will follow on March 25, and Rhode Island's on June 3. The results will depend, as always, on who can win the Brahmins and the Yankees, the rural frontiersman and the urban sophisticate, and above all the old Irish and the New Immigrants.

---

[30] See Charles Brereton's published study, *First Step to the White House: The New Hampshire Primary, 1952-1980.*

Selected Bibliography

Books

Brooks, Van Wyck, *The Flowering of New England*, Dutton, 1936.
Handlin, Oscar, *Boston's Immigrants*, Athenium, 1971.
Huthmacher, J. Joseph, *Massachusetts, People and Politics, 1919-1933*, Harvard University Press, 1959.
Miller, Perry, *Errand into the Wilderness*, Harvard University Press, 1956.
—— *Nature's Nation*, Harvard University Press, 1967.
Peirce, Neal R., *The New England States*, W. W. Norton and Co., 1976.
Solomon, Barbara Miller, *Ancestors and Immigrants: A Changing New England Tradition*, University of Chicago Press, 1972.
Turner, Frederick Jackson, *The Frontier in American History*, Robert E. Krieger Publishing Co., 1976 edition.
—— *The Significance of Sections in American History*, Peter Smith (publisher), 1959.

Articles

Federal Reserve Bank, Boston, *Economic Indicators*, selected issues.
—— *New England Economic Review*, selected issues.
Lockridge, Kenneth, "Land, Population and the Evolution of New England Society: 1630-1790," *Past and Present*, No. 39.
Maine Times, selected issues.
New Hampshire Times, selected issues.

Reports and Studies

Brereton, Charles, *First Step to the White House: The New Hampshire Primary 1952-1980.*
Editorial Research Reports: "Resurgence of Regionalism," 1977 Vol. I, p. 143.
Northeast-Midwest Congressional Coalition/Northeast-Midwest Institute, *New England State Profiles*, Washington, D.C., September 1978.
—— *The State of the Region: Economic Trends of the 1970s in the Northeast and Midwest*, Washington, D.C., January 1979.
The Conference Board, *Regional Outlook 1979-1980*, June 1979.

THE SOUTH:
CONTINUITY
AND CHANGE

by

Sandra Stencel

Mar. 7
1 9 8 0

THE SOUTH: CONTINUITY AND CHANGE

"Of BOOKS about the South there is no end," V. O. Key wrote in the preface of his classic work, *Southern Politics* (1949). "Nor will there be as long as the South remains the region with the most distinctive character and tradition." Key was right. Writers have never tired of examining the South and all its vices and virtues. Perhaps no other region of the country has been analyzed in such minute detail. But the unique characteristics and history of the region are no longer the principal preoccupations of Southern historians. In fact, many books and articles written about the South in recent years have shared a totally different theme: that the South has become in most matters virtually indistinguishable from other sections of the United States.

The theme of "the vanishing South" is not new. It was nearly 10 years ago that journalist Joseph B. Cumming Jr. declared: "The South is over."[1] Harry Ashmore, the Pulitzer Prize-winning editor of the *Arkansas Gazette*, wrote his *Epitaph for Dixie* in 1957.[2] The latest round of discussions on the South's place in the Union began when Jimmy Carter was elected president in 1976. Carter was the first American president born and raised in the Deep South.[3] His victory was said to symbolize the South's absorption and acceptance by "mainstream America."

As the 1980 presidential campaign moves into high gear and the focus of the presidential selection process shifts from the snowy hills of New England to the southern primaries, Americans undoubtedly will notice that not all traces of Dixie have disappeared. But most observers agree that the South never again will be, as W. J. Cash described it nearly 40 years ago in *The Mind of the South*, "another land, sharply differentiated from the rest of the American nation. . . ."[4]

No one who visits the South today can deny that the region has undergone profound changes. A generation ago John Gun-

---

[1] Joseph B. Cumming Jr., "Been Down Home So Long It Looks Like Up To Me," *Esquire*, August 1971, p. 84.
[2] Ashmore won the Pulitzer Prize in 1958 for his editorials on the school integration crisis at Little Rock, beginning in September 1957. He is now a member of the National Advisory Council of the Robert Maynard Hutchins Center for the Study of Democratic Institutions, associated with the University of California at Santa Barbara.
[3] Lyndon B. Johnson of Texas became, in 1963, the first president since Andrew Johnson (1865-68) to come from a Southern state. But LBJ was not identified with the Deep South, as Carter was.
[4] W. J. Cash, *The Mind of the South* (1941), p. vii.

ther called the South the "problem child of the nation."[5] By almost any measure, the South was the nation's poorest section — in cash income, in housing, in health and nutrition, in education, in job skills. It was also overwhelmingly rural with only a few large cities and numerous small towns.

In recent years, however, the South has undergone a steady urbanization and industrialization that has tended to iron out differences between it and the rest of the nation.[6] The influx of millions of "Yankees" and other outsiders further diluted regional differences. Between 1970 and 1977, according to the Southern Growth Policies Board, over six million people moved into the South — more than double the number of Southerners who moved to other sections of the United States.[7]

'Americanization' Evokes Mixed Response

"The Americanization of Dixie," as journalist John Egerton called it,[8] did not eliminate all vestiges of the so-called southern way of life. Southerners retain certain distinctions besides their accents. As a group they are poorer, blacker, less educated, less culturally mixed, less unionized, more conservative, more patriotic and more religious than other Americans. But the old pluralism that made a Southerner entirely different from his Western or Northern counterpart has disappeared.

Of all the factors that characterize this latest version of the new South, one stands out — the elimination of race as an all-consuming issue. Jimmy Carter is fond of saying the civil rights movement freed Southern whites as well as blacks. No one would deny that serious race problems remain in the South and elsewhere. But, novelist Walker Percy wrote, "the South and Southerners . . . white and black . . . no longer suffer the unique onus, the peculiar burden of race that came to be part of the very connotation of the word South."[9] What freed the South was not the elimination of racial prejudice in the region, but the growing recognition that racial problems did not stop at the Mason-Dixon line. "When South Boston exploded with the same fury as South Georgia, there came the slow realization that racial prejudice wasn't buried behind soft Southern accents," wrote journalist Reg Murphy.[10]

---

[5] John Gunther, *Inside U.S.A.* (1947), p. 658.
[6] In 1970, 68.6 percent of the U.S. population resided in metropolitan areas, while in the South the figure was 55 percent. By 1976, the percentages were 72 and 62.4. See "Small Cities and Rural Communities in the South: An Analysis of Recent Trends and Policy Needs," issued by the Southern Growth Policies Board, November 1979, p. 3.
[7] Southern Growth Policies Board, "A Profile of the Southern States," December 1978, p. 4. The Southern Growth Policies Board is a non-profit agency formed in 1972 to foster regional cooperation. It now embraces 13 Southern states.
[8] Title of a book he authored in 1974.
[9] Walker Percy, "Southern Comfort," *Harper's*, January 1979, p. 80.
[10] Reg Murphy, "Not Since Jefferson and Madison . . ." *Saturday Review*, Sept. 4, 1976, p. 11. Murphy, now editor and publisher of the *San Francisco Examiner*, observed Carter's formative political years as editor of *The Atlanta Constitution*.

The Unsolid South

For the purposes of this report, the South is defined as Alabama, Arkansas, Florida, Georgia, Kentucky, Louisiana, Mississippi, North Carolina, South Carolina, Tennessee, Texas and Virginia — unless otherwise stated. The South, however, is a fluctuating entity that is difficult to delineate precisely. Perhaps that is why so many people consider the South a state of mind.

One conventional definition is that the South consists of the 11 states of the old Confederacy. This would exclude Kentucky. V. O. Key Jr., who adhered to this 11-state listing in his analysis of Southern politics, noted another common link — they were the only states in the nation that "did not go Republican more than twice in the presidential elections from 1876 to 1944."

Historian André Siegfried, in his *America Comes of Age* (1927), excluded from the South the entire Allegheny region because so few blacks lived there. By his definition, only seven states were purely Southern — South Carolina, Georgia, Alabama, Florida, Mississippi, Louisiana and Arkansas.

Professor Howard W. Odum of the University of North Carolina divided the United States into six big regions — the Northeast, Middle States, Northwest, Far West, Southeast and Southwest. Included in Odum's definition of the Southeast were Virginia, North Carolina, South Carolina, Georgia, Florida, Alabama, Kentucky, Tennessee, Mississippi, Arkansas and Louisiana. John Gunther followed Odum's listing, except that he excluded Kentucky from his discussion of the South in *Inside U.S.A.*

The U.S Census Bureau divides the South into three regions: the South Atlantic states (Delaware, Maryland, the District of Columbia, Virginia, West Virginia, North Carolina, South Carolina, Georgia and Florida); the East South Central states (Kentucky, Tennessee, Alabama and Mississippi); and the West South Central states (Arkansas, Louisiana, Oklahoma and Texas).

Southerners express mixed feelings about the changes the region has undergone. C. Vann Woodward, the Yale historian from Arkansas, once said that only "a blind sentimentalist" would mourn the passing of many of the things that once stood "as indisputable fact that the South was different . . . the one-horse farmer, one-crop agriculture, one-party politics, the sharecropper, the poll tax, the white primary, the Jim Crow car, the lynching bee."[11] But even those who for years spoke out against the more pernicious aspects of Southern distinctiveness believe something has been lost in the rush to rejoin the Union.

"Since World War II . . . the region has become urbanized, standardized and neonized," wrote Jack Temple Kirby. "Visu-

---

[11] Quoted by Neal R. Peirce in *The Deep South States* (1974), p. 14.

ally there is little difference between the superhighways and streetscapes of Ohio and Alabama. Cars, gasoline stations, subdivision architecture, glass-faced office towers and gaudy fast food stands are the same."[12] Similar thoughts were expressed by John Egerton. "The South and the nation are not exchanging strengths as much as they are exchanging sins; more often than not, they are sharing and spreading the worst in each other, while the best languishes and withers," he wrote.

Race Relations: New Faces, Old Problems

Birmingham, Ala., the city Dr. Martin Luther King Jr. once described as "the most thoroughly segregated in the United States," last fall elected its first black mayor, Dr. Richard Arrington, a two-term city councilman and educator. Arrington, the son of a Depression-era sharecropper, said his election showed "more about how far Birmingham has come than all the public relations we can do." It also underscored the growing political strength of Southern blacks *(see p. 44)*.

Ironically, it was a racial incident that prompted Arrington to enter the mayoral race. In June 1979 a white Birmingham policeman who was answering a robbery call fatally shot an unarmed black woman. Although a citizen review committee ruled that the officer was not justified in killing the woman, the mayor, David Vann, refused to fire him.[13] Vann's decision prompted the biggest protest demonstration in the city since the demonstrations led by Dr. King in the early 1960s. The July 20 march was organized by a coalition of black groups, including the Southern Christian Leadership Conference and the National Association for the Advancement of Colored People (NAACP).

The Birmingham shooting was one of several racial incidents in the South in the past year. Perhaps most disturbing to civil rights advocates is the increasing number of incidents involving the Ku Klux Klan. In Greensboro, N.C., last November five persons were killed and several others wounded when shooting broke out between Klan members and demonstrators attending an anti-Klan rally organized by a Marxist group called Workers Viewpoint. Four persons were wounded on May 26 in a shootout between Klansmen and black demonstrators in Decatur, Ala. In June 1979 a federal court in Birmingham convicted nine Klansmen of firing into the homes of two black civil rights activists and two racially mixed couples.

The increased visibility of the Ku Klux Klan is seen by some as evidence that the "Old South" still lives. Ron Harris wrote in

---

[12] Jack Temple Kirby, *Media-Made Dixie* (1978), p. 160.
[13] Vann said July 17 that his reason for not firing the officer was that Birmingham police had been trained to fire quickly. Vann did order a change in police training and firearm regulations. The Fraternal Order of Police had threatened to strike if the officer was dismissed. Vann ran for re-election, but was defeated in a seven-man primary in October.

Home to Dixie

For Southern blacks, the search for a better life has historically taken a northern direction. Thousands of blacks continue to flee the South, but today even greater numbers are leaving other sections of the country to settle south of the Mason-Dixon line. Between 1975 and 1978, according to U.S. Census Bureau estimates, 270,000 blacks moved to the South compared to an out-migration of 244,000.

The blacks moving to the South were described by Larry Long, chief of the Census Bureau's population study division, as "the cream of the crop." They are fairly young — average age about 30 — and have higher than average levels of education. Two out of every three blacks moving South are returnees who were born in the region.

The return-to-Dixie movement was first noticed in the early 1970s. *Ebony* magazine reported in August 1971: "Many blacks, returning South to avoid Northern crime and pollution problems, are enthusiastic with praise about the area's progress."

The primary reason for the black re-migration is the South's new prosperity. New opportunities have opened up for skilled workers of both races. But the South still has little to offer the poor and the untrained. Blacks in these categories are likely to remain in the North where welfare payments are higher.

the February 1979 issue of *Ebony* magazine: "Despite all of the talk about the new 'right-thinking' South, about 'racial change,' about the increased number of black elected officials and 'smooth integration of schools' and 'more black employment' — despite this, to be black in the South is, for the majority of black people, still to be poor, undereducated and isolated from the white community; to live in substandard, segregated housing; to be underrepresented on juries; to be shut out from meaningful participation in the elective process; and to be excluded from employment in all but the lowest-paying, most menial jobs."[14]

The lingering traces of the "Old South" are most evident in the small- and medium-sized towns that once epitomized the Southern way of life. "The places that are the most repressive can almost be pinned to those areas where blacks are a noticeable part of the population but not enough to have real political, social or economic power — those areas with, say, 12 to 25 percent blacks," observed Steve Suitts, director of the Southern

---

[14] Ron Harris, "The Myth of the 'New South,' " *Ebony,* February 1979, p. 56.

Regional Council in Atlanta. "These kinds of areas are where the civil rights activities of the '60s were seen from a distance by most blacks and whites. There was no baptism by fire, so there was no need to create biracial committees and the like, no politics of accommodation."[15]

Rising Concern Over KKK's New Visability

The Department of Justice reports that in the year that ended last Sept. 30, there were 44 serious racial incidents in the nation involving the Ku Klux Klan, up from just eight the year before. A report issued in November by the B'nai B'rith's Anti-Defamation League estimated Klan membership nationwide at 10,000 — up from 8,000 in March 1978. During the same period, it estimated, the number of Klan sympathizers grew from 30,000 to between 75,000 and 100,000. The growth was attributed to a rising white backlash to advances made by blacks and other minorities in recent years and to worsening economic conditions.

According to the league's study, much of the growth in Klan membership has been in the South, where new Klan leaders, openly espousing violence and staging well-publicized confrontations with black groups, have succeeded in attracting many recruits even as Klan membership in the North has declined. These new Klansmen, the study found, are generally younger and more prone to violence than other members. In contrast to northern Klansmen, those in the South are generally less isolated and find greater support in their communities. This support encourages the Klan to take a more active role in politics. Much of the Klan's success in the South is attributed to the emergence of vocal new leaders, especially David Duke and Bill Wilkinson, who head separate and rival organizations based in Louisiana.

Despite its reported growth and increased visibility, it would be wrong to conclude that the Klan and its doctrine of white supremacy represent the feelings of most Southerners. "The publicity has been disproportionate to the Klan's influence," said Charles Wittenstein of the Anti-Defamation League's Atlanta office. "The Klan is entirely outside the mainstream of Southern life. We attribute the membership increases to the more effective huckstering by Klan leaders such as Wilkinson."

But even a minor surge in Klan activity is cause for concern, in view of the organization's violent history. Founded as a social club in 1866 by demobilized Confederate soldiers in Pulaski, Tenn., it soon became a far-flung vigilance committee. The common goal of the Klan and such allied groups as the Knights

---

[15] Quoted in *The New York Times*, July 5, 1979. The Southern Regional Council is a non-partisan, privately funded research and action center with a deep interest in racial matters. It was founded in 1944.

of the White Camellia, the White League, the Invisible Circle and the Pale Faces was to curtail or eliminate black political power and return control of the South to its antebellum leaders. When the Klan's leader ordered it disbanded in 1877, its mission had been largely accomplished. The second coming of the Klan began in 1916 and lasted well into the 1920s. In addition to being anti-black, the new Klan was anti-Catholic, anti-Semitic, anti-foreign-born, and anti-radical. At the peak of its strength during this period, it had a membership estimated at four million nationwide.

The 1954 Supreme Court decision outlawing school segregation set in motion the third era of widespread Klan activity, which reached a climax in 1965 when four Klansmen were arrested in connection with the shooting death of Viola Liuzzo, a white civil rights worker, on an Alabama highway. Public outrage over this incident led to a decline in the Klan's strength. In its current incarnation, the Klan cannot count on the tacit or even active support of Southern law-enforcement officials. The attitude of Southern blacks has changed, too. Blacks "are no longer afraid of the Klan," said Ozell Sutton, southeastern regional director of the Justice Department's Community Relations Service. ". . .[I]f blacks are struck first, they're going to strike back."[16]

Southern Economic Advances

IN 1938 President Roosevelt took a long, appraising look at the South and declared the region "the nation's No. 1 economic problem."[17] Although various New Deal agencies had pumped large amounts of money into the area during the 1930s, the South, and especially the Deep South, remained mired in poverty. The average annual income of the region was only about half that of the country as a whole. The rest of the United States also was suffering from the effects of the Depression, but the South was so much worse off, Roosevelt said, that its poverty produced an "economic unbalance in the nation as a whole."

The South's economic problems long antedated the national economic crisis of the 1930s. They originated with the destruction of the Southern economy by the Civil War. A report by the President's National Emergency Council in 1938 attributed the perpetuation of the section's poverty to a high degree of absentee ownership of its resources, high interest rates, disadvantageous freight rates and a protective tariff policy which, by

---

[16] Quoted by Jeff Prugh of the *Los Angeles Times,* June 17, 1979.
[17] In a letter to the Conference on Economic Conditions in the South, July 5, 1938.

holding down imports, made it harder to sell abroad agricultural commodities the South had for export. Noting, however, that the region was rich in population and natural resources, the council called it "the nation's greatest untapped market and the market in which American business can expand most easily."

Since 1938 the South has come a long way toward fulfilling its economic potential. *Business Week* magazine in 1972 compared the South to a developing country that had reached the "take-off" stage of its economic development. The magazine acknowledged some unaddressed and unsolved problems in the region — growing disparities in the distribution of wealth, increasing pollution and congestion and urban sprawl — but on the whole it sketched a glowing profile. "The South today means economic growth . . . a still pleasing environment and rich new markets for all sorts of goods and services." The influx of people and industries into the region, it said, was producing social as well as economic benefits:

> New people bring fresh skills and bigger consumer markets. New business diversifies and broadens the economic base, upgrades the labor force, raises wages and creates new regional capital markets. Together, they spin off growing cities and suburbs, engender a strong middle class, shatter traditional social and political attitudes, homogenize the region and build myriad bridges to the rest of the country.[18]

Tangible evidence of the South's economic transformation can be seen by anyone driving down Interstate Highway 85 from southern Virginia through the Piedmont sections of the Carolinas and northern Georgia to Atlanta. I-85 starts south of Richmond, the capital of the old Confederacy and headquarters of Virginia's major economic interests. Along the I-85 corridor in North and South Carolina is the largest textile-producing area in the United States. New factories making chemicals, transportation equipment and electrical equipment have also sprung up there in recent years. Durham is the home not only of Duke University but of a large and sophisticated black community. Raleigh, the nearby state capital, is the site of North Carolina State University. These two cities and Chapel Hill, home of the University of North Carolina, form the legs of the Research Triangle, a collection of "think tanks" and corporations, including such giants as IBM, Burroughs, Chemstrand and Hercules.

Only a few miles away, at Greensboro, is the headquarters of Burlington Industries, the nation's largest textile company. The neighboring city of High Point is one of the largest furniture manufacturing centers in the nation. Western Electric has a big plant nearby. At Winston-Salem, in the center of the state's to-

---

[18] "The Rich New South: Frontier for Growth," *Business Week,* Sept. 2, 1972, p. 34.

The South

Map labels: Frankfort, Louisville, KENTUCKY, Richmond, VIRGINIA, Nashville, TENNESSEE, Chapel Hill, Durham, Raleigh, NORTH CAROLINA, Memphis, ARKANSAS, Little Rock, Amarillo, SOUTH CAROLINA, Columbia, Birmingham, Atlanta, Charleston, ALABAMA, GEORGIA, Savannah, El Paso, Fort Worth, Dallas, MISSISSIPPI, Jackson, Montgomery, Plains, ATLANTIC OCEAN, TEXAS, LOUISIANA, Austin, Houston, Baton Rouge, New Orleans, Tallahassee, FLORIDA, San Antonio, Rio Grande River, Mississippi River, GULF OF MEXICO, Miami, Statute Miles 0 100 200 300

bacco industry, is the headquarters of R. J. Reynolds Industries, the state's biggest company. Charlotte, North Carolina's largest city, is second only to Atlanta as a southeastern distribution, transportation and office center.

Across the border in South Carolina, I-85 passes through Spartanburg and Greenville, two other big textile centers. The area around the two cities has been called "one of the most industrialized and most blue-collar parts of the nation."[19] I-85 passes through Atlanta, the hub of the entire Southeast. The city has come a long way since the 1930s when it was known principally as the corporate home of Coca-Cola or, more likely, the hometown of Margaret Mitchell, whose novel (and later movie) *Gone With the Wind* brought fame to her and her city.

Among American cities, only New York and Chicago attract more convention visitors. Atlanta's airport, now being vastly expanded, is second only to Chicago's O'Hare in passenger traffic. The mayor, Maynard Jackson, is black and throughout the city blacks sit in positions of power. Since the late 1940s, racial liberalism has been witnessed in Atlanta politics. During the 1960s, when riots tore apart many other cities in the North and South, Atlanta remained relatively calm, advertising itself as "the city too busy to hate."

World War II as Catalyst for Development

"The South has considerably more industry than most people give it credit for having," John Gunther wrote in 1947. But until the 1960s, the South had considerably less than the rest of the nation. In the early days of the Republic, the South developed a number of small, consumer-goods industries which produced almost solely for local markets. The first cotton mills were established in North Carolina and Georgia around 1810, and by 1860

[19] Michael Barone, Grant Ujifusa and Douglas Matthews, *The Almanac of American Politics 1980*, p. 800.

there were 160 mills with an $8 million annual output. But industrial growth came to a standstill after the Civil War and did not pick up until the 1880s, when *Atlanta Constitution* Editor Henry W. Grady launched the first of many campaigns for a "new South" based on diversified agriculture and industry.

Using the incentives of cheap labor, low taxes and a warm climate, the South began to woo northern manufacturers. Many took the bait. The region's cotton manufacturing industry grew steadily until by the mid-1920s the South surpassed New England in number of spindles in operation. Factory employment advanced rapidly in the South after World War I and held up better there than elsewhere during the Depression years of the 1930s. Most of the Southern manufacturing employment, however, was in relatively low-paying industries: textiles, lumber and wood products, food, apparel and tobacco.

World War II was the great catalyst for economic growth. The South, with its climate for year-round training and the political clout of its senior members in Congress, landed scores of military bases. They provided good-paying jobs for thousands of Southerners and pumped vast sums into the local economies. The federal govenment spent billions for constructing or expanding chemical, ammunition and shipbuilding industries in the South. Hundreds of thousands of new manufacturing jobs were added.

The South was emerging from World War II, historian H. Clarence Nixon wrote in 1944, "with more social change and more unfinished business than any other part of the country," with fewer sharecroppers but more pipefitters and welders, with less plowing and hoeing but more mowing and sowing, with less rural isolation and more urban sophistication, with nearly a million people in the ranks of organized labor and a growing movement for anti-union laws, with veterans returning from new experiences beyond the seven seas and with "a standard of living for the common man that was undreamt of in its prewar philosophy."[20]

The surge of growth continued without letup. Between 1939 and 1958 the value of manufacturing output in the southern states rose from $9.8 billion to $65 billion, faster than in the rest of the country. In the same period, the number of workers in manufacturing increased from 1.3 million to 3.5 million. New industries set off new growth of commercial enterprises; retail trade rose from $9.2 billion in 1939 to $54.5 billion in 1958, also faster than elsewhere.[21]

[20] H. Clarence Nixon, "The South After the War," *Virginia Quarterly Review*, Vol. XX, 1944, pp. 321-334.
[21] "The Blue Book of Southern Progress," *Industrial Development and Manufacturers Record*, May 1959, pp. 27, 30.

Centers of Population in the South

(U.S. rank in parentheses)

Metropolitan Area	Population	Metropolitan Area	Population
Dallas-Fort Worth (10)	2,610,800	New Orleans (33)	1,136,800
		San Antonio (37)	996,100
Houston (11)	2,422,000	Louisville (40)	887,000
Atlanta (18)	1,804,800	Memphis (41)	876,000
Miami (21)	1,449,800	Birmingham (46)	799,700
Tampa-St. Petersburg (25)	1,366,700	Norfolk-Virginia Beach (49)	782,000

* 1976 Census Bureau estimates

This diversification of industry accelerated during the 1960s. Employment in such industries as rubber and plastics, transportation equipment, electrical parts and petrochemicals rose, while employment in the traditional industries of textiles, tobacco and furniture declined. The number of southern chemical workers, for example, increased by about one-third during the decade. By the end of the 1960s that industry accounted for more than 6 percent of the manufacturing work force of the region.

The South's economy also benefitted from a diversification in agriculture. It involved a switch from almost total dependence on commodity crops like tobacco and cotton, with volatile prices, to more profitable ventures such as livestock, poultry and eggs, and dairy products. The mid-South rivals the Pacific Northwest in timber production, and cattle raising on a big scale has moved as far eastward as Florida. In Arkansas, where poultry is king, the farmer's henhouse has given way to the mass marketing and production techniques of agribusiness.

Among the millions of people who flocked to the South in the 1960s and early 1970s were many experienced professionals, businessmen and technicians. Some came to staff or open headquarters or regional offices of large companies. Others worked in aerospace facilities in such cities as Huntsville, Ala., Cape Canaveral, Fla., and Houston, Texas. These workers helped narrow the wage gap between the South and the rest of the nation. Per capita income in the Deep South states increased by over 100 percent between 1961 and 1971, compared to a national increase of 83.5 percent. "But the people were still badly off," Neil Peirce recounted. "Five of the . . . states — Mississippi, the lowest, plus Arkansas, Alabama, South Carolina and Louisiana — ranked at the absolute bottom of the 50 states in actual per capita income. Georgia at 34th place among the states and Florida

at 24th place were somewhat better off, but even the Florida figure was 5 percent behind the national average."

'Sun Belt' Gains and 'Snow Belt' Losses

Southern industrial growth remained strong in the 1970s.
Non-agricultural employment in the region grew by 27.4 percent
in the period 1970-77, compared to a 15.8 percent increase
nationwide.[22] As in the rest of the nation, the biggest job gains
were in state and local governments and in service industries
such as banking, real estate and retail trade. The southern
states were better able than their northern neighbors to absorb
workers leaving the agricultural sector, to provide jobs for the
large number of young people entering the work force and to
accommodate workers migrating from other regions. The
South's annual average unemployment rate remained below the
U.S. average throughout the 1970s,
although the gap has been narrowing.

Between 1970 and 1976 corporate
or regional headquarters of 55 domestic and foreign companies moved to
Georgia, most of them to Atlanta.
About 450 companies shifted headquarters or major divisions to Tennessee during the same period, while
180 corporation headquarters,
subsidiaries or major divisions relocated in the Houston area.[23] In *Fortune* magazine's latest annual listing
of the nation's largest 500 companies,
56 were based in the South.[24]

The South's prosperity in the 1970s was in sharp contrast to
the economic decline that plagued many states in the industrial
"Snow Belt." Accusations surfaced in the mid-1970s that of the
billions in public funds that are transferred annually from the
federal to state and local governments, a disproportionate
amount was going to the Sun Belt states.[25] Others charged that
the southern states were unfairly offering a wide variety of
incentives to attract industries from other sections.

The notion that the Sun Belt prospered mainly by stealing
from its neighbors was disputed by a study released in Novem-

---

[22] Southern Growth Policies Board, "A Profile of the Southern States," December 1978, p.
16.
[23] Figures quoted in *U.S. News & World Report*, Aug. 2, 1976, p. 45.
[24] See *Fortune*, May 7, 1979, pp. 268-289, and *Fortune*, May 15, 1969, pp. 166-184. See also
Gurney Breckenfeld, "Business Loves the Sunbelt (and Vice Versa)," *Fortune*, June 1977,
pp. 132-146.
[25] See Joel Havemann, Neal R. Peirce and Rochelle L. Stanfield, "Federal Spending: the
North's Loss is the Sunbelt's Gain," *National Journal*, June 26, 1976, p. 878.

ber 1976 by the Commerce Department's Economic Development Administration.[26] During a three-year period of study (1969 to 1972), the report said, only 1.5 percent of the job losses in the North was caused by companies moving, while more than half the losses occurred because companies went out of business. During that period over 2.6 million new jobs appeared in the 13 southern states (the old Confederacy plus Kentucky and West Virginia). Of that number, 35 percent were created by the founding of new companies, 64 percent by the expansion of existing companies and a mere 1 percent by in-migration.

The migration of people and industries to the South appears to be slowing, according to an economic survey published in *The New York Times*, Jan. 6, 1980. "Many states of the Northeast are providing tax benefits and other incentives for companies and their jobs to stay put, and, to a great extent, these incentives have been effective," said Wendell Rawls Jr., author of the survey. As a result, Southern governors have begun courting foreign investors and have been having "considerable success." In Atlanta alone there are nine full-time foreign consulates, four foreign trade and government offices, and honorary consulates representing 23 countries. Miami, Fla., is a magnet for Latin American trade and investment. About half a million Latin Americans visited Miami in 1978 and spent an average of more than $1,000 each. The city's economy also has been bolstered by the thousands of Cubans who have settled there since Fidel Castro came to power in 1959.

Lingering Poverty in Rural, Black Areas

Amidst the towering office buildings, shiny new factories and other signs of the South's economic boom, many pockets of poverty remain, especially in the black rural sections of the Deep South and the isolated hollows of Appalachia. In 1975, the latest year for which complete statistics are available, almost 10 million people in 14 southern states (Oklahoma and West Virginia in addition to Kentucky and the old Confederacy), nearly 16 percent of their total, lived below the officially defined poverty line.[27] According to an official report, 60 percent of the nation's rural poor lived in the South in 1977.[28] Another study found that 22 percent of the counties in the South had 25 percent or more of their families living below the poverty line. Of the 295 counties, 284 were in rural areas.[29]

---

[26] Carol L. Jusenius and Larry C. Ledebur, "A Myth in the Making: The Southern Economic Challenge and Northern Economic Decline," November 1976.

[27] In 1975, the federally defined poverty threshold was $5,500 for a non-farm family of four and $4,695 for a farm family of four. See U.S. Bureau of the Census, "Money, Income and Poverty Status in 1975 of Families and Persons in the United States and the Southern Region," Series P-60, No. 112, June 1975.

[28] National Commission for Employment and Unemployment Statistics, "Rural Employment and Unemployment Statistics," Background Paper No. 4, May 1978, p. 3.

[29] Institute for Policy Analysis, "Estimated Children in Poverty for U.S. Counties," June 1978.

Southern States
at a Glance

State	1978 Pop. Estimates *(add 000)*	Increase* Since 1970	Pct. of Pop. in Poverty	Per Capita Income**
Ala.	3,742	8.6%	16.4%	$6,247
Ark.	2,186	13.6	18.5	6,183
Fla.	8,594	26.5	14.4	7,505
Ga.	5,084	10.8	18.0	6,700
Ky.	3,498	8.6	17.7	6,615
La.	3,966	8.8	19.3	6,640
Miss.	2,404	8.4	26.1	5,736
N.C.	5,577	9.7	14.7	6,607
S.C.	2,918	12.6	17.2	6,242
Tenn.	4,357	11.0	15.8	6,489
Texas	13,014	16.2	15.2	7,697
Va.	5,148	10.7	10.5	7,624

*National average: 7.0%
**National average: $7,810

Source: Bureau of the Census; all figures for 1978 except percentages of population in poverty, which are 1975 figures.

The incidence of poverty among Southern blacks is three times as high as that among Southern whites — although in absolute numbers there are more poor whites than poor blacks. In 1978 the median income for black families was just over half (57 percent) as much as for white median families.[30] Some of the South's poorest blacks can be found in the unpainted shacks that dot the Mississippi Delta — the crescent-shaped area of fertile land and Faulknerian novels[31] stretching along the Mississippi River southward from Memphis.

About 60 percent of the Delta's population is black and, according to Mississippi's State Department of Public Welfare, 43.5 percent of the area's inhabitants are on some form of welfare. "When the plantation aristocracy decided to mechanize their farms, it wreaked spectacular havoc throughout the whole system," Tony Dunbar wrote in 1971. "The black tenant farmer and sharecroppers had nothing of their own to fall back on, no alternate sources of employment, no land, no history of diverse occupation." The result, Dunbar said, was "a poverty unparalleled in this country today."[32]

---

[30] National Urban League, "The State of Black America," 1980.
[31] William Faulkner lived at Oxford, Miss., at the edge of the Delta. Greenville, Miss., in the heart of the Delta, was the boyhood home of Walker Percy, one of today's leading Southern novelists.
[32] Tony Dunbar, *Our Land Too* (1971), p. 214.

**Educational Attainment of Persons
25 and Older, 1970-75**

	1970		1975	
All Races	**U.S.**	**South**	**U.S.**	**South**
8th grade or less	27.7%	33.3%	21.9%	27.8%
Some high school	17.1	18.1	15.6	16.5
High school graduate	34.0	29.0	36.2	31.7
Some post high				
school education	21.2	19.6	38.6	24.0

Columns may not add to 100 due to rounding

Source: Southern Growth Policies Board

Large pockets of poverty also remain in Appalachia. Congress in 1965 approved an aid and development program for this mountainous region stretching across 13 states, most of them southern.[33] Some 2.7 million of the 19 million inhabitants live in poverty, according to the Appalachian Regional Commission. In only six of the region's 397 counties was average per capita income above the national average in 1978. Recent evidence suggests, however, that Appalachia is slowly turning itself around. By the late 1970s its poverty population had decreased to about 14 percent, down from 31 percent in 1960. Between 1965 and 1976 per capita income climbed from 78 percent to 85 percent of the national average. Perhaps the most telling indication of an economic turnaround was the reversal of out-migration. In the 1970s there was a net increase of people coming — or coming back — to the Appalachian region.[34]

Labor's Struggle to Make Bigger Inroads

Although income growth in the South outpaced the national average in the 1970s, it still remained below national levels.[35] One reason is that the South remains the least unionized region in the United States.[36] About 29 percent of the nation's workers are members of unions or employee associations, according to the Department of Labor. But in the 12 southern states the percentages are much lower. They range from a high of 29 percent in Kentucky to just 10 percent in North and South Carolina. Between 1963 and 1974 union membership declined in all the southern states except Georgia, Alabama and South Carolina.

---

[33] The Appalachian region designated by Congress includes all of West Virginia and parts of Alabama, Georgia, Kentucky, Maryland, Mississippi, New York, North Carolina, Ohio, Pennsylvania, South Carolina, Tennessee and Virginia.

[34] Figures quoted by Doris Deakin in "Appalachia — On the Way," *Appalachia,* March-April 1979, pp. 1-12. *Appalachia* is published by the Appalachian Regional Commission, an agency set up by the 1965 legislation.

[35] The regional per capita income for the South in 1977 ($6,217) was 89.6 percent of the national average ($7,019), according to the Southern Growth Policies Board. For 1978 comparisons, see table *(opposite page).*

[36] See "Labor's Southern Strategy," *E.R.R.,* 1978 Vol. I, pp. 221-240.

In recent years organized labor has been trying to turn this trend around. It has focused especially on the textile industry, one of the least organized segments of the economy. Of the 700,000 textile workers in the South, only about 10 percent are union members. Textile workers also are among the lowest paid in the country, according to Sol Stettin, president of the Amalgamated Clothing and Textile Workers Union.

A primary target of labor's southern organizing campaign is J. P. Stevens, the New York-based textile company which employs 45,000 workers at 85 plants in the South, most of them in the Carolinas. Only Burlington is larger. Stevens has managed to delay bargaining with textile unions for years despite representation election results, orders from the National Labor Relations Board and findings of unfair labor practices. Labor's persistence was illuminated by George Meany, the late president of the AFL-CIO, in a television interview in 1977. "I think if we crack J. P. Stevens in the South, quite a few other firms will come along," Meany said.

Changing Southern Politics

NOT SINCE the creation of the American nation 200 years ago, through the skillful negotiations and writings of such Southerners as Thomas Jefferson and James Madison, have Southerners been so influential as they are this summer," Reg Murphy wrote in 1976, shortly after Jimmy Carter won the democratic presidential nomination. Carter's nomination (and subsequent election) was seen as a symbol of the South's return to good grace. Discussions of Carter's rural Southern background frequently dominated press coverage of the 1976 election. Four years later, as Carter seeks renomination for another term, his background is not a significant issue. In fact, three of the Republican presidential hopefuls are from the South. John Connally of Texas and Howard Baker of Tennessee are native-born and George Bush, though a son of New England, has lived most of his adult life in Texas.

Black Voters and 'New Breed' Politicians

Of all the changes that have transformed the South, the mounting political power of blacks is perhaps most striking. In 1960, 61 percent of the voting-age whites in the South and 29 percent of the blacks were registered to vote.[37] By 1976 the

---

[37] These figures, provided by the Voter Education Project in Atlanta, do not include voter registration in Kentucky.

percentages were 68 (white) and 63 (black). In Mississippi, the black registration rate had risen from 5 to 61 percent, while in Georgia it was greater (75 percent) than white registration (66 percent).

"It used to be Southern politics was just 'nigger' politics — a question of which candidate could 'outnigger' the other," civil rights leader Andrew Young said in 1976. "Then you registered 10 percent to 15 percent in the community, and folks would start saying 'Nigra.' Later you got 35 percent to 40 percent registered, and it was amazing how quick they learned to say 'Nee-grow.' And now that we've got 50 percent, 60 percent, 70 percent, of the black votes registered in the South, everybody's proud to be associated with their black brothers and sisters."[38]

"I say to you quite frankly that the time for racial discrimination is over."

Gov. Jimmy Carter
Inaugural Address, 1971

The Voting Rights Act of 1965 is credited with bringing about this change. The 1965 law suspended literacy tests and other qualification devices in states where less than 50 percent of the population of voting age had been registered by Nov. 1, 1964. It also provided for the appointment of federal examiners with authority to register voters in areas covered by the legislation.[39]

Southern politicians quickly recognized and responded to the change. With the help of newly registered blacks, a group of moderate Southern governors was elected in the early 1970s — among them Dale Bumpers of Arkansas, Reubin Askew of Florida and Jimmy Carter of Georgia, all Democrats, and Linwood Holton of Virginia, a Republican. "I say to you quite frankly that the time for racial discrimination is over," Carter said in his January 1971 inaugural address. "Our people have already made this major and difficult decision."

That first generation of "new breed" governors has since spawned a second: Forrest (Fob) James of Alabama, Lamar Al-

---

[38] Quoted in *Time*, Sept. 27, 1976, p. 40. Young, then a congressman from Atlanta, campaigned for Carter and became his ambassador to the United Nations.
[39] The areas affected were Alabama, Georgia, Louisiana, Mississippi, South Carolina, Virginia, 39 counties in North Carolina, one county in Arizona and one county in Hawaii.

exander of Tennessee, William Winter of Mississippi, Richard W. Riley of South Carolina, Robert Graham of Florida and Bill Clinton of Arkansas. All except Alexander are Democrats. "Many of those white moderate contenders ... might never have gotten into politics at all before the black vote began to 'open up' the political process in the region," observed Neal Peirce.[40]

But what about those who long had been associated with the race-baiting politics of the past? They, too, have responded to the South's vastly expanded and changed electorate. Gov. George C. Wallace of Alabama first took the oath of office as governor in 1963 proclaiming: "Segregation now, segregation tomorrow, segregation forever." When he took the oath again 12 years later, he pledged: "The people in government in this state are concerned with all our citizens, whether they be black or white. It shall continue this way." Sen. Strom Thurmond, R-S.C., like Wallace, had a national reputation as a diehard segregationist. In the early 1970s, however, Thurmond started hiring black staff members and making his constituency services available to black South Carolinians.

Southern Blacks Holding Elective Offices

The growth of black voting in the South has been accompanied by a rising number of blacks seeking and winning elective office. Fewer than 25 blacks held elective office in 1962 and fewer than 250 in 1968. The number had increased to 1,457 in April 1974; by July 1979 there were 2,332 black elected officials in 12 southern states *(see box, opposite)*. According to the 1979 edition of the *National Roster of Black Elected Officials,* published by the Joint Center for Political Studies, a Washington research group, these officials account for over half of all black elected officials in the nation, 37 percent of all black state legislators, 52 percent of all black municipal officials, 45 percent of all black judicial and law enforcement officials, and 48 percent of all black education officials.

When Richard Arrington took office as mayor of Birmingham last November, he became the fourth black mayor of a big Southern city, joining Maynard Jackson of Atlanta, Ernest Morial of New Orleans and Henry Marsh of Richmond. Tennessee is now the only state of the old Confederacy that does not have at least one elected black mayor. Maynard Jackson in 1973 became the first black to become the chief executive of a major Southern city. Four years later, Atlanta voters returned Jackson to office in a landslide victory made possible by significant bi-racial support.

---

[40] Peirce, *op. cit.,* p. 23.

Black Elected Officials in the South

	July 1979	April 1974
Alabama	208	149
Arkansas	226	150
Florida	91	73
Georgia	237	137
Kentucky	76	59
Louisiana	334	149
Mississippi	327	191
North Carolina	240	159
South Carolina	222	116
Tennessee	109	87
Texas	174	124
Virginia	88	63
Total	2,332	1,457

Source: Joint Center for Political Studies

Jackson lost the distinction of being the black elected official with the largest constituency in the South when Ernest Morial was elected mayor of New Orleans in November 1977. Morial received 20 percent of the white vote. Black voters then accounted for about 43 percent of the city's electorate. At least 10 percent of Richard Arrington's votes came from whites, despite pre-election predictions that Birmingham's 55 percent white majority would line up solidly behind Arrington's opponent, lawyer-businessman Frank Parson. The South's improved racial climate extends beyond the big cities. Thebaud Jeffers, the black mayor of Gastonia, N.C., a small mill town that is 85 percent white, was returned to office with 62 percent of the vote against two white opponents.

Despite their recent political gains, blacks remain grossly underrepresented in Southern politics as in national politics. In Mississippi, for example, blacks make up almost 37 percent of the population, but only 10 percent of the state legislature. However, these numbers compare favorably with the nation as a whole. Overall, blacks hold only 1 percent of the elective posts. Charles V. Hamilton, professor of government at Syracuse University, predicts that in the 1980s "the Southern states will provide the most fertile ground for developing black electoral politics, linking local action with national politics."[41]

Louis Martin, a longtime Democratic Party activist who was an adviser to Presidents Kennedy and Johnson, believes there is "a new breed of black politician in the South. He's not just interested in electing blacks; he's interested in which white per-

[41] Quoted in *Ebony*, January 1980, p. 36.

sons get elected and in working with them." A similar observation was made by John Lewis, a leading black activist of the 1960s as chairman of the Student Non-Violent Coordinating Committee and now associate director of ACTION, a federal anti-poverty agency: "You go to New York City or Chicago or Detroit . . . and you don't see the interaction between blacks and whites that goes on now among Southern politicians . . . I have a greater sense of hope and optimism about the Southern states than about any other part of the country."[42]

Breakup of Once-Solid Democratic South

The Republican Party was dormant in the South from the end of Reconstruction until recent decades. On the presidential level, the Republicans have done well in the South since 1952, when Florida, Tennessee, Texas and Virginia voted for Dwight D. Eisenhower. Barry Goldwater in 1964 got virtually unanimous support from the Southern delegates to the Republican National Convention and then went on to capture Alabama, Georgia, Louisiana, Mississippi and South Carolina.

In 1968 the South divided its electoral votes between Richard M. Nixon and George C. Wallace, who ran as the candidate of his own American Independent Party. Wallace took Alabama, Arkansas, Georgia, Louisiana and Mississippi; Nixon carried the seven other Southern states. Nixon's "Southern strategy" — his pledge to various Southern politicians that he would ease up on federal pressures forcing school desegregation — served him better in 1972. By runaway margins, Nixon took the 11 states of the old Confederacy plus all the border states. It was the first Republican sweep of the South since Reconstruction.

Republican gains have been slower to materialize at lower levels, but in 1978 three conservative Republican senators — John Tower of Texas, Strom Thurmond of South Carolina and Jesse Helms of North Carolina — won re-election over strong challengers who received help from President Carter. For the first time since the post-Civil War period, Mississippi elected a Republican senator (Thad Cochran) and Texas a Republican governor (William Clements). A year later, in December 1979, Louisiana also elected its first Republican governor since Reconstruction (David C. Treen).

It is still too soon to tell whether those Republican victories in the South foreshadow greater Republican gains in November. But they do emphasize the rebirth of the two-party system in the once solid South and are further proof that politicians like other Americans can no longer afford to take the South for granted.

---

[42] Martin and Lewis were quoted by Jack Nelson of the *Los Angeles Times,* June 3, 1979.

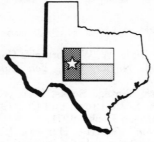

Texas
the
Superstate

For many people Texas remains the quintessential American state. Perhaps it is because the state is too big, too diverse, "too much of a world of its own," as John Gunther wrote in *Inside U.S.A.*, to be categorized as belonging to one region or another.

Texas lies in the center of the "Sun Belt," the southern rim of states running from Virginia to Southern California. Like the other Sun Belt states, Texas has experienced an unprecedented influx of people and industry in recent years. Since 1960 the state's population has grown by about 36 percent, to over 13 million. Reapportionment after the 1980 census is expected to give Texas two additional seats in the U.S. House of Representatives.*

Houston, the ultimate boom town, is now the fifth largest city in the nation, with a population in excess of 1.5 million. Of the 500 largest corporations in the United States, as listed by *Fortune* magazine, 18 have headquarters in Houston or Dallas. Oil and associated service industries have contributed greatly to urban growth in the state. Equally important, however, have been high technology industries such as electronics, semiconductors and aerospace.

Even with its large cities and thriving industries, Texas still somehow seems a rural state, with many small farming towns with names like Muleshoe, Kerrville, Sweetwater, Ozona and Levelland. Texas remains by far the biggest livestock-producing state in the nation. But the character of the beef industry has been changing, especially in the Panhandle region.

Since the early 1960s, traditional cow-calf ranches have given way to stocker operations that import yearling calves from other regions — East Texas, Louisiana, Alabama, Florida, Georgia — where more rain falls and grasses grow lusher. Stocker ranches keep the calves through the winter, fattening them by 200 pounds or so, then selling them to feedlots clustered around Amarillo. There they are prepared for market on grain sorghums grown on the High Plains.

The residents of Texas have not shared equally in the state's new wealth. About one-sixth of the population lives below the poverty line. Poverty is especially prevalent among the state's Mexican-Americans, who account for at least 18 percent of the population.

* All the gains are projected for Southern and Western states. The Census Bureau expects added seats for Arizona (1), California (2), Colorado (1), Florida (3), New Mexico (1), Oregon (1), Tennessee (1), Texas (2), Utah (1) and Washington (1).

Selected Bibliography

Books

Ashmore, Harry S., *An Epitaph for Dixie*, W. W. Norton & Co., 1957.

Ayers, H. Brandt and Thomas H. Naylor, eds., *You Can't Eat Magnolias*, McGraw-Hill, 1972.

Cash, W. J., *The Mind of the South*, Vintage Books, 1941.

Cole, Robert, *Farewell to the South*, Little Brown and Co., 1972.

Dunbar, Tony, *Our Land Too*, Pantheon Books, 1971.

Egerton, John, *The Americanization of Dixie*, Harper's Magazine Press, 1974.

Gunther, John, *Inside U.S.A.*, Harper & Brothers, 1947.

Key, V. O. Jr., *Southern Politics*, Vintage Books, 1949.

Kirby, Jack Temple, *Media-Made Dixie*, Louisiana State University Press, 1978.

Peirce, Neal R., *The Border South States*, W. W. Norton & Co., 1975.

——*The Deep South States*, W. W. Norton & Co., 1974.

Reed, John Shelton, *The Enduring South*, Lexington Books, 1972.

Watters, Pat, *The South and the Nation*, Pantheon Books, 1969.

Woodward, C. Vann, *The Burden of Southern History*, Louisiana State University Press, 1960.

Articles

Breckenfeld, Gurney, "Business Loves the Sunbelt (and Vice Versa)," *Fortune*, June 1977.

Harris, Ron, "The Myth of the 'New South,' " *Ebony*, February 1979.

Matthews, Tom, "The Southern Mystique," *Newsweek*, July 19, 1976.

Percy, Walker, "Southern Comfort," *Harper's*, January 1979.

Proffitt, Nicholas, "Texas: The Superstate," *Newsweek*, Dec. 12, 1977.

"The Ku Klux Klan," *Ebony*, October 1979.

"The New Rich South: Frontier for Growth," *Business Week*, Sept. 2, 1972.

"The New South: Pushing Forward on all Fronts," *U.S. News & World Report*, Aug. 2, 1976.

"The Second War Between the States," *Business Week*, May 17, 1976.

"The South as the New America," *Saturday Review*, Sept. 4, 1976.

"The South Today," *Time*, Sept. 27, 1976.

Reports and Studies

Commission on the Future of the South, "The Future of the South," report to the Southern Growth Policies Board, November 1974.

Editorial Research Reports: "Labor's Southern Strategy," 1978 Vol. I, p. 221; "Resurgence of Regionalism," 1977 Vol. I, p. 143; "Minority Voting Rights," 1975 Vol. I, p. 141; "Changing Southern Politics," 1966 Vol. I, p. 41; "Changing South," 1959 Vol. I, p. 421.

Southern Growth Policies Board, "A Profile of the Southern States," December 1978.

——"Small Cities and Rural Communities in the South: An Analysis of Recent Trends and Policy Needs," November 1979.

——"Southern Urban Trends 1960-1977," December 1978.

ROCKY MOUNTAIN WEST: AN UNFINISHED COUNTRY

by

Tom Arrandale

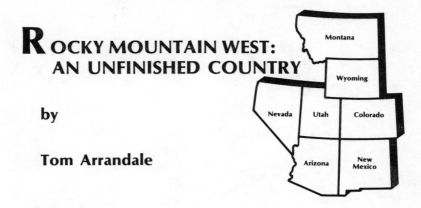

**Mar. 14
1 9 8 0**

ROCKY MOUNTAIN WEST

T HE Rocky Mountain West remains a raw, empty land 90 years after the frontier era ended.[1] Western communities lie hundreds of miles apart, all but lost in the boundless sweep of granite mountain facades, rolling sagebrush plains and barren deserts. For the West has never filled up with the farms, cities and towns that cover long-settled coastal and prairie regions. It remains an unfulfilled land, economically and culturally unfinished. The wide open spaces set the West apart — and give the mountain states of Montana, Wyoming, Colorado, Utah, Nevada, New Mexico and Arizona both promise and problems that are much different from more crowded parts of the country.

"Emotionally, the West retains its image as the future of America," University of Wyoming historian Gene M. Gressley has observed.[2] The Northeast, Midwest and California now contend with decaying cities, sagging economies and environmental damage. But the Rocky Mountain West, even after three decades of fast growth, remains hopeful that it can preserve its matchless scenery, clear air and easy-going life. "The West feels it has time to avoid a lot of mistakes," said Louis D. Higgs, executive director of the Four Corners Regional Commission. "We're not playing catch-up football like the East."

Wild horses still roam through Wyoming's Red Desert and Nevada's sagebrush plains. Deer and antelope are still plentiful on Montana and New Mexico plains, and bighorn sheep scramble up Colorado, Utah and Arizona mountains. Cowboys still round cattle up in the spring, and herders drive sheep to mountain meadows. The Rocky Mountains still hold a wild, frontier flavor, long vanished from other regions. For most Westerners, many of them recent migrants from other states, the West remains a good place to live because it is different from other parts of the country.

The snowy mountains against the big brilliant sky remain as alluring to Americans today as to 19th century trappers, explorers and settlers. Since World War II, Americans have been mov-

---

[1] Historian Frederick Jackson Turner, in an 1893 essay, "The Significance of the Frontier in American History," concluded that the expansion onto the western frontier had been completed. He based his study on the 1890 census; the census director reported that settlers had reached the farthest extent of the nation's western territories.

[2] Gene M. Gressley, "Regionalism and the Twentieth Century West," in *The American West, New Perspectives, New Dimensions* (1979), p. 197; Jerome O. Steffen, ed.

ing west in growing numbers to live in the mountains and deserts. Cow towns, railroad depots and health resorts have grown into vibrant cities. And the region has begun to shake off its historic role as a distant, inhospitable colony supplying resources to the rest of the nation. "Once termed 'the great American desert,' these states are now becoming the most desirable locations in which to live and work," proclaimed a 1979 Hudson Institute study of Arizona's future. "Arizona may indeed be a development prototype for post-industrial society."[3]

With roughly 10 million people, less than the New York metropolitan population, the Rocky Mountain states would seem to have plenty of room for expansion. But in fact the West is already approaching hard choices on how to divide up its land. Except for the high, snow-capped mountains — and the narrow, sometimes dry, rivers that carry melting snows off to distant seas — most of the region's 780,000 square miles are chronically short of water. The nation's drive to tap huge coal, uranium, oil shale and other energy reserves causes fear of ecological damage and the onset of a boom-and-bust cycle. "Once distance, space and remoteness were our economic curse," Montana historian Ross Toole points out. "Now they are our economic blessing. What awesome irony and tragedy it would be if we were to turn our curse into a blessing only to turn it again into a curse."[4]

Prevailing West-Against-Rest Mentality

When 1980 primary campaigns move westward,[5] the candidates will find the Rocky Mountain West increasingly at odds with the rest of the country. The customary Western concerns about land, water and mineral development still dominate Rocky Mountain politics. More than ever, Westerners resent the power that outsiders wield over their future. And President Carter's land and water policies of the last three years have convinced many that the federal government neither understands nor cares about western conditions. Western tempers have flared in response, and the West has replaced the Deep South as the region most alienated from the rest of the country. "A new Mason-Dixon line is being drawn at the 100th meridian," Colorado Gov. Richard D. Lamm has warned.[6]

The true West begins at the 100th meridian, the longitudinal benchmark running north-south from the Dakotas down through the Texas Panhandle. West of the line, average rainfall dwindles

[3] Paul Bracken, with contributions by Herman Kahn, "Arizona Tomorrow," prepared by the Hudson Institute for Arizona Tomorrow Inc., 1979.

[4] Quoted by Wallace and Page Stegner, "Rocky Mountain Country," *Atlantic*, April 1978, p. 45.

[5] Wyoming caucuses are held during March; Arizona caucuses (for Democrats only) follow on April 12; Colorado caucuses on May 5 and Utah caucuses on May 19; Nevada holds its primary May 27, followed by Montana and New Mexico June 3.

[6] Quoted in "The Angry West vs. the Rest," *Newsweek*, Sept. 17, 1979, p. 31.

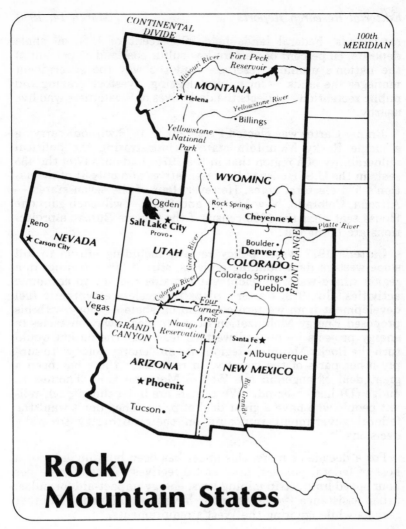

Rocky Mountain States

below 20 inches a year, except on mountain formations. The Rocky Mountain states are actually part mountain, part plains, part desert basin and plateau. But all are several thousand feet above sea level, in contrast to the humid East and the Pacific slope.

Historically, western resource development has been controlled by faraway corporate boardrooms — in New York, San Francisco, even London. They financed railroads, mines and huge cattle ranches. Now, the West's fate more and more is determined in Washington, D.C., in the halls of Congress and the federal agencies that manage the government's vast western land holdings. The federal government owns about half the land in the West, in national parks, wilderness, forests and public

53

rangelands. Federal lands hold 80 percent of U.S. oil shale deposits, 60 percent of western low-sulfur coal and 35 percent of the nation's uranium reserves. And the way the government manages the lands — for mining, logging, livestock grazing and public recreation — affects the daily lives of Westerners who live nearby.

Jimmy Carter was elected President in 1976 without carrying a single Rocky Mountain state, demonstrating the political vulnerability of a region that in the 1970s had only 17 of the 435 seats in the U.S. House of Representatives and only 31 of the nation's 535 electoral votes. However, four of the seven states — Arizona, Colorado, New Mexico and Utah — will each gain one House seat after the 1980 census if the Census Bureau's projections are borne out.

Carter's 1977 water policy review, including efforts to kill some western dam-building projects, stirred bitter feelings in a region where water development remains the key to economic activities.[7] In 1979, Carter's plans to accelerate synthetic fuel development from western coal and oil shale — along with his proposed Energy Mobilization Board to clear away obstacles to energy projects — revived western fear that the nation would turn the Rocky Mountain region into an "energy colony" to supply other parts of the country. In response, "there has been a great deal of anger in the West," Montana Gov. Thomas L. Judge (D) has observed. "Westerners are independent, self-reliant people who have a great deal of pride. They don't want the federal government imposing on their authority to make decisions."[8]

For a decade or more, this anger has been building against a host of federal policies, laws and directives — the 55 mile per hour speed limit, strip mining laws, energy impact-aid formulas, urban assistance — that they feel have been tailored to fit other regions while ignoring the West's requirements.

'Sagebrush Rebellion' Over Federal Land

That long-building anger broke out in 1979 in Nevada's "Sagebrush Rebellion" against the Interior Department's Bureau of Land Management. BLM, the agency that manages 174 million acres of federally owned lands in 11 western states,[9] had long been staffed mainly by western natives sympathetic to the ranchers and miners who used public lands. Since the early 1960s, in response to an environmental movement based mainly in the East and on the West Coast, the agency has been operat-

---

[7] See "Western Water: Coming Crisis," *E.R.R.*, 1977 Vol. I, pp. 21-40, and "Western Land Policy," *E.R.R.*, 1978 Vol. I, pp. 81-100.

[8] Interview on ABC-TV's "Good Morning America," Sept. 13, 1979.

[9] Arizona, California, Colorado, Idaho, Montana, Nevada, New Mexico, Oregon, Utah, Washington and Wyoming.

Land in Federal Ownership

State	Area (sq. mi.)	Federally Owned	State	Area (sq. mi.)	Federally Owned
Ariz.	113,417	42.8%	Nev.	108,889	86.6%
Colo.	103,766	36.1	N.M.	121,412	33.6
Mont.	145,587	29.7	Utah	82,096	66.1
			Wyo.	98,203	47.8

Source: Bureau of Land Management

ing under congressional mandates to toughen its control over public rangelands. BLM's budget and staff have increased, and "many of the best natural resource students from the Earth Day era ended up employed by the BLM," Utah State University Professor Bernard Shanks has said.[10]

As a result of these changes, ranchers who graze livestock on public lands now must contend with grazing fee increases, BLM directives as to where sheep and cattle may be placed, and 144 court-ordered environmental impact statements bearing on overgrazed lands. Mining engineers and oil-well drillers also are faced with the agency's regulations to protect archeological sites, lessen soil disturbances and preserve wildlife habitats. Conflicts inevitably have risen. "If things continue in the pattern of the last 10 years, it's now a matter of having to stand and fight," Idaho State Senator Larry Craig maintains.

The Nevada Legislature enacted a law asserting state control over the 49 million acres that BLM manages in the state. The law's proponents argued that Congress, by forcing Nevada to give up any claim to federal lands in order to achieve statehood, violated the constitutional requirement that all states enter the Union on an equal basis. Nevada officials are seeking a U.S. Supreme Court test, but Interior Department attorneys profess to find little merit in the state's position. Nor is Congress likely to give up energy-rich western lands. BLM Director Frank Gregg suggests that the ownership debate is diverting attention from "the real issue, which is how to manage the land, and what kind of management system can best respond to the needs of the West itself."

Western environmental groups, which typically have more influence with federal agencies than with state governments, dismiss the rebellion as a "sagebrush rip-off" by selfish interests. They maintain that state land offices cannot properly manage environmentally sensitive range, and note that state constitutions tend to require state lands be managed to achieve the

---

[10] Bernard Shanks, "BLM Back in the Spotlight After Years of Neglect," *High Country News*, Jan. 26, 1979.

highest possible profit. "It would be a financial catastrophe to Nevada if the sagebrush rebellion were successful," contends Nevada State Sen. Cliff Young, one of three senators to vote against the measure.

Philip M. Burgess, executive director of the Western Governors Policy Office in Denver, terms the sagebrush rebellion "probably a huge misstep — in the right direction." For the rebellion at least has called national attention to the impact of federal land ownership on state economies. Nevada, with 87 percent of its land in federal hands, has been trying to diversify its gambling-based economy with mineral and agricultural development. But many Nevada towns, even Las Vegas, are surrounded by BLM holdings.

The West itself is divided over the sagebrush rebellion — and a host of public land issues such as wilderness preservation and wildlife protection. Rapidly growing western cities are edging out toward federal lands, and their residents more and more make use of federally owned parks, forests and rangelands for camping, hiking, rock-hounding and motorbiking. "There's a certain freedom we have in the fact that the federal government owns those lands," Young said.

Demands for access to public lands are sure to grow as western cities keep growing. All the while environmental groups are gaining strength in western cities as newcomers join efforts to preserve the natural surroundings that drew many from other regions. James W. Curlin, deputy assistant to the secretary of the interior, told a group of New Mexico environmentalists in January: "It's the raw backwoods West vs. the more urbane cities."

The Urban Oasis Civilization

MAN'S PRESENCE still seems impermanent over much of the western landscape. Crumbling adobe walls, caving mine shafts, rusting windmills and rotting stage station timbers all testify to how tenuous settlement has been. Wyoming, with roughly four persons per square mile, is the emptiest state except Alaska. Wyoming has no cities classified by the Census Bureau as metropolitan — a city of 50,000 people or more and its environs. Cheyenne, the capital and the state's largest city, is now at the 50,000 mark. Montana has no cities of 100,000, and all other Rocky Mountain states have large sections where few people live. Authors Wallace and Page Stegner, father and son, observe that "much of Utah is almost as empty as it ever was."[11]

[11] "Rocky Mountain Country," *op. cit.,* p. 75.

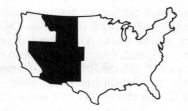

Population Growth and Urbanization

State	1979 Pop. (est.) (add 000)	Gain Since 1970*	Metropolitan Population**
Arizona	2,450	38.0%	74.5%
Colorado	2,772	25.5	80.6
Montana	786	13.2	24.4
Nevada	702	43.6	80.9
New Mexico	1,241	22.1	33.6
Utah	1,367	29.0	78.8
Wyoming	450	35.3	0.0

*National average: 8.3%
**For 1976

Source: Bureau of the Census

Together, the Rocky Mountain states average less than 12 persons per square mile, according to 1977 population estimates, roughly one-fifth of the national population density of 61.2. But Walter Prescott Webb, the late University of Texas historian, observed nearly a quarter-century ago, "One of the paradoxes of the West is that with its excess of land and dearth of people, it is already an urban society." In Webb's view, "the West is today [1957] virtually an oasis civilization." It is built around burgeoning cities where water is siphoned from rivers, underground wells or impoundments, often at great distances, in the midst of a predominantly desert region.[12]

The oasis pattern steadily grows more evident. Not only is the West growing rapidly but in Colorado, Arizona, Utah and Nevada, three-fourths of the people are concentrated in metropolitan areas *(see box, above)*. Since 1950, more than 1,250,000 have moved into Colorado's Front Range area stretching south from the Wyoming border through Denver to Colorado Springs and Pueblo. Eighty-one percent of the state's population lives in this corridor, roughly 50 miles wide and 200 miles long. Another 1,250,000 are expected to arrive in the next 20 years.

---

[12] Walter Prescott Webb, "The American West, Perpetual Mirage," *Harper's* magazine, May 1957, p. 25.

Denver has emerged as a regional center for transportation, communications, trade and high-technology industries. More than 2,000 energy-related companies make the Front Range their headquarters for developing oil, gas, uranium, coal and oil-shale resources throughout the Rocky Mountain region.·Phoenix has experienced similar growth, mushrooming from a city of 80,000 at the end of World War II into the center of a metropolitan area of more than 1.2 million. Tucson, whose population stood at 40,000 in 1945, now is the center of an area approaching 500,000. Albuquerque in 35 years has grown from 50,000 to nearly 400,000. And in Utah, more than three-quarters of the state's 1.2-million residents live within 45 miles of Salt Lake City's Mormon Temple Square in an urbanized strip extending from Ogden south to Provo between the Wasatch Mountains and the Great Salt Lake. Since World War II, Reno and Las Vegas, Nev., have become gambling-based tourist centers.

Energy-Related Jobs and Sun Belt's Lure

The development of Western energy reserves is accelerating the growth of Rocky Mountain cities, especially Denver. Gulf, Texaco and Standard Oil Co. of California, among other energy-producing companies, have set up offices in Denver as they prepare to tap oil and gas from Utah and Wyoming's Overthrust Belt, coal from New Mexico's Four Corners area and Wyoming's Powder River Basin, oil shale from the Piceance Creek Basin of northwestern Colorado, and uranium from the Four Corners and Wyoming's Red Desert. A Colorado Energy Research Institute study in 1979 calculated that there were 28,000 energy-related jobs in the Denver area, including 11,000 that had been created since 1970.[13]

Important though they are, energy companies in the Denver area provided less than a third of the new employment in 1970-78. Tourism was also important to the local economy, while federal and state government offices, light manufacturing and the region's traditional trade and agricultural businesses together contributed substantially to a growing economic base. Such companies as IBM, Hewlett-Packard, Eastman Kodak, Sunbeam, Frito-Lay, Johns Manville and AMAX have opened Denver area plants and offices, and the Front Range has begun to rival the San Francisco Bay area's "Silicon Valley" and Boston's Route 128 as a center for high-technology companies. "The technology companies are here probably because of the amenities and general market growth," observed Denver economist David Bramhall. "They're also here for the skilled labor, and because executives and their wives like to live out here."[14]

---

[13] "Impacts of Energy Resource Development on the Denver Metropolitan Area," June 1979.
[14] Quoted in "More Elbowroom for the Electronics Industry," *Business Week,* March 10, 1979, p. 94.

In Arizona and New Mexico, service industries and clean, light manufacturing are replacing mining and agriculture as economic mainstays. Arizona draws 15 million tourists a year, six times the state's permanent population, and the Phoenix area is swollen by about 100,000 people who live there only part of the year. Affluent older people flock to Arizona to live in posh retirement communities and travel trailer campgrounds. Yet more migrants to Arizona are young, well-educated and well-paid. According to the Hudson Institute report on Arizona, "a picture emerges of men early in their prime years making a decision to move in order to make a new start in their careers and lives."

Downtown Phoenix

As they grow, western cities are shaking off their cow-town image. In January, Denver opened a $13-million theater complex as part of the new Denver Center for the Performing Arts. Congresswoman Patricia Schroeder, who represents Denver, has said Denver is "becoming much more sophisticated almost hourly. . . . We're becoming a major cosmopolitan city." Denver and Salt Lake City support symphony orchestras, and Salt Lake City boasts of two professional dance companies. In Albuquerque, growth has meant "a richer cultural life," said Mayor David Rusk, son of former Secretary of State Dean Rusk.

Old West in Time of Change

NO OTHER region lies as close to its past as the Rocky Mountain West. Much of it has been settled for only three or four generations. In the last 30 years, electric power lines, telephones and even television signals have penetrated into remote mountain valleys, desert ranches and Indian reservations. Pickup trucks, many equipped with citizen band radios, have brought families in closer touch with neighbors and isolated towns. Yet many Westerners — ranchers, farmers, Indians, small-town merchants — live much the same way that their parents, grandparents and even great-grandparents did.

Continuity has nurtured conservatism, a fundamentalist belief in the old self-reliant ways. The Old West romance of gunfights, saloon brawls and cowboys riding off into the sunset was perhaps more a product of eastern imagination than of western reality. But the underlying attitudes — independence, determination, a constant battle with the land and elements — remains valid to this day. Now, however, the old values are encountering new challenges.

Ranching's Old Values, New Uncertainty

No occupation has been more emblematic of the West — and perhaps indeed of the whole country — than that of ranching. The huge 19th century cattle spreads were long ago broken up, and livestock raising in recent years was often identified with tax shelters for oilmen and other absentee owners. But throughout the Rocky Mountain states, cattle and sheep ranching remains a family occupation, with fathers and sons sharing the work of branding, round-ups and wool shearing. For many, the Stegners wrote, "ranching is both a business and a way of life — the most authentic and cherished way of life that has developed in the West."

But traditional western ranching is a risky venture. Beef, lamb and wool markets are volatile, while the cost of labor, vaccines, supplemental feed and equipment has climbed upward. A rancher who runs 150 cows and their calves could clear $20,000 one year and less than half that two years later. In *The Last Cowboy,* a study of Texas Panhandle ranching first published in *The New Yorker,* Jane Kramer noted that "Ranching lately had less to do with an individual's adventure with a herd of cattle than with that global network of dependencies and contingencies that people had taken to calling 'agribusiness.' "[15]

In Texas, still the leading beef-producing state, Panhandle ranchers now import calves from East Texas and the southeastern states for fattening and then sale to Amarillo feedlots. Farther west in the Rocky Mountain states, most ranchers still run traditional cow-calf operations; they maintain a basic herd of cows and sell their calves to feedlots. But in the last few decades western ranchers have faced increasing competition from the Southeast, where heavier rainfall produces lush grass that supports more cattle per acre. In 1978, Florida produced more beef than any Rocky Mountain state except Montana; Georgia, Alabama and Louisiana ranked as high as the traditional ranching states of New Mexico, Utah and Wyoming.

Rocky Mountain ranchers depend heavily on obtaining grazing rights on national forest and BLM public range lands. Much

---

[15] Jane Kramer, *The Last Cowboy* (1977), p. 48.

of those lands, overgrazed in the past, have been declining in forage production. But when the BLM tries to reduce grazing, the agency encounters resistance from ranchers. Montana and Wyoming ranchers feel threatened by the strip mining of coal from beneath the grazing lands. Some sell their ranches and leave, but others resist and even form Sierra Club chapters in the fight to preserve the land. In the long run, however, traditional ranching seems destined to vanish gradually as older men retire and die. Their sons quite often are unwilling to take over the operations. "Strictly on economics, they have 50 years left," predicts Brant Calkin, the Sierra Club's Southwest representative. "It's not something I wish, but they're [doomed] just like buggy whips."

Western farmers also face an uncertain future mainly because water is so critical in a region where rainfall is minimal. Western agriculture generally is limited to a relatively few areas where rivers, federally financed reservoirs and underground water aquifers provide a dependable water source for irrigation. Carter's water policies make it clear to Rocky Mountain farmers that the era of expensive federal dam-building projects to store water for irrigation is coming to an end. In the meantime, groundwater irrigation may be ebbing as underground water tables drop, pumping costs rise, and cities expand onto surrounding farmland.

On the Texas High Plains, intensive irrigation since World War II has been mining the Ogallala Aquifer groundwater resource that rainfall cannot replenish. In central Arizona, where irrigated agriculture accounts for 89 percent of water consumption, the growth of Phoenix and Tucson is increasing competition for limited surface and groundwater supplies. Farther north, "Colorado is rapidly approaching an agricultural crossroads," a state Department of Agriculture study declared in 1979. Groundwater reserves are declining on the state's eastern plains and energy projects compete for water on the West Slope, as the western side of the Rocky Mountain range is called.[16]

Mineral Extraction on Indian Reservations

No Westerners face more drastic changes, perhaps, than the region's impoverished Indian tribes. From the Crow and Northern Cheyenne reservations on the Montana plains to the mesas and mountains of the huge Navajo lands in New Mexico, Utah and Arizona, western tribes possess valuable coal, uranium and oil and gas resources that energy companies want to develop. Twenty-five western tribes, members of the Denver-based Council of Energy Resource Tribes (CERT), claim 15 percent of the

---

[16] Colorado Department of Agriculture, *Agricultural Land Conversion in Colorado*, Vol. I, 1979, p. xi.

nation's strippable coal, 4 percent of its known oil and gas reserves and as much as half of the U.S. uranium resources. Peter MacDonald, chairman of both the Navajo Tribal Council and CERT, has said energy-rich tribes "have come to realize that our resources can — if carefully managed — become the foundation for overall economic development for a sector of American society that has been overlooked and underdeveloped for more than 200 years."

Since its formation in 1975, CERT has won $2 million in federal grants to hire economists, lawyers and engineers to advise the tribes so they can negotiate their own deals to develop mineral resources. CERT members now are trying to renegotiate low-paying contracts previously negotiated on their behalf by the federal Bureau of Indian Affairs. Tribal leaders hope that rising energy revenues will provide the economic muscle to bring about independent, self-governing status. "When you think of where the tribes were three years ago, it's almost like a miracle," declared LaDonna Harris, president of Americans for Indian Opportunity.[17]

New Mexico's Acoma Pueblo Indians and the Northern Cheyenne tribe reject energy projects on religious grounds. Many Indian traditionalists fear that coal or uranium mining will scar the lands they revere. Radical Native American groups, allied with white anti-nuclear activists, are protesting uranium mining on Navajo and Pueblo lands in New Mexico. Navajo ranchers say that "Anglo" — white — drilling crews leave debris scattered over rangelands. One company has canceled its plans to build a coal gasification plant on Navajo lands because tribal opposition blocked approval by the tribal council.

Energy revenues may be the Navajos only hope of providing for a tribal population that is expected to double to 300,000 people during the next 20 years. MacDonald wants to set tribal energy funds aside to finance agricultural, craft, tourist and light industrial projects on the 25,000-square-mile reservation. But with unemployment running at 30 percent and the tribal work force growing by 5,000 people a year, "we really have a pretty big job ahead," Navajo economist Al Henderson commented.

Social Problems in Western Boom Towns

The change overtaking the Rocky Mountain West has been most visible and tragic in the small western towns near booming energy fields. Sleepy railroad towns and agricultural trade centers have been overwhelmed by an influx of people who have come to reopen mines, explore for minerals and build power plants. Rock Springs, Wyo., growing rapidly since a power plant

---

[17] Mrs. Harris, a Commanche, is wife of a former U.S. senator, Fred Harris, D-Okla.

was built near the town in the early 1970s, has drawn national attention as a notorious example of the social problems that accompany rapid energy development.

The towns of Craig, Colo., Gillette and Jeffrey City, Wyo., and Grants, N.M., are going through coal or uranium booms that overload schools, sewers and other public services. The northwestern Colorado towns of Meeker, Rifle and Rangely await oil shale development with mixed fear and anticipation. Gene M. Gressley, the Wyoming historian, writes that in energy-impacted areas "a cloud of foreboding has affected the Westerner's belief in the future. He is beginning to have a tremendous feeling of powerlessness."[18]

To some long-time residents, energy development offers a chance for profit and economic improvement that will bring jobs for children who otherwise would be forced to move away. But for many, especially the elderly, the flood of outsiders and the surging local prices disrupt the quiet, familiar life they had always known. Colorado officials have given priority to providing housing for elderly residents who are forced to give up their homes but cannot afford rising rents.

Mormon, Hispanic Concern About Change

As migrants arrive, chances increase for conflict with long-established religious and cultural groups who have dominated parts of the Rocky Mountain region. In rapidly growing Utah, at least 85 prcent of the Salt Lake City residents still are Mormons, members of the Church of Jesus Christ of Latter-day Saints who founded the state and dominate its economy and social structure. But non-Mormons ("gentiles") have been flocking to Utah for mountain scenery, skiing, economic opportunity and the appeal of a low-crime area. Historic bitterness between Mormons and gentiles has disappeared, but secular newcomers may be increasing the opposition to Utah's strict liquor laws and Mormon leaders' conservative views on morals and family life.

In New Mexico, Arizona and southern Colorado, meanwhile, the influx of Anglos from other regions is reducing the once-dominant economic and political power of Hispanics whose ancestors colonized the Southwest nearly 400 years ago. Spanish-speaking domination continues in impoverished and isolated counties of northern New Mexico and southern Colorado. In the cities, young Hispanics are resentful of the affluent Anglo newcomers who seem to reap most of the economic benefits of growth. And many U.S. citizens of Spanish and Mexican descent are concerned by calls for a crackdown on illegal aliens from Mexico now living in the Southwest.

---

[18] Greesley, *op. cit.*, p. 217.

It is not known with any certainty how many Mexican nationals are in this country illegally. The Census Bureau believes the number is below three million and possibly is between 1.5 and 2.5 million, although estimates from other sources tend to run higher. A Census Bureau official notes that most Mexican nationals who enter the country illegally tend to return to Mexico for at least part of the year, and thus are less likely than others to take up permanent residence in the United States. Separate studies indicate that about half of the Mexicans in this country — illegally and legally — are in California and about one-fifth in Texas. Curiously, perhaps, the same studies indicated that there were likely to be more Mexicans in Illinois than in New Mexico, Arizona and Colorado combined.[19]

Shaping a Regional Destiny

A S THE frontier fades, the Rocky Mountain West is bracing for continued rapid change in the last two decades of the century. With the spread of big cities, the miseries of boom towns and a troubled outlook for western agriculture, the region has shifted away from its traditional faith that all-out growth would fulfill its destiny. "Until recently," Greesley observed, "the West assumed that, under the spell of growth . . . all of its major difficulties would be solved by a larger regional economic product. Now the West, in common with the rest of the nation, must select from alternative futures."

In the early 1970s, no-growth sentiment was rife in the Rocky Mountain states. Colorado voters in 1972 rejected the state's plan to hold the 1976 Winter Olympics and in 1974 elected Richard D. Lamm, the leader of the fight against the Olympic Games, as governor on a strong environmentalist platform. Since then, however, Lamm and other regional leaders have shifted back toward positions that acknowledge that growth is inevitable as the nation develops domestic energy supplies and Americans keep moving westward. "I see nothing short of an energy depression that will alleviate our growth rate," Lamm commented in an interview. "Colorado is just a boom state, growing three times [as fast as] the national average. That's highly likely to continue."

Recent Unity Aims of Western Governors

That prospect is spurring the Rocky Mountain states to develop a united front in dealing with federal resource agencies and energy companies. The West's strong individualism and

---

[19] See "Census Taking, 1980," *E.R.R.*, 1980 Vol. I, pp. 144-147.

states' rights philosophy in the past have thwarted most joint regional action, except for New Deal development programs and river compacts that allocated water resources among states. Rocky Mountain congressional delegations, often split evenly between Republicans and Democrats, have had little success in forming a united caucus such as northeastern and midwestern members have developed on regional issues. And during the 1970s, several senior Democrats from the Rocky Mountain states left Congress either in defeat or retirement. The list includes Sen. Mike Mansfield of Montana, the Majority Leader; Rep. Wayne N. Aspinall of Colorado, chairman of the House Interior Committee; and Clinton P. Anderson, a leading congressional advocate of nuclear energy development.

But as the scope of potential energy projects became evident, the governors stepped up efforts to coordinate their responses to development pressures. The governors of the seven Rocky Mountain states, currently all Democrats, in 1977 joined with the governors of Alaska, Nebraska and the Dakotas to form the Western Governors Policy Office (WESTPO) in an attempt to speak with a unified voice on energy development questions. With so much of the region's energy reserves owned by the federal government, U.S. agency decisions on coal leasing, synthetic fuel projects and environmental law waivers could shape the whole region's future.

Gov. Lamm

These 11 states have enjoyed some success toward that end. WESTPO spokesmen opposed giving Carter's proposed energy mobilization board the power to waive state and local environmental laws, and they have urged the administration to take a step-by-step approach to the development of oil shale and other synthetic fuels. State agencies have reached cooperative agreements with BLM state offices that make resource development decisions for federal lands. The Interior Department's new coal leasing procedures give the governors a voice in recommending where, on federal lands, coal should be mined. In a meeting with Carter in 1979, the governors won a pledge from him that the administration's energy planners would not try to override state water laws.

Coping With Urban Expansion, Air Pollution

As the "Sun Belt" migration continues, the Rocky Mountain region will encounter more urban problems of the kind many newcomers have recently fled. Being relatively young, western

Income in the Rockies

Per capita personal income in three of the seven Rocky Mountain states was above the $7,810 national average in 1978, the latest year for which U.S. Commerce Department statistics are available. Wyoming ($9,096), Nevada ($9,032) and Colorado ($8,001) rose above the national average. Arizona ($7,374), Montana ($7,051), Utah ($6,622) and New Mexico ($6,505) fell below that mark.

However, the non-farm income in all seven states rose faster than in the nation as a whole in the five-year span between the last quarter of 1973 and the last quarter of 1978, according to further Commerce Department findings.* The national growth in that time was assigned an index value of 100 points by department statisticians. In relationship to that numerical value, here are how the Mountain States performed:

Wyoming	173	Arizona	117
Nevada	139	Colorado	114
Utah	133	Montana	112
New Mexico	130		

*See *Survey of Current Business*, April 1979, pp. 22-24.

cities have been spared many of the problems of urban decay that the older cities of the Northeast and Midwest have faced for years. But Rocky Mountain cities, like Los Angeles before them, have grown haphazardly, with housing developments leapfrogging across empty desert and farmland, often spreading in thin lines along the interstate highways built since the 1950s. The resulting low-density living, favoring single-family ownership, has maintained a spacious feeling. But it is proving costly: for water and sewer lines and for gasoline in driving to work. And the thin air at high altitudes is susceptible to automobile exhaust pollution.

Denver's air pollution produced 157 "unhealthful" days a year in 1975-77, according to a report issued Feb. 19 by the White House Council on Environmental Quality, more than such industrial cities as Houston (54), Toledo (21) or Jersey City (74). Among 42 cities surveyed, only four — New York (273), Los Angeles (264), Cleveland (225) and Riverside, Calif. (193) — recorded more days in which the governments's air pollution index topped 100. Smog often blocks the view of nearby mountains for which Denver was famous. The federal Environmental Protection Agency on March 1 ordered $300 million in federal funds withheld from Colorado, effective March 14, because the state General Assembly (legislature) missed a thrice-extended federal deadline for enacting an automobile emission inspecting and control program.

Albuquerque, too, has had air-pollution problems. This winter Albuquerque officials asked homeowners to stop using wood stoves; they were adding smoke to auto-polluted air during temperature inversions. Along Utah's Wasatch Front, auto exhaust contributes as much pollution as a nearby copper smelter and steel plant. Southwestern cities that 30 years ago were essentially health resorts now have increasing humidity and pollen counts because newcomers have planted and watered grass, shrubs and trees. Arizona Gov. Bruce Babbitt has asked, "How do you have growth without destroying the values that brought people here in the first place?"

Tucson, Albuquerque and Colorado Springs have annexed surrounding areas as development reached them. But Phoenix and Denver already are surrounded by fast-growing suburban towns. Phoenix Mayor Margaret Hance has pushed "infilling" policies to develop areas within the city that have been passed over. In Colorado, Governor Lamm has launched an ambitious Colorado Front Range Project to help local governments in the 13-county area prepare for the new residents expected in the next two decades.

Visions of a Balanced Regional Economy

As they deal with energy development and urban growth, Rocky Mountain officials remain mindful of the region's boom-and-bust past that left mining towns and regions with no continuing economic base once the mines played out. "The late 1900s are going to look like the late 1800s," Louis D. Higgs remarked. "We'll have all the problems they had in the late 19th century but were ignored. Back then, the boom-and-bust cycle was just allowed to run. I don't think we're going to allow that this time."

If the emergence of urban centers amid the mountains is a mixed blessing, it also may offer the Rocky Mountain states a chance to break out of the colonial economic status that has limited its past development. Always before, northern states like Montana and Wyoming looked east to Minneapolis and Chicago or west to Seattle for venture capital to finance resource development. To the south, Colorado, New Mexico, Arizona and Utah were dependent on Dallas and Houston to the east or Los Angeles and San Francisco to the west. But now Denver and Phoenix are reaching sufficient size to put together much of the needed financing. "The biggest change in the West is that it's developing its own capital centers," Higgs said. "It's now developed the beginnings of home-grown capitalism."

This financial power may be essential as the region strives to develop a broader economic base — one that will remain in place after the energy boom has run its course. In the meantime, region officials want to make sure that the still-important tourism and agriculture are not swept away by the demands of energy projects and urban expansion. In Lamm's words, "One of the problems of having energy come on is that it's a one-time harvest." Despite good intentions and even the best efforts, growth will nonetheless take its toll on the region's unique institutions. "Whatever the West is, a lot of it is going to vanish," Calkin of the Sierra Club has predicted. "It can and will be a fine place to live," he added, "but it isn't going to be the frontier."

Selected Bibliography

Books

Athearn, Robert G., *High Country Empire, The High Plains and Rockies,* University of Nebraska Press, 1960.

Boorstin, Daniel J., *The Americans, the Democratic Experience,* Vintage Books, 1973.

Kramer, Jane, *The Last Cowboy,* Harper & Row, 1977.

Nash, Gerald D., *The American West in the Twentieth Century,* University of New Mexico Press, 1977.

Steffen, Jerome O., ed., *The American West, New Perspectives, New Dimensions,* University of Oklahoma Press, 1979.

Articles

"The Angry West vs. the Rest," *Newsweek,* Sept. 17, 1979.

"Denver's Mile-High Energy Boom," *Time,* Aug. 13, 1979.

"Is Colorado Helpless Against Land Blight?" *Conservation Foundation Letter,* May 1979.

Parrish, Michael, "The Saints Among Us," *Rocky Mountain Magazine,* January-February 1980.

Stegner, Wallace and Page, Stegner, "Rocky Mountain Country," *Atlantic,* April 1978.

Webb, Walter Prescott, "The American West, Perpetual Mirage," *Harper's,* May 1957.

Reports and Studies

Bracken, Paul, with contributions from Herman Kahn, "Arizona Tomorrow," a study prepared by the Hudson Institute for Arizona Tomorrow Inc., 1979.

Colorado Department of Agriculture, "Agricultural Land Conversion in Colorado," 1979.

Colorado Energy Research Institute, "Impacts of Energy Resource Development on the Denver Metropolitan Area," June 1979.

Colorado Office of the Governor, "Front Range Project, the First Year," Nov. 12, 1979.

Editorial Research Reports: "Western Water: Coming Crisis," 1977 Vol. I, p. 23; and "Western Land Policy," 1978 Vol. I, p. 83.

Four Corners Regional Commission, "Regional Development Plan," March 1979.

G REAT LAKES STATES: TROUBLE IN AMERICA'S INDUSTRIAL HEARTLAND

by

William Sweet

**Mar. 28
1 9 8 0**

GREAT LAKES STATES

BOUND on virtually all sides by major waterways, situated at the heart of the nation's land and air transportation routes, and blessed in some sections with the richest soil found anywhere in the world, the Great Lakes states owe their enormous economic power to a happy conjunction of natural resources, markets and Yankee ingenuity. The combination of iron from Lake Superior to the northwest and coal from the Appalachian fields to the southeast made the Great Lakes region the home of U.S. heavy industry.

It was here, in the late 19th century, that an application of industrial machinery to family farming began to revolutionize agriculture. Today the region's agricultural and industrial products are transported to the world via the St. Lawrence Seaway to the north, the Ohio River to the south, and the Mississippi to the west. Chicago, the world's greatest rail center at the height of the railroad era, today has the world's busiest airport, O'Hare.

Ever on the move, the Great Lakes states typically inspire money-making and only occasionally nourish achievements of the more refined kinds. This is a region populated by business people big and small, workers, and farmers, but not — generally — artists. Chicago's industrial squalor provided themes for naturalist and muckraking writers at the turn of the century, to be sure, but its most celebrated writer, Ernest Hemingway, already was in Paris when he wrote his first stories about fishing and hunting in upper Michigan. He soon found more glamorous places to fish and hunt. Sherwood Anderson, similarly, already had left the Midwest when he published his powerful vignettes of stunted lives, broken ambitions and fantasies in a small Ohio town.[1]

Jazz flourished briefly during the Twenties in Chicago, having migrated up the Mississippi from New Orleans, but it soon moved on to mature in Harlem's more vibrant culture. Perhaps the most enduring contribution made by the Great Lakes states to American high culture, the Chicago school of architecture, was in the field of artistic endeavor closest to industry, craft and money.

Like the great Chicago architects — Daniel H. Burnham, Louis Sullivan and Frank Lloyd Wright — the people most

---

[1] See Sherwood Anderson, *Winesburg, Ohio* (1919), which was based on Elyria, Ohio.

71

remembered for their achievements in the industrial Midwest are people who built or invented things. Thomas A. Edison and the Wright brothers came from Ohio (though they did much of their work elsewhere); Henry Ford was born in Michigan, where he built his great auto plants; the McCormick brothers established their farm machinery company, now known as International Harvester, in Chicago; the Armour family built its meat-packing empire in the Midwest. These are the kinds of people who made the Great Lakes states the heart of America's machine-tool, auto manufacturing, steelmaking, farm machinery and food-processing industries.

Today, however, these states seem to have stopped producing or attracting the great inventors and industrial empire builders. Since World War II, new industry has tended to locate elsewhere, in the South and West, and the region's traditional industries have fallen on hard times. Many of the region's workers, who once had hoped to raise themselves or at least their children out of assembly-line work, now fear falling back into unemployment. Whole communities struggle with the threat of stagnation and decay.

Many cities dissolved in racial turmoil during the Sixties, only to face pressing fiscal problems in the Seventies. First Cleveland, then Chicago, saw its municipal credit ratings slashed. Now Chicago's residents, according to one of them, "shudder at comparisons to New York and Cleveland" and wonder whether their city "is still, as many Easterners always suspected, little more than a crossroads town, its evening clothes borrowed and its gleaming jewels due back to the pawnshop before dawn."[2]

Legacies of the Old Northwest Territory

Though the people of the Great Lakes may be suffering from a crisis of identity today, they occupy a region strongly molded not only by natural geographic boundaries but also a highly coherent historic tradition. What is called the Great Lakes states or, as designated by the U.S. Census Bureau, the "East-North Central Region," was known in the early days of the American nation as the Old Northwest. This was a territory the British had wrested from France in the Seven Years War (1756-63), and after the Revolution the territory remained for a while under England's *de facto* control, while various states and land companies struggled for recognition of their own claims.

After Virginia's cession to the Union of its claims in 1784, Congress enacted the Northwest Ordinances of 1785 and 1787, which provided for surveying and subdivision of the Northwest into rectangular townships, the establishment of territorial self-

---

[2] Eugene Kennedy, "Hard Times in Chicago," *The New York Times Magazine,* March 9, 1980, p. 22.

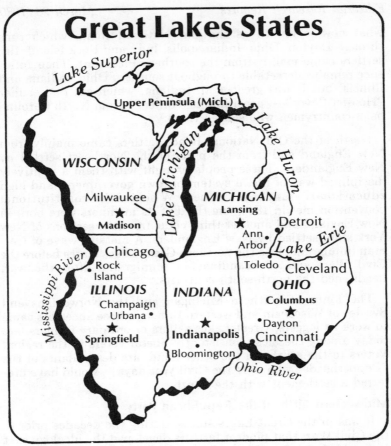

Great Lakes States

Lake Superior

Upper Peninsula (Mich.)

Lake Huron

WISCONSIN

Milwaukee
★
Madison

Lake Michigan

MICHIGAN
Lansing
★
Detroit
Ann
Arbor

Lake Erie

Mississippi River

Chicago
Rock
Island

Toledo Cleveland

ILLINOIS

INDIANA

OHIO
Columbus
★

Champaign
Urbana
★
Springfield

★
Indianapolis

Dayton
Cincinnati

Bloomington

Ohio River

government with the advance of settlement, and a procedure for entry of the territories into the Union as new states. In effect, the late historian Frederick Jackson Turner frequently stressed, Congress rejected the idea of systematically exploiting the territories for the benefit of the 13 original colonies in favor of a land-grant system and local self-government. Equally important, the Ordinance of 1787 prohibited slavery in the Northwest.

During the early decades of the 19th century eager pioneers poured into the Northwest, pushing back the native Algonquin Indians, and before long the region was being stripped of its forests as farmers began to till the rich glacial and alluvial soils. The census of 1820 determined that one-fourth of the U.S. population already was west of the seaboard states, and by 1850 one-half the people were living outside the original 13 colonies. Ohio achieved statehood in 1803, Indiana in 1816, Illinois in 1818, Michigan in 1837, and Wisconsin in 1848.

Two distinct patterns of migration in this period left an enduring mark on the region's social geography. To the south of what now is known as the Old National Road, which runs through Dayton, Ohio, Indianapolis, Ind., and Rock Island, Ill., settlers came mainly from the southern Piedmont. Their influence remains detectable throughout southern Ohio, Indiana and Illinois, but it was greatest in Indiana, which got its peculiar "Hoosier flavor" — according to Turner — from North Carolina back-countrymen who settled there.[3]

North of the Old National Road, settlers came mainly from New England and from the parts of the Northeast settled by New Englanders. These people brought with them a relatively disciplined way of life, a system of town government, and high educational standards. When Wisconsin's constitutional convention met in 1846, one-third of its members were born in New England and another third came from the sections of New York state settled by New Englanders. A massive wave of German immigrants into the northern Great Lakes states before the Civil War, and of Scandinavian immigrants after the war, heightened the north-south contrasts.

The Finns of northern Michigan and the Norwegians and Swedes of Wisconsin and western Illinois, whose ancestors came to work as loggers, Great Lakes sailors or ordinary farmers, are today among the most consistently liberal voters in the region. Voters to the south, on the other hand, are descendants of the "Copperheads" who — in the Civil War days — would have preferred a settlement with the South.

Midwestern Birth of the Republican Party

It was in the Great Lakes states, during the decades prior to the Civil War, that pioneer farmers developed the ideology that has guided the Republican Party down to the present day: It was the ideology of free labor, free soil and free men — in short, free enterprise. The westward movement that peaked in the 1850s was essentially a movement of landed small businessmen, who believed that hard work was the one true path to improvement of self and society. Increasingly, these settlers came to believe that the dignity or honor of free labor could not be reconciled with the institution of slavery.

As the Republican governor of Wisconsin put it in 1860, "Free labor languishes and becomes degrading when put in competition with slave labor, and idleness, poverty, and vice, among large classes of non-slaveholders, take the place of industry and thrift and virtue."[4] Republicans detected the debilitating effects of the slave mentality not only in the South but even in the sec-

---

[3] "The Middle West" (1901), in Frederick Jackson Turner, *The Frontier in American History* (1976 edition), p. 134. According to one derivation, the word "Hoosier" comes from a word in the Cumberland dialect which denotes anything very big.

[4] Alexander W. Randall, quoted by Eric Foner, in *Free Soil, Free Labor, Free Men* (1970), p. 57.

Great Lakes States at a Glance

State	1979 Pop. Estimates (add 000)	Pop. Rank Among States	Pop. Increase Since 1970*	Per Capita Personal Income**
Illinois	11,230	5	1.1%	$8,745
Indiana	5,400	12	3.9	7,696
Michigan	9,208	7	3.7	8,442
Ohio	10,731	6	0.7	7,812
Wisconsin	4,720	16	6.8	7,597

*National average: 8.3%
**National average: $7,810
Source: Bureau of the Census; per capita personal income figures are for 1978.

tions of the Great Lakes states settled by southern migrants, which were frequently compared unfavorably with the New England sections such as Connecticut's Western Reserve in northern Ohio.

The opening of the Erie Canal in 1824 strengthened commercial ties between the Old Northwest and the Northeast, led to the rise of New York City as the nation's largest metropolis, and established the New York-Midwest axis that was to dominate the United States after the Civil War. Ohio, however, and not New York, generally controlled the Northeast-Midwest's political machinery both before and after the war. Ohio's leading statesman in the pre-war period, Salmon P. Chase, was instrumental in converting abolitionism from a quasi-religious cause into a successful political movement.

In the early part of the 19th century, interest in abolitionism had grown strong among the revivalist denominations in the Midwest and among northeastern Congregationalists and Unitarians.[5] Chase, who was to become U.S. chief justice during the Civil War, developed the argument that growing "slave power" had thwarted the Founding Fathers' intention to see slavery gradually eliminated.[6] Repeated extensions of slavery to the West gradually convinced Northerners of slave power's insidious designs, and over a period of decades Chase was able to guide a series of third party efforts toward the formation of the GOP.

Defections of northern Democrats and "conscience Whigs" over the issue of slave power led to the creation of the Liberty Party and the Free Soil Party in the 1830s and 1840s and culminated finally in the sudden emergence of the Republican Party in 1854. When the sectional crisis came to a head in 1860 it was a son of Illinois, Abraham Lincoln, who proved acceptable

[5] See W. W. Sweet, *Revivalism in America* (1965 edition) and Peter Brock, *Radical Pacifists in Ante-Bellum America* (1968). In New England, especially, abolitionist sentiment often was closely allied with pacifist beliefs.

[6] The Ordinance of 1787, which barred slavery in the Old Northwest, figured prominently in Chase's argument.

to all wings of the new party — northeastern radicals, and midwestern Free Soilers of southern, northern and foreign origin. Another son of Illinois, U.S. Grant, led the northern troops to victory.

From the Civil War to the early 1920s midwestern Republicans were at the zenith of their influence. Seven of the ten presidents in this period came from the Great Lakes States. Ohio accounted for five (Hayes, Garfield, McKinley, Taft and Harding), and Illinois (Grant) and Indiana (Benjamin Harrison) one each. Even after Great Lakes' Republicans began to lose power relative to politicians from other regions they remained a formidable force in the counsels of the GOP. During the 1930s and 1940s Robert A. Taft of Ohio led the Republican Party's isolationist wing, while Arthur H. Vandenberg of Michigan presided over the internationalists during World War II and afterward.

During the 1950s and 1960s Ray Bliss of Ohio, like Mark Hanna at the turn of the century, was the party's most important chairman. Gerald R. Ford, representing the largely Dutch constituency that produced Vandenberg, rose in the party's House leadership in the Fifties and Sixties, while Everett M. Dirksen of Peoria, Ill., moved into the top Senate position. Rep. Robert H. Michel, the House minority whip who now represents Peoria, and Rep. Guy Vander Jagt, from Michigan Dutch country, are currently considered the two likeliest candidates to succeed Minority Leader John Rhodes some day.

New Migrants and Their Political Impact

In the latter part of the 19th century hordes of migrants from eastern and southern Europe came to work in the factories springing up around the Great Lakes, and there they provided the foundation for the Democratic Party's city machines. While Republicans retained control in such southern-area cities as Columbus and Cincinnati, the northern metropolises fell to the Democrats, and the fight was on between business and labor for the allegiance of the swing "downstate" (Illinois) or "out-state" (Michigan) constituencies.

In some areas, notably in Wisconsin and western Illinois, a Lincolnesque Republicanism retained a strong grip and repeatedly generated reactions against the wing of the party oriented to the interests of big business. Late in the last century, for example, Wisconsin's Robert M. LaFollette perceived the GOP as corrupted by years of unquestioning loyalty. He wrote in his autobiography:

> It had fought a desperate war for a great and righteous cause. It had behind it the passionate enthusiasm of a whole generation of men. It was the party of Lincoln and Grant and Sherman. I

remember well the character of the ordinary political speech of those years. Even well down into the eighties they all looked backwards to fading glories, they waved the flag of freedom, they abused the South, they stirred the war memories of the old soldiers who were then everywhere dominant in the North.[7]

In his struggles with the railroads and the monopolies in Wisconsin, "Fighting Bob" relied heavily for support on "those hard-headed old pioneers from New England and from northern Europe who thought as they plowed," and especially on the Scandinavians, "an independent, liberty-loving people."[8] He also received invaluable assistance from people at the University of Wisconsin in Madison, the type of land-grant state university which plays a very big role in the culture and politics of every Great Lakes state.

LaFollette eventually bolted the Republican Party, forming the Progressive Party. Though his party, after some initial success, has long ceased to function, some of Wisconsin's leading politicians today are heirs to many of the Progressive ideals. Sens. William Proxmire and Gaylord Nelson and Rep. Henry S. Reuss, all Democrats, reflect many aspects of the Progressive tradition. Within Republicanism, it is again a man of Scandinavian descent from western Illinois, John B. Anderson, who has risen to challenge the party's right wing. Anderson and the Wisconsin Democrats share liberal views on social questions and conservative views on fiscal matters, and in many ways they are more in tune with each other than with their own colleagues.

In contrast to the progressive political tendencies found mainly among rural people of northern European descent in the Great Lakes states, a quite different dissenting movement has manifested itself repeatedly in the southern and urban areas. Here a reaction occasionally has set in among the more established white people against the eastern- and southern-European immigrants, largely Catholic or Jewish, and against southern blacks who migrated north. Before the Civil War midwesterners of German origin were instrumental in beating back nativist impulses in the Republican Party, but in the 1920s a revived Ku Klux Klan established a strong hold in the southern tier of the Great Lakes states and for a few years had a formidable presence in Chicago, Detroit, and Milwaukee.

Indiana and Ohio, at that time, were "the leading Klan states in the nation."[9] In Michigan, Henry Ford made a newspaper he distributed via his dealerships a major organ for anti-Semitic propaganda (he associated Jews with eastern financial power, which he feared); in the 1930s Father Charles Edward Coughlin

---

[7] Robert M. LaFollette, *LaFollette's Autobiography* (1913), p. 15.
[8] *Ibid.*, pp. 18, 177.
[9] John Higham, *Strangers in a Strange Land* (1972), p. 297.

spread anti-Communist and anti-Semitic views over his Radio
League of the Little Flower, based in Royal Oak, Mich.

As late as 1918 Turner was still able to express an unreserved
optimism about the midwestern melting pot: "In the midst of
more or less antagonism between 'bowie-knife Southerners,'
'cow-milking Yankee Puritans,' 'beer-drinking Germans,' 'wild
Irishmen,' a process of mutual education, a giving and taking,
was at work."[10] But Turner wrote before the Klan's revival in
the Twenties, the race riots of the Sixties, and the strong presidential campaign that George C. Wallace mounted in the Great
Lakes states in 1968 and 1972. Recent commentators on the
industrial Midwest tend to take a much harsher view of the
melting pot. Chicago columnist Mike Royko, for example, has
described ethnic neighborhoods in the following terms:

> With their tote bags, the immigrants brought along all their old
> prejudices, and immediately picked up some new ones. An Irish-
> man who came here hating only the English and Irish Protestants
> soon hates Poles, Italians and blacks. A Pole who . . . arrived
> hating only Jews and Russians . . . soon learned to hate the Irish,
> the Italians, and the blacks. That was another good reason to stay
> close to home and in your own neighborhood-town and ethnic
> state. Go that way, pass the viaduct, and the wop will jump you, or
> chase you into Jew town. . . . And who can tell what the niggers
> might do?[11]

Even today, some of Chicago's most impoverished blacks live in
prison-like housing projects, where it is not uncommon at mid-
day to see the police running around with rifles. In some of the
Italian neighborhoods, on the other hand, the police are not in-
vited in; vigilante groups patrol the streets instead, and no black
would make the mistake of being seen there after dark.

Industrial Labor's Midwest Base

THE World's Columbian Exposition of 1893 marked the coming of age of the Old Northwest. It was here at the Chicago
fair that Turner delivered his celebrated lecture on "The Significance of the Frontier in American History." What Turner presented to the assembled historians was not merely a new and
highly provocative interpretation of U.S. history, but in fact a
manifesto of sorts. Turner proclaimed that the West and not the
East accounted for America's most distinctive, most important
and best traits, contrary to what eastern-bred intellects had always imagined.

---

[10] Frederick Jackson Turner, "Middle Western Pioneer Democracy," in *The Frontier in American History* (1976 edition), p. 349.
[11] Mike Royko, *Boss* (1971), pp. 31-32.

Just blocks away from the Exposition fairground, John D. Rockefeller had recently established the University of Chicago to be a great new center of learning of America's heartland. And on the university campus, in the part of Chicago known as "the Plains," Frank Lloyd Wright would soon build Robie House, which came to be called the first ranch-style home. Wright said at that time he was betting on the car rather than the elevator, and sure enough, within decades, families all over the country would be driving cars built in the Great Lakes states and living in ranch-style homes.

Robie House

But behind the glittering skyscrapers that lined Chicago's waterfront and the elegant homes that architects like Wright were building in the suburbs, the great masses of immigrant workers were stirring, and for the next decades the history of the Great Lakes states centered on a struggle between business and labor for economic and political power. It was often violent. In 1886, 11 persons were killed and 66 wounded at Chicago's Haymarket Square in a riot that grew out of the McCormick Harvester Co. strike.

In 1894 a strike at Chicago's Pullman works prompted President Cleveland to send in federal troops, and again many deaths resulted. After the strike, Eugene V. Debs, a native of Indianapolis and the leader of the Brotherhood of Locomotive Firemen, became a convert to socialism. From the 1890s down to World War II Debs was at the heart of a serious effort to create a politically oriented labor movement based on the organization of all workers — both skilled and unskilled — in each industry.

Opposed to Debs was Samuel Gompers, head of a cigarmakers' local in New York City and the ascendant leader of the American Federation of Labor, which was founded in 1886 in Columbus, Ohio. Gompers preached a British-style trade unionism, based on strong central control over locals, organization by craft rather than by industry. Gompers had the advantage of appealing to highly skilled and well established workers, while the industrial unionists had to contend with unskilled and often foreign-born workers, who could easily be tarred as "un-American" importers of foreign ideologies.

Despite such disadvantanges, one union, the Industrial Workers of the World ("Wobblies"), made some headway up to World War I, and a labor movement based on socialist thought appeared to have some chance of taking hold. Debs got only 97,000 votes for president on a Socialist Party ticket in 1900; but when he ran with Emil Seidel, the Socialist mayor of Milwaukee, in 1912, he got 897,000 votes or 5.9 percent of the total. The craft organization of the AFL proved to be by far the more successful approach in this period, however, and by World War I the federation had over two million members. World War I provided the occasion for suppressing all flirtation with foreign ideas and effectively wiped out the AFL's competition for a decade.

In May 1917 the government raided the Socialist Party's Indianapolis offices, and in February 1918 there was a mass trial in Chicago of Socialists accused of obstructing the war effort. Victor Berger, a Marxist elected to Congress from the Milwaukee district now represented by Henry Reuss, was convicted and twice barred from taking his seat. In the spring of 1918 over 100 Wobblies were tried in Chicago, and 92 were convicted. Deportation of foreign-born radicals followed. Meanwhile, the Senate censured Sen. LaFollette for his opposition to the war. In 1924 La Follette ran for president as the candidate of the Progressive Party and he won 17 percent of the vote.

Rise and Decline of Industrial Unionism

Despite the setbacks suffered by industrial unionists at the time of World War I, vast economic changes already were laying the foundation for a renewed attempt at organizing the unskilled. In 1900 the first fully integrated steel corporation had appeared in the form of U.S. Steel, and while the immediate effect was to wipe out all vestiges of labor organization in the steel industry and in steel-controlled Great Lakes shipping, the long-term effect was to stiffen labor's resolve.

Steel production increased fourteenfold in 1890-1929. From 1896, when the first automobiles were sold in the United States, production of motor vehicles increased to nearly one million in 1915 and to more than five-and-a-half million in 1929. By then, roughly 30 percent of the goods manufactured in the United States were made in the Great Lakes states.[12]

With the onset of the Depression in 1929, unemployment soared throughout America's industrial heartland, moving Congress in the 1930s to enact several laws favorable to labor organizing.[13] In this new climate, industrial unionism flourished. After the AFL refused at its 1935 convention to give up the

[12] Joseph G. Rayback, *A History of American Labor* (1966), pp. 189-191.
[13] The Norris-LaGuardia Anti-Injunction Act of 1932 and the National Labor Relations (Wagner) Act of 1935 were of primary importance to labor. The Wagner Act guaranteed employees the right to organize and strike, created the National Labor Relations Board and spelled out "unfair labor practices" by employers. The 1932 act limited the use of court injunctions against peaceful union activities and strikes.

crafts principle and to launch an industrial organizing drive, eight labor leaders — of whom John L. Lewis of the United Mine Workers was the most powerful — set up the Committee for Industrial Organization.

Lewis had become convinced that coal could be managed adequately only if steel also was organized. By the end of 1937, the Steel Workers Organizing Committee had acquired 300,000 members, and by 1941 it was recognized by both "Big Steel" (the top four companies) and "Little Steel" (all the others) as the bargaining agent for the steel workers.

In the auto industry, which was virtually untouched by unionism on the eve of the Depression, labor made equally impressive gains. In 1936 the newly formed United Auto Workers joined the CIO, and the famous "sit down" strikes soon broke out in the big automobile factories, with the Reuther brothers, Walter and Victor, playing prominent roles. Organization of the closely allied rubber industry also proceeded apace.

By 1938, when the Committee for Industrial Organization became the Congress of Industrial Organizations, the CIO had nearly four million members. Unlike their AFL counterparts, the ambitious CIO leaders did not hesitate to get involved in the political fray. Their support for Franklin D. Roosevelt was unequivocal, and the Political Action Committee which they set up in 1943 with Sidney Hillman as chairman fought hard in the 1944 election for the candidates deemed sympathetic to labor.

Industrial labor, especially in the Great Lakes states, appeared to be poised for major new gains at the end of World War II. In retrospect, however, labor's political influence was at its peak in 1945, and its story since then has been on the whole one of decline. The strident demands made by Lewis during the war, and the known presence of many Communists among CIO organizers, had alienated much of the public. So, apparently did a heavy wave of strikes immediately following the war, reflecting labor's desire to "catch up" after years of wage controls. When the Republican Party took control of Congress in 1946 it lost no time in enacting legislation, notably the Taft-Hartley Act of 1947, placing restraints on union activity.[14] From that time forward, labor was on the defensive. The exposure during the 1950s of racketeering among labor leaders led to the expulsion of the Teamsters from the AFL and to a further drop in labor's prestige.

Many critics of labor, including some who are sympathetic to its basic objectives, have accused union leaders of failing to keep pace with changes in the work force since 1945: a shift from

---

[14] For background, see Congressional Quarterly's *Congress and the Nation*, Vol. I (1965), pp. 565-587.

manufacturing to services, the entry of many minority-group members and women into the job market, and an increase in employment in the South and West relative to the old industrial heartland. Whatever the exact causes, the proportion of non-farm workers who are union members declined from 35.5 percent in 1945 to less than 25 percent in 1978.[15] Between 1964 and 1976, union membership declined in the Great Lakes states at rates close to the national average.

Stagnation in Region's Economy

O N DEC. 2, 1942, on the University of Chicago campus, the first self-sustaining nuclear reaction took place under the direction of Enrico Fermi. Had midwesterners understood the full implications of Fermi's experiment, they might have been tempted to brand the Italian scientist an importer of foreign ideas. For Fermi ushered in the atomic age. One side effect would be the birth of a technology that took root outside of the auto-and-steel-centered industrial belt.

The great factories that soon were built for the production of atomic bombs were located not in the old industrial heartland but rather in Tennessee, New Mexico, Washington state and South Carolina. As for the planes that would carry these bombs, they were built primarily in the Southwest and Southeast. When guided missiles matured, they were produced mainly in the West, while nuclear submarines and carriers naturally had to be built along the nation's seacoasts.

The high-technology precision instrumentation that was increasingly essential to the operation of advanced weaponry tended, like the planes and the missiles and the ships, to be made mainly in the Southeast, the Southwest, and New England. Ironically, the man who presided over a major shift from reliance on conventional weapons to weapons for mass destruction was a former president of General Motors, Charles E. Wilson. Wilson was famous for remarking, as President Eisenhower's secretary of defense, "What's good for the country is good for General Motors and vice versa." What Wilson actually did as secretary of defense was not especially good for General Motors or the industrial Midwest generally.

With the nation's most advanced high-technology industries leading the way in a movement out of the industrial heartland, other industries found plenty of reasons to follow suit. Whereas in the North businesses must contend with high taxes, more

[15] Jeremy Rifkin and Randy Barber, *The North Will Rise Again* (1978), p. 16.

unionization and a decaying infrastructure, in many sections of the South and West they are able to build from scratch under favorable tax incentives and draw on pools of lower-paid labor. Especially since energy prices began to soar in 1973, businesses have had a strong motive to locate in the sunnier regions of the country.

Not only have the Great Lakes states seen businesses move funds earned in the industrial heartland into other regions of the country, but they have had to put up with the indignity of subsidizing the out-migration. Largely because three-quarters of all federal expenditures for procurement go to the defense industries, and because in a typical year the Great Lakes region receives only about 10 percent of the prime contract awards, it suffers the nation's largest net loss of tax dollars each year. In 1976, according to the congressional Northeast-Midwest Coalition, the Great Lakes states sent the federal government about $20 billion more than they got back, while the South showed a net gain of over $20 billion and the West of $12 billion.[16]

National Policy Effects and Fiscal Strains

Recent major policy moves taken by the Carter administration are virtually certain to aggravate the industrial heartland's economic woes. The large increases slated for the defense budget will worsen inflation, according to most economists, because more weapons will be produced relative to consumer goods.[17] In addition, proceeds from the windfall profits tax may be allocated largely to energy development projects such as synfuels, to the detriment of conservation projects such as mass transit in the heartland.[18] Representatives of the Great Lakes states may succeed in getting what they consider a fair share of the tax revenues, but even so, the energy-rich states in the Southwest and West could reap over $100 billion in added energy severance taxes over the next 10 years as a result of oil decontrol.[19]

Since World War II the economic growth of the Great Lakes states has been well below the national average.[20] From 1950 to 1975, manufacturing employment in the region grew 4.3 percent, compared with 76 percent in the Southeast, 141 percent in the

---

[16] Northeast-Midwest Coalition, *The State of the Region* (1979), Appendix P, p. 29. See also Dr. James R. Anderson, *The Pentagon Tax: The Impact of the Military Budget on Major American Cities,* March 1979. Some scholars argue plausibly that advocacy groups such as the Northeast-Midwest Coalition exaggerate the negative impact of defense expenditures on the Great Lakes states, but they do not dispute the character of the general trend.

[17] Workers are paid to produce the weapons, but because fewer consumer goods are manufactured, more dollars will chase fewer goods. The effects of higher defense spending on employment also are widely expected to be unfavorable. See Michael Edelstein, *The Economic Impact of Military Spending* (1977).

[18] For final provisions of the windfall profits tax legislation, see *Congressional Quarterly Weekly Report,* March 8, 1980, pp. 668-669.

[19] Interview with Bill Hogan of the Northeast-Midwest Coalition, March 21, 1980.

[20] See Howard Z. Friedenberg, "Regional Differences in Personal Income Growth, 1929-77," *Survey of Current Business,* October 1978, pp. 27-31.

Southwest and a national average of 20 percent.[21] Though the Great Lakes states generally are thought to be exceptionally sensitive to recessions, because of their dependence on durable goods industries which are the first to suffer in times of economic downturn, the region — apart from Michigan — has not suffered higher-than-average joblessness *(see opposite).*[22]

It is clear, though, that the "redistribution of manufacturing and related activities away from these highly industrialized regions led to the rapid growth of public assistance and unemployment compensation payments," and that these payments have generated considerable fiscal difficulties "because they increased faster than the state and local tax base."[23] Since the population of the region did not grow significantly during the 1970s, these states stand to lose five seats in the U.S. House of Representatives after the 1980 census. According to Census Bureau projections, Illinois and Ohio will probably lose two seats apiece, and Michigan one.[24]

Steel and Automobile Industries in Crisis

It is no secret that serious problems afflict the steel and auto industries, the two industries on which the Great Lakes states depend most heavily. U.S. steel production peaked at 111.4 million net tons in 1973, and by 1978 it had dropped to 97.9 million tons. Steel imports, just 146,000 tons in 1946, amounted to 24 million tons in 1978.[25] The last big steel mill was built in the United States at Burns Harbor, Ind., during the 1960s, and about a quarter of America's steel capacity is said to be outdated today. U.S. Steel, still the nation's largest steel manufacturer, has shelved plans for a giant integrated plant at Conneaut, Ohio, is diversifying its investments out of steel, and has laid off thousands of workers. Some of the specialty steel manufacturers are thought to be in better shape, and many U.S. producers hope to improve their equipment by importing Japanese technology. Pressure is very high for stronger government restrictions on steel imports.[26]

American steelworkers, whose wages average over $10 per hour, are among the best paid of any manufacturing workers. But the United States has lost about 100,000 steelmaking jobs over the last 20 years, and it is quite likely that many more will be lost in the years ahead. Last Nov. 27, U.S. Steel announced plans to close 16 plants — including facilities in Gary, Ind., and Youngstown, Ohio — and to lay off 13,000 workers. This was the

[21] "The Second War Between the States," *Business Week*, May 17, 1976, pp. 97-98.
[22] See Robert B. Bretzenfelder, "Sensitivity of State and Regional Income to National Business Cycles," *Survey of Current Business*, April 1973, pp. 2-27.
[23] Vernon Renshaw and Howard I. Friedenberg, "Transfer Payments: Regional Patterns, 1965-1975," *Survey of Current Business*, May 1977, p. 15.
[24] See "Census Taking, 1980," *E.R.R.*, 1980 Vol. I, p. 158.
[25] American Iron and Steel Institute, *Annual Statistical Report, 1978*, Tables 14 and 21.
[26] For background, see "Job Protection and Free Trade," *E.R.R.*, 1977 Vol. II, p. 953.

Unemployment Rates

	1975	1976	1977	1978	1979
Illinois	7.1%	6.5%	6.2%	6.1%	5.5%
Indiana	8.6	6.1	5.7	5.7	6.4
Michigan	12.5	9.4	8.2	6.9	7.8
Ohio	9.1	7.8	6.5	5.4	5.9
Wisconsin	6.9	5.6	4.9	5.1	4.5
U.S. Average	8.5	7.7	7.0	6.0	5.8

Source: U.S. Bureau of Labor Statistics

second big blow to Youngstown steel workers in just a few years. In 1977 the Lykes Corp. closed its Campbell facility at a cost of 5,000 jobs. A church-supported group called the Ecumenical Coalition attempted unsuccessfully to obtain federal subsidies to open the Campbell works under a worker-ownership plan.[27]

The auto industry, which purchases about a quarter of the nation's steel production each year, appears to be in little better shape than steel. Last year nearly a quarter of the cars sold in the United States were imports, and the nation's second and third biggest car producers — Ford and Chrysler — both showed huge losses on their domestic operations. The Chrysler Corp.'s $1.1 billion loss was the largest ever by an American company, sending its management to Congress to plead for aid in an attempt to avert bankruptcy.[28] Ford's domestic losses were also large, but profitable foreign operations helped offset them.

General Motors has greatly improved its position against domestic competitors in recent years, basically — it seems — because it was first to recognize the fuel-efficient car as the wave of the future and to start down-sizing its models. Ford is widely expected to do better after it introduces, this year and next, a new line of compact cars that the company's highly successful German engineers have helped to design. American Motors, No. 4 in the industry, has been making a profit since it acquired Jeep and associated itself with Renault, the gigantic French company; some industry analysts believe that a similar association recently established between Chrysler and another big French company, Peugeot-Citroen, may save Chrysler. Douglas Fraser, head of the United Auto Workers, has worked hard in recent months to get Japanese and European makers to build facilities in the United States and — in the meantine — voluntarily to reduce exports to this country.[29]

---

[27] See *Time*, March 17, 1980, pp. 66-67, and *Business Week*, Sept. 17, 1979, pp. 78-96.
[28] Last Dec. 21, Congress cleared legislation providing Chysler with $1.5 billion in loan guarantees.
[29] See *The Wall Street Journal*, Feb. 15, 1980, *U.S. News & World Report*, Aug. 27, 1979, pp. 21-24, and *Business Week*, March 26, 1979. See also "Auto Research and Regulation," *E.R.R.*, 1979 Vol. I, pp. 145-164.

The world steel industry as a whole is suffering from over-capacity, and for that reason domestic manufacturers are not likely to get much relief from foreign competition in the coming years. In the auto industry, foreign manufacturers have had much more experience than their U.S. counterparts in producing energy-efficient cars, and the American industry may have trouble matching the quality of imported vehicles. America's heavy industry plainly is in for a long period of painful readjustment, at best, and some fear that its problems may feed on each other and plunge the Great Lakes states and cities into a deep economic slump.

Federal Intervention vs. Belt-Tightening

Last May the United Auto Workers, the United Steel Workers and the International Association of Machinists joined in publishing a study based on an "intensive study of policies and practices to cope with economic dislocation in three highly industrialized countries, Sweden, West Germany, and the U.K. [Britain]."[30] On the basis of these findings, the three industrial unions recommended the adoption of national planning to assure full employment, advance notice of industrial layoffs, federal procurement and credit allocations to prevent job dislocations. To stop the flight of capital south and west and the migration of poverty north, they also recommended federalized unemployment insurance and workers compensation, repeal of "right-to-work" legislation and abolition of state and local tax abatements to lure industry from one region to another.

In contrast to that position, the advocacy of more federal intervention, there are those who argue that regions like the Great Lakes can solve their problems only by tightening their belts and making themselves more attractive to business. That has been Cleveland's goal since its populist mayor, Dennis Kucinich, was defeated last year and replaced by George V. Voinovich. The city recently ran the following ad in several major newspapers: "There's a new frame of mind in Cleveland. This new frame of mind recognizes ... that the financial community must have confidence and understanding before they can extend the credit necessary for a smoothly running city; and that businessmen, large and small, must have the hope of making a profit before they will venture the money and effort which creates new jobs, wealth and needed tax revenues."

Mayor Jane Byrne of Chicago also appears eager to restore her city's attractiveness to business, but her efforts to curb the power of the city unions already have led to bitter confrontations with transit workers, teachers, and fire-fighters.[31] At the

---

[30] *Economic Dislocation,* Joint Report of Labor Union Study Tour Participants, 1979, p. 5.
[31] See Sidney Lens, "The City that Doesn't Work Anymore," *The Progressive,* April 1980, pp. 34-38.

Centers of Population

Chicago's skyline

City	1977 Pop.* (add 000)	Rank U.S. Cities	% Change Since 1970	1977 Metro. Area Pop.* (add 000)
Chicago	3,063	2	− 9.1	7,017
Detroit	1,290	6	−14.7	4,370
Indianapolis	705	12	−4.0	1,144
Milwaukee	653	17	−8.9	1,427
Cleveland	609	19	−18.1	1,950
Columbus	532	22	−1.5	1,087
Cincinnati	403	31	−11.0	1,375
Toledo	359	39	−6.5	777
Akron	244	58	−11.3	661
Dayton	198	66	−18.9	833

*Bureau of the Census estimates

same time, the city's poor blacks — for whom the Irish-run city never worked very well — have been increasingly outspoken in demanding more rather than fewer services. At a time when urban tax bases are shrinking, while many inner-city neighborhoods remain impoverished ghettos, belt-tightening can be a difficult and risky business.

Even though growth trends have favored other regions of the country in recent decades, average per capita income still is higher in most Great Lakes states than in the Southeast and Southwest. While some areas in the industrial Midwest have experienced serious economic difficulties, and while many neighborhoods have become miserable places to live, many people nonetheless have managed to make a lot of money. These people typically have moved to the affluent suburbs. Chicago's suburbs, for example, include three of the five richest congressional districts in the United States. One of them, DuPage County, "regularly produces higher Republican percentages than Orange County, California."[32]

Throughout the Great Lakes states the suburban vote, when combined with "downstate" and "out-state" vote, often tips the balance against the city- and industry-based Democrats. Generally, the Great Lakes states are much more conservative than many people would expect this highly urbanized area to be. This

[32] Michael Barone et al., *Almanac of American Politics, 1980*, p. 261.

helps account for the victories of Ronald Reagan and Jimmy Carter over more liberal candidates of their parties in the Illinois presidential primary elections. In boosting Republican and Democratic nominations, the March 18 primary showed that Illinois remains a key state in presidential politics, despite the declining power and prowess of the Chicago Democratic machine. Indeed the entire bloc of industrial midwestern states remain a formidable power — if not always in the primaries then in November.[33] This clout is attested by the Republicans' choice of Detroit for their party's convention this summer.

[33] Wisconsin's primary is April 1, followed by Indiana's on May 6, Michigan's on May 20, and Ohio's on June 3.

Selected Bibliography

Books

Anderson, Sherwood, *Winesburg, Ohio,* The Viking Press, 1960 edition.
Foner, Eric, *Free Soil, Free Labor, Free Men,* Oxford University Press, 1970.
Higham, John, *Strangers in a Strange Land,* Atheneum, 1972.
Jackson, Kenneth T., *The Ku Klux Klan in the City,* Oxford University Press, 1967.
La Follette, Robert M., *La Follette's Autobiography,* The Robert M. La Follette Co., 1913.
Rayback, Joseph G., *A History of American Labor,* The Free Press, 1966.
Royko, Mike, *Boss: Richard J. Daley of Chicago,* Signet, 1971.

Articles

In These Times, selected issues.
Kennedy, Eugene, "Hard Times in Chicago," *The New York Times Magazine,* March 9, 1980.
Lens, Sidney, "The City that Doesn't Work Anymore," *The Progressive,* April 1980.
"The Second War Between the States," *Business Week,* May 17, 1976.
Survey of Current Business, selected issues.

Reports and Studies

Economic Dislocation, Joint Report of Labor Union Study Tour Participants, United Auto Workers, United Steelworkers, International Association of Machinists, Washington, D.C., May 1, 1979.
Edelstein, Michael, *The Economic Impact of Military Spending,* Council on Economic Priorities, New York City, 1977.
Editorial Research Reports: "Census Taking 1980," 1980 Vol. I, p. 141.
Northeast Midwest Coalition-Northeast Midwest Institute, *A Case of Inequity: Regional Patterns in Defense Expenditures, 1950-1977,* Washington, D.C., August 1977.
—— *The State of the Region: Economic Trends of the 1970s in the Northeast and Midwest,* Washington, D.C., January 1979.

MIDDLE ATLANTIC STATES: FIGHT AGAINST STAGNATION

by

Marc Leepson

**April 4
1 9 8 0**

MIDDLE ATLANTIC STATES

THE DIFFERENT regions of the United States have not fared equally during the economic turbulence of recent years. For the "Sun Belt" states of the South and Southwest, the Seventies brought unprecedented economic growth. For the Middle Atlantic region, the decade featured high unemployment, low growth in population, employment and income, and low rates of capital investment. Were these economic problems caused by the gains in the Sun Belt? One theory is that the industries that deserted the industrial North — especially New York, Pennsylvania and New Jersey — were enticed by the South's favorable economic climate, which included low taxes on businesses, a preponderance of "right to work" laws and the overall weakness of organized labor. In short, the Sun Belt region was thought to be "booming in great part because it's pro-business and the northern cities, by and large, aren't."[1]

Business Week magazine in 1976 characterized the situation as a "civil war between the states," with the economic arena as the battlefield in a "struggle for income, jobs, people and capital."[2] That "war" continues, as perceived by a number of business writers and even sociologists. In recent years there has been an outpouring of articles, studies and reports, and at least two books,[3] chronicling a shift of economic power from North to South. Lobbying groups like the Northeast-Midwest Congressional Coalition and the Council for Northeast Economic Action were set up to advance the economic interests of the North.

By some accounts, the North's economic slippage has been going on for decades and — except for New England where an economic revival of sorts is taking hold[4] — has worsened since the 1974-75 recession. But not everyone accepts the thesis that the Sun Belt's success has come at the expense of the northern states. James Lothian, a senior consultant with the Fantus Co., an industrial location consulting firm, calls it "a myth" that "all the industries in the North are relocating in the South." Although many northern plants have expanded their capacity in the South, "there have been very few instances where a plant in the North packs up totally and moves to the South."[5]

---

[1] Gurney Breckenfeld, writing in *Fortune*, June 1977, p. 136.
[2] "The Second War Between the States," *Business Week*, May 17, 1976, p. 92.
[3] *Power Shift* (1975) by Kirkpatrick Sale and *The North Will Rise Again* (1978) by Jeremy Rifkin and Randy Barber.
[4] See "New England's Regionalism and Recovery," pp. 1-24.
[5] Interview, March 12, 1980.

A U.S. Department of Commerce study reinforces Lothian's view. The study, issued in 1976, found that during a previous three-year period only 1.5 percent of job losses in the North was caused by companies moving; more than half the losses occurred because companies went out of business.[6]

Moreover, the states in the Middle Atlantic region, like those in the Sun Belt, have begun to offer business incentives, including tax benefits to provide more favorable business conditions. Maryland, for example, recently began a campaign to attract new industry and to encourage existing industry to expand. The campaign included a 15-page special advertising section in the March 24 issue of *Business Week*. "In Maryland," the ad said, "we offer you a solidly pro-business attitude that's here today and here tomorrow." Wendell Rawls Jr. had observed earlier in *The New York Times* that "to a great extent these types of incentives have been effective."[7]

Losses of Manufacturing Jobs; Old Facilities

The economic concern of the Middle Atlantic states is real, even if it is sometimes in danger of being overstated. In this region — New York, New Jersey, Pennsylvania, Maryland, Delaware, West Virginia and the District of Columbia for purposes of this Report — unemployment since the 1974-75 recession has averaged about one percentage point above the national average. The Middle Atlantic has lost more manufacturing jobs than any other section of the country.

The U.S. Department of Labor reported that from 1970 to 1978 the nation showed a 5.4 percent increase in the number of people employed in manufacturing. But each of the Middle Atlantic jurisdictions lost manufacturing workers during that time. The District of Columbia led with a loss of 19.3 percent, reflecting a sizable population decline in the nation's capital *(see p. 251)*. The other losses were:

New York	15.7%	New Jersey	8.5%
Maryland	10.7	Delaware	2.9
Pennsylvania	10.5	West Virginia	1.5

In this region where heavy manufacturing — along with mining — has been dominant since the 19th century, the current stagnation is all the more obvious. One problem today, possibly the main one, is that many of the industrial facilities are old and cannot function efficiently. Competitors using the latest equipment, whether they are in Germany, Japan or the South, have a built-in advantage.

---

[6] The study, written by Carol L. Jusenius and Larry C. Ledebur, "A Myth in the Making: The Southern Economic Challenge and Northern Economic Decline," dated November 1976, dealt with the period 1969-72.

[7] *The New York Times*, Jan. 6, 1980.

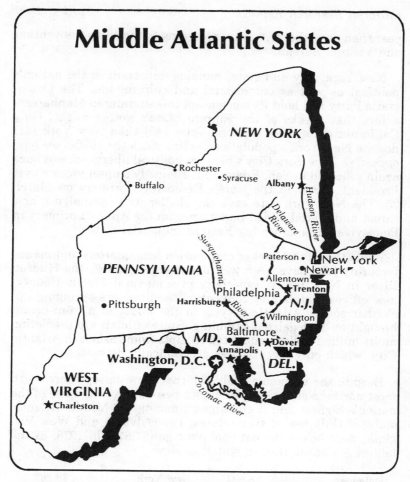

Middle Atlantic States

NEW YORK

• Rochester
• Syracuse
• Buffalo
Albany ★

Delaware River
Hudson River
Susquehanna

Paterson •
PENNSYLVANIA
• Allentown
New York
Newark ◄
• Pittsburgh   Harrisburg ★
Philadelphia •
N.J.
Trenton ★
River
• Wilmington
Baltimore
MD. •
Annapolis ★
Dover ★
**WEST
VIRGINIA**
Washington, D.C. ★   **DEL.**
★ Charleston
Potomac River

"The best way to appreciate this is to take an Amtrak ride through the once great workshop cities of Pennsylvania, New York, Ohio or Illinois," columnist Nicholas von Hoffman wrote recently. " . . . [W]hen you see Reading, or Altoona, or Youngstown, or Schenectady you'll think you are touring a museum showing the Birth of the Industrial Revolution. These places look like the English Midlands and the factories are often as old." In western Pennsylvania are "sudsy, sooty montages of the Edwardian era, iron work barns wherein the old ways of forge and open hearth are passed down from father to son."[8]

Instances of Success in City Revitalization

The overall picture, however, is not one of unrelieved gloom. New York City, for example, despite fiscal ills, remains the nation's banking, cultural and communications center. Tourism continues to boom, attracting more visitors (17.5 million) last

[8] Writing in *The New York Review of Books,* April 3, 1980, p. 16.

year than any other U.S. city, according to the city's Convention and Visitors Bureau.

New York, city and state, remains important in the nation's political as well as commercial and cultural life. The Democratic Party will hold its convention this summer in Manhattan, a fact that speaks of the Empire State's voting might. Only California casts more electoral votes (45) than New York (41) despite New York's population decline since the 1940s *(see box, opposite)*. New York City's bent for political liberalism was once again reflected in Sen. Edward M. Kennedy's upset victory over President Carter in the state's Democratic primary on March 25. The New York vote gave the challenger's campaign a new thrust and placed added importance on the April 22 primary in Pennsylvania, another big Eastern industrial state.[9]

While the city's losses of corporation headquarters and manufacturing jobs have been well documented, across the Hudson River in New Jersey, especially in semi-rural Morris County, new offices, hotels and convention facilities are springing up. Farther south, Atlantic City is in the midst of a mini-boom, brought on by legalized gambling. State officials are predicting multi-million-dollar annual tax receipts from casinos in Atlantic City, which only recently was economically depressed.

Despite the economic problems that New Jersey shares with most northern states, its per capita pesonal income is one of the nation's highest and is the highest among the Middle Atlantic states.[10] Only two of these states, Pennsylvania and West Virginia, were below the national average ($7,810) in 1978, as the following Census Bureau statistics show:

Delaware	$8,604	New York	$8,267
Maryland	8,306	Pennsylvania	7,733
New Jersey	8,818	West Virginia	6,456

Pennsylvania, the nation's second most populous state for more than a century, is now fourth, behind California, New York and Texas. But its two biggest cities, Philadelphia and Pittsburgh, both have experienced some degree of revitalization in recent years. Pittsburgh, the "Steel City," now advertises itself as the "City of Champions," in recognition of the national attention devoted to its professional baseball and football teams, the Pirates and Steelers. They play in Three Rivers Sta-

---

[9] Other presidential primaries in the Middle Atlantic region are: Delaware, April 1; District of Columbia, May 6; Maryland, May 13; and New Jersey and West Virginia, June 3.

[10] Personal income for residents of Washington, D.C., is higher than in any state. It was $10,022 in 1978. Income tends to be higher in urban centers, and the nation's capital is entirely urban.

Population and Redistricting

New York, Pennsylvania and the District of Columbia will hold the distinction of being the only major jurisdictions in the nation to lose population in the past decade — if the 1980 census confirms mid-1979 estimates made by the Census Bureau *(see below)*.

Among the other Middle Atlantic states, only West Virginia's estimated growth rate (7.7 percent) was above the national average (7.0 percent) in the 1970-79 period. However the 43.9 million people whom the census takers expect to count in the Middle Atlantic region will still constitute 20 percent of the nation's total.

Census Bureau projections indicate that the three most populous states in the region — New York, New Jersey and Pennsylvania — will continue to lose seats in the U.S. House of Representatives as a consequence of a dwindling or stagnant population. On the basis of reapportionment after the 1980 census, New York is expected to lose four seats, Pennsylvania two and New Jersey one. New York lost two seats after each of the previous three censuses. Pennsylvania lost three seats in 1950, three in 1960 and two in 1970. West Virginia lost one seat in 1960 and another in 1970.

State	1979 Pop. Estimates (add 000)	Pop. Change Since 1970
Delaware	582	+ 6.5%
District of Columbia	656	−13.1
Maryland	4,149	+ 6.7
New Jersey	7,332	+ 2.7
New York	17,649	− 3.2
Pennsylvania	11,731	− 0.5
West Virginia	1,878	+ 7.7

dium at the edge of Pittsburgh's gleaming downtown area, the site of one of this country's most noticed urban renewal areas.

In many places, downtown urban renewal did not bring new life to the city. But Baltimore, like Pittsburgh, appears to be one of the success stories. Baltimore's vitality is measured not only by the eye appeal of its new architecture and the restoration of old residential sections but also in reams of statistics on trade and commerce. In nearby Washington, where federal employment cushions the shock of recession, a building and restoration boom is also under way. In Delaware and Maryland came the news of budget surpluses last year. In Maryland, where the General Assembly mandated a balanced budget, the surplus was $300 million. In Delaware, where there is no sales tax, the General Assembly enacted an income tax cut last year, only two years after overcoming a budget deficit.

West Virginia's economic future has brightened considerably since the rapidly increasing cost of imported oil has given greater importance to coal — the state's primary natural resource.[11] For example, President Carter announced a plan March 6 naming 31 utilities, mostly in the Northeast, that would have to reduce their use of oil and burn coal instead. According to the National Coal Association, coal represents 80 percent of the nation's total energy reserves. The U.S. Geological Survey estimates that at least 1.7 trillion tons of coal lie beneath American soil. A significant portion is in western Pennsylvania and West Virginia. Bituminous coal, the soft coal used in making steel and other industrial products, long was the economic cornerstone of the two areas. Northeastern Pennsylvania, moreover, is the site of large deposits of anthracite, the hard coal used for home heating.

Steel's Decline and Coal's Disappointment

But coal's heralded comeback has so far been disappointing in the eastern United States. There is fear in the industry that coal remains "the fuel of last resort" because of the soaring costs of mining and shipping it and abiding by anti-pollution rules in burning it. The future of coal is not in the East, analysts say. According to the brokerage firm of Dean Witter Reynolds, the eastern states will supply the nation's utilities with 50 percent of their coal in 1985, compared to 78 percent in 1975. The gap will be filled by coal mined, especially strip-mined, in the West where the coal-mining companies are owned primarily by the nation's large oil corporations. "The West will be dynamic, and the East stagnant," in coal production in the 1980s, said Joel Price, a vice president of Dean Witter Reynolds.[12]

About two-thirds of all coal shipments now move by rail; the rest is hauled by barge or truck. One reason for the coal industry's problems in the East is that the highways and railways used to transport coal are in need of repair. Pennsylvania Gov. Richard L. Thornburgh told a meeting of the Coalition of Northeastern Governors, held Feb. 26 in Washington, D.C., of his state's "desperate need" to upgrade and rejuvenate coal-haul roads, railroads and port facilities in Philadelphia. A recent Pennsylvania Department of Transportation study found that $1.1 billion would be needed to improve 2,500 miles of coal-haul highways and 700 bridges.

The Federal Highway Administration estimates that about $7.3 billion would have to be spent to upgrade coal roads nationwide. All but $900 million would be needed in the Appalachian states. It reported in 1978 that "the projected increase in coal

---

[11] See "America's Coal Economy," *E.R.R.*, 1978 Vol. I, pp. 281-300.

[12] Quoted in *Business Week*, Sept. 24, 1979, p. 106.

production will place unprecedented demands upon trucks and highway systems, especially in the East ... Appalachia's coal road problems could well become so severe as to become a bottleneck on coal production."[13]

Another of western Pennsylvania's vital industries, steel, suffered a decline in the 1970s. U.S. Steel, the nation's largest steel company, last year reported its largest quarterly loss ever — $561.7 million in the October-December period. While some steel companies did fare well last year, the industry faces an uncertain future primarily because of foreign competition, especially from Japan and West Germany, and because of the industry's unwillingness or inability to rebuild old, antiquated mills.[14]

U.S. Steel last November layed off 13,000 workers in outmoded plants at 16 locations in eight states. At some of the steel fabrication plants, workers were given the option of accepting a three-year wage freeze or having the plants shut down. Some 1,270 workers at two U.S. Steel plants near Pittsburgh — Ambridge and Shiffler — voted to accept the freeze rather than lose their jobs.

Fiscal Ills of New York and Other Cities

Economic problems are not confined to private enterprise in the Middle Atlantic region. New York City has repeatedly faced the specter of municipal bankruptcy in recent years. When the city was unable to borrow money to meet and pay debts in 1975, it was bailed out by loan guarantees from New York state and later from the federal government. Moreover, the city was forced to give much of its control over fiscal affairs to a state-created Municipal Assistance Corporation (MAC) as a condition for receiving aid from Albany and Washington.

New York City's fiscal problems today have by no means been solved. A U.S. General Accounting Office report last year seconded MAC's recommendation of immediate budget cuts as a first step for the city to eliminate budget deficits and return to fiscal health.[15] But city officials say President Carter's proposed cuts in revenue sharing (see p. 262) would make any attempts at balancing the city's budget futile.

New York's fiscal problems are not unique. Observers say symptoms of fiscal insolvency — increasing costs of social services, education and city salaries that are unmatched by revenues — are evident in a number of large cities in the nation,

---

[13] U.S. Department of Transportation, Federal Highway Administration, "Transporting the Nation's Coal — a Preliminary Assessment," January 1978, pp. 11-12.

[14] For background on steel's foreign competition, see "Job Protection and Free Trade," *E.R.R.*, 1977 Vol. II, pp. 964-971.

[15] U.S. General Accounting Office, "New York City's Fiscal Problems: A Long Road Still Lies Ahead," Oct. 31, 1979.

including Philadelphia and Washington. The city government in the nation's capital faces a 1980 budget deficit estimated at some $172 million. Mayor Marion Barry has proposed a mid-year tax increase of $20.2 million and requested a $66.2 million supplemental appropriation from Congress, which controls more than half the land in the city and pays a significant portion of its expenses. The city's school system will be forced to lay off about 700 teachers this year, increase the number of children in each class and cut back on adult education programs in order to trim its budget. In Philadelphia, the city's municipal and school system budgets are expected to run a deficit of $93 million by mid-1981.

From Colonies to Megastates

THE MIDDLE ATLANTIC states is a term of convenience used to designate a group of states that lack such unifying historic ties as the New England and southern states share. There is no precise agreement as to just what this geographic designation embraces. Maryland, West Virginia or the District of Columbia are often left out of this grouping — sometimes all three are.

Before the American Revolution the "middle colonies" referred to New York, New Jersey, Pennsylvania and sometimes Delaware — once an appendage of Pennsylvania. Maryland, below the Mason-Dixon line, was generally considered southern. West Virginia had not yet been separated from Virginia,[16] and Washington, D.C., had not yet been created. The four middle colonies lay between "the wilderness Zion of the Puritans and the plantation colonies of the South" without "any common characteristics save their intermediate location."

And yet the authors of a *Literary History of the United States* go on to say that not being "dominated like New England in a single theological system or like the southern colonies by a peculiar [slave-owning] social system, was itself a significant common characteristic." The middle colonies, "by virtue of their linguistic and cultural variety, their relatively democratic social and political institutions, their easy tolerance, and their material prosperity . . . were the typically American region."[17]

Few areas of the earth embraced such a conglomerate population [the authors added]. There were Dutch patroons on the Hudson; Anglican, Jewish, Huguenot, and Dutch Calvinist merchants in

---

[16] This occurred during the Civil War. Virginia's western counties opted to stay in the Union and were admitted in 1863.

[17] *Literary History of the United States* (1974 ed.), p. 82; Robert E. Spiller et al., eds.

New York; English Quakers and transplanted New England Puritans on Long Island and in New Jersey; English and Welsh Quaker merchants and farmers in Philadelphia and the surrounding counties; industrious German sectarians farming the fertile hinterland of Philadelphia; hardy Scots-Irish on the frontiers; descendants of Swedish and Finnish traders along Delaware Bay; Negro servants and slaves; Iroquois, Delaware and Susquehanna Indians. . . . Here were the people from whom, as Crèvecoeur was to write, "that race now called American have arisen."

The most distinctive note was contributed by the Quakers, a religious minority whose central figure in America was William Penn, perhaps the greatest of colonial statesmen. Receiving from Charles II sole possession of a vast tract, which in 1682 he began to organize as a haven for persecuted European Quakers and any other religious group, Penn founded Pennsylvania.

". . . [B]y virtue of their linguistic and cultural variety, their relatively democratic social and political institutions, their easy tolerance, and their material prosperity [the Middle Colonies] were the typically American region."

"Pennsylvania was a portent of the America to be," wrote the late historian Samuel Eliot Morison. "Maryland had tried religious toleration but repealed her famous law in 1692; Rhode Island made religious liberty work on a small scale among English people only; but Pennsylvania was the first large community since the Roman Empire to allow different nations and religious sects to live under the same government on the basis of equality."[18]

But Penn's "holy experiment" was not as successful as he had hoped. Quarrels broke out among the colony's leaders, and in 1701 the "Three Lower Counties" — a parcel which Penn owned but was overlooked in the royal charter he received — became the separate colony of Delaware. The second Lord Baltimore, who in 1663 had begun to settle Maryland as a refuge for English Catholics, carried on a vexatious boundary dispute with Penn. It was resolved only when English astronomers Charles Mason and Jeremiah Dixon, in 1763-67, surveyed the famous line, which still today marks the border between Pennsylvania and Maryland.

New Netherlands had meanwhile been claimed by the Dutch, with their scattered settlements from the tip of Manhattan Is-

---

[18] Samuel Eliot Morison, *The Oxford History of the American People* (1965), p. 131.

land (New Amsterdam) on up the Hudson River and along the Delaware. But the Dutch were more interested in the fur trading than in permanent settlement and they soon fell prey to the English. The English captured New Amsterdam in 1664, and renamed it New York. The Dutch recaptured it in 1673, but gave it up for good when the Dutch trading empire in America dissolved.

The ex-Dutch territory between the Hudson and Delaware Rivers was ceded to Sir George Carteret and Lord Berkeley in 1664, but 74 years elapsed before this future colony of New Jersey attained a royal government. The Dutch inhabitants of northwestern New Jersey — near New York — and the Puritans of the southern part of the colony — near Philadelphia — could not agree on how the territory was to be ruled. New Jersey has never ceased to feel the strong gravitational pull of New York on one side and Philadelphia on the other.

New York's Meteoric Ascent in the 1800s

However, neither the city nor the state of New York became a commanding presence until early in the 19th century. New York was still one of the smaller states in population at the time of the Revolutionary War, outranked not only by Massachusetts and Virginia but — if colonial censuses can be trusted — also by Pennsylvania, Maryland and North Carolina. While early figures may be suspect, there is no doubt that at the outbreak of war with England, Philadelphia surpassed New York City in size and refinement.

Penn's city of brotherly love then had 30,000 people, making it the second-biggest city in the English-speaking world. The new nation declared its independence in Philadelphia and made it the capital — except for brief intervals — until the new city of Washington was ready to receive the government. In her classic, *American Cities in the Growth of the Nation,* Constance McLaughlin Green gives this account of Philadelphia:

> During the decade of the 1790s when she was the seat of the national government, official society had given life here a brilliance and extravagance far removed from the Quaker simplicity of earlier years. Along her wide streets, lined with harmoniously proportioned houses and public buildings, had rolled the fine coaches of federal dignitaries and foreign ministers, and at the President's levees the brocaded coats, silk hose, and powdered wigs of the aristocrats of the new republic had astonished Europeans looking for a gathering of rustics.

> With the removal of the federal government to the new capital at Washington in the summer of 1800, Philadelphia returned to many of her former sedate ways; traces of her Quaker origins had in fact remained in evidence all through her days of worldly splendor.

Quaker merchants, if overshadowed for a time by the statesmen and hangers-on of the national government about Independence Hall, had continued to direct from their counting houses the commercial affairs upon which the city's wealth rested.[19]

As a center of commerce, finance and population, Philadelphia was destined to give way to New York City. By the time of the first federal census in 1790, New York was bigger. Moreover, "New Yorkers seemed to be endowed by nature with the capacity to amass and use capital wisely," Green observed. Their harbor, by far the best on the Atlantic Coast, attracted enterprising merchants from all parts of the country, while the state's liberal auction laws allowed shippers privileges denied them elsewhere and encouraged European vessels to dock in New York. Above all, the city's rise to commercial pre-eminence in the 19th century can

Wall Street in the 19th Century

be traced to the opening of the Erie Canal in 1825, connecting New York City by water to Buffalo and linking the city commercially to the developing old Northwest Territory around the Great Lakes.

The sobriquet "Empire State" had now replaced the plain old "York State," reflecting the reality of the times. New York, with 1,372,812 inhabitants in 1820, became the nation's most populous state, a distinction it would hold through subsequent censuses until 1970, when California pushed ahead. The city passed the 100,000 mark in 1820, 300,000 in 1840 and 500,000 before mid-century. "The city's increase in population was phenomenal," Morison remarked. "There has been nothing like it since, even in California."

The Middle Atlantic States played a pivotal role in the nation's transformation from a largely agricultural and commercial society into a modern industrial nation after the Civil War. The North's industrial and financial sectors emerged from the war in healthy economic shape. Republican-dominated Congresses enacted a series of measures boosting tariffs, lowering taxes, giving away public lands for railroad building — all to protect U.S. (especially Northern) business and to promote the nation's westward expansion. Expand it did, opening up the

---

[19] Constance McLaughlin Green, *American Cities in the Growth of the Nation* (1957), p. 10.

frontier and creating financial empires out of railroading, steel-making, coal-mining and banking.

This was "Gilded Age," giving rise to "the robber barons" whose excesses would become the target of muckraking writers at the turn of the century. In this age J. P. Morgan, the New York financier, challenged the Rothschilds' pre-eminence as international bankers. In the last decades of the century, New York City began to rival London as the economic capital of the world.

Lingering Ethnic Influence of Immigration

America's industrial expansion created a great demand for labor, which tended to be filled increasingly by foreigners. During the last part of the 19th century and the first of the 20th century, there was an unprecedented inflow of immigrants — more than 23 million from 1871 until the outbreak of World War I in 1914. Most of them settled in or near the port cities where they arrived, giving those urban areas an ethnic identity which lasts to this day. This is especially true for New York, where Ellis Island was a main entry point.

The immigrants who flocked to the East Coast cities came mostly from peasant stock. In some cases, they were fleeing intolerable conditions at home — religious persecution in the case of eastern European Jews; famine in the case of the Irish after 1845. In an earlier period, 1820-60, the immigrants tended to be Scots, Irish, Welsh, and Germans from the Upper Rhine Valley. The second wave, in 1860-90, featured Prussians, Saxons, Bohemians and Scandinavians.[20]

The massive arrivals of Jews, other eastern Europeans and Italians and Greeks in the third wave, 1890-1914, were, like the Irish, Germans and Scandinavians before them, largely from rural areas. But they were more likely than their predecessors to be destitute and never got beyond the port cities. Great numbers of them were packed into big city tenements. New York's Lower East Side was the crowded home of 1.5 million poor Jewish immigrants in the early part of this century. It is estimated that 35 percent of New Jersey's population is of Italian descent.

Many of the immigrants settled in small industrial cities, including the cotton-mill towns of the Delaware Valley and manufacturing areas near Pittsburgh, New York City and Albany. The 1850 census recorded only 26 cities with more than 25,000 people; 50 years later there were more than six times as many, and most of them were in the Middle Atlantic region. Mary Procter and Bill Matuszeski wrote in their book *Gritty Cities:* "Even as the big cities grew bigger because of industri-

---

[20] See "Ethnic America," *E.R.R.*, 1971 Vol. I, pp. 54-57.

Centers of Population

City	1977 Pop.* (add 000)	Rank U.S. Cities	% Loss Since 1970	1977 Metro. Area Pop.* (add 000)
New York	7,298	1	7.6	9,387
Philadelphia	1,778	4	8.8	4,794
Baltimore	804	8	11.3	2,147
Washington	685	13	9.5	3,033
Pittsburgh	442	28	15.0	2,294
Buffalo	390	33	15.8	1,313
Newark	324	44	15.2	1,969
Rochester	256	57	13.5	970
Jersey City	232	61	12.1	564
Syracuse	178	79	9.7	648

*Bureau of the Census estimates

alization, many small towns had become middle-sized cities. This growth came to an end after World War I when the large cities and their surrounding metropolitan areas once again took on the dominant role in industrial growth."[21]

Fast Growth Among Small, Industrial Cities

Smaller cities that had enjoyed such fast growth — such as Paterson, N.J., Wilmington, Del., and Troy, N.Y. — typically had the advantage of nearby canals, railroads or navigable rivers and were able to use coal or water power to supply their industries. The roots of Paterson's development date from 1701 when Alexander Hamilton founded the Society for Establishing Useful Manufactures. It chose Paterson's Passaic River's great falls as the site for the U.S. government's first attempt to sponsor an American industry.

Cities like Reading, Allentown, Bethlehem and Lancaster, Pa., not only were located near coal seams and other raw materials, but they also had the advantage of being situated on main transportation routes. These cities were centers of the iron and steel industries, and produced brass, clocks, locomotives, ships and in the case of Paterson, railroad cars and silk.

These smaller cities began to decline economically by the end of World War I. Their goods "were directly usable in an agrarian economy," Procter and Matuszeski wrote. But "with rapid industrialization, capital goods became the more valuable manufactured goods; steel companies, for example, shifted production from steel rails to structural steel. A big city location was a definite advantage in marketing these goods to other manufacturers."[22]

[21] Mary Procter and Bill Matuszeski, *Gritty Cities* (1978), p. 8.
[22] *Ibid.*, p. 11.

103

The large cities themselves underwent significant changes. During the first three decades of the 20th century, more than two million blacks left the rural South for what they hoped would be better lives in northern cities, and they would be followed by millions more in the next three decades. By the turn of the century most large cities in the country had become economically and socially stratified. The affluent were living in comfortable townhouses and the poor — many of whom were newly arrived immigrants or from rural areas — worked long hours for low wages in surrounding ethnic ghettos. The middle classes tended to move to the less-expensive outlying areas.

The prosperity of the 1920s, along with the growing number of automobiles, gave new impetus to suburban development. It was not until after World War II, though, that the flight to the suburbs intensified. By 1960, the U.S. population was divided almost equally among the central cities, suburbs and non-metropolitan areas — each with about 60 million people. But by 1970, the population of the suburbs had grown to 76 million, compared to 64 million in the cities. New York City lost 9.7 percent of its jobs in the 1960s while its suburbs gained 24.9 percent. This pattern was repeated in one big city after another in the industrial North.

Outlook for the Eighties

MANY of the older cities of the industrial North are suffering from wear and tear. Buildings, streets, sewer and water lines typically are aged and overused. These cities also tend to be the ones that have been hurt most by the departure of the white middle class, leaving behind a lower tax base and a heavier welfare load.

Thus the financial resources to mend physical deterioration and care for the social ills have shrunk as the needs have increased. While there are success stories here and there — Baltimore's downtown revitalization, for example — most of the cities continue to be haunted by the same litany of problems they have faced for two decades or more, those of racial polarity, crime, declining revenues and municipal services.

One set of physical problems on the horizon in the urban North, which so far has received relatively little attention, was pointed up recently in a report prepared for the Consortium of Northeast Organizations.[23] It is the deteriorating condition of

---

[23] Consortium of Northeast Organizations, "Water Resource Priorities for the Northeast," Oct. 9, 1979.

many of the municipal water-delivery systems. These systems are wearing out and there are not enough funds to replace them.

Another serious and growing water problem involves the disposal of hazardous wastes. New Jersey, for example, the nation's most densely populated state, also leads the nation in chemical manufacturing. Nearly all of its main waterways are polluted. The consortium report said that 11 northeastern states[24] will generate about 28 percent of all hazardous wastes in the nation this year. Improper hazardous waste disposal has brought severe environmental and health problems in the Middle Atlantic region. The toxic chemical contamination in Love Canal near Buffalo, N.Y., and illegal chemical dumpings in New Jersey's Meadowlands have attracted national attention.[25]

The consortium study estimated that in order to meet federal anti-pollution goals, many cities in the Northeast will need to install expensive advanced waste-water treatment facilities at a total cost of $5 billion. The price tag to repair outmoded sewer systems was put at $10 billion.

Heavy Reliance on Mass Transportation

A price tag of the same order, when fully calculated, could be applied to mass transit needs in the Middle Atlantic states. As the New York City transit strike on April 1 made clear, urban dwellers in the Northeast, more than in other parts of the country, depend heavily on public transportation. According to statistics compiled by the Coalition of Northeast Governors, the transit systems in the 11 northeastern states carried some 1.4 billion riders in 1979, about half of the nation's total. Like the region's water and sewage system and its highway and ports, many of the mass transit systems are old and in need of refurbishing. The cost to do so in the Middle Atlantic region alone would run to the tens of billions of dollars.

The biggest problems involve declining revenues, increasing costs and the growth in transit operating subsidies. In Maryland — the only state which helps to finance two major metropolitan rapid transit systems, in Baltimore and Washington — the state's share of operating subsidies is scheduled to grow from about $41 million in the current fiscal year to more than $133 million by fiscal year 1989.

Commuter railways and buses run by the New Jersey Department of Transportation handle some 400,000 passengers daily, the state government estimates. But much of the mass transportation system is old and in need of significant rehabilitation.

---

[24] The five Middle Atlantic states plus the six New England States: Connecticut, Maine, Massachusetts, New Hampshire, Rhode Island and Vermont.
[25] See "Toxic Substance Control," *E.R.R.*, 1978 Vol. II, p. 741.

The state government currently is working on a seven-year, $4.5 billion capital improvement program designed to repair bridges, widen and resurface roads, upgrade rail lines and replace buses and rail cars. New Jersey transportation officials say they cannot rehabilitate their system without significant help from the federal government — about $1.3 billion in the next seven years.

New York has similar problems with old yet heavily used transportation facilities. New Yorkers account for about 35 percent of all transit riders and 50 percent of all transit passenger miles in the nation. Yet New York receives only about 20 percent of the total allocation of federal transportation funds. In Pennsylvania, state officials say the highway system is deteriorating much more quickly than it is being repaired. They estimate that it will take about $1.5 billion to restore and modernize over 1,000 miles of interstate highways in Pennsylvania.

Demand for 'Fair Share' of Federal Funds

Officials in the Middle Atlantic states say that one reason for their water, transportation and economic problems is that they do not receive a fair proportion of federal funds. The Northeast-Midwest Congressional Coalition, in fact, was set up three-and-a-half years ago to address the issue of "fiscal disparity" among the regions of the nation. "We are not trying to stem the flow of funds to the South," said John Moriarity, the coalition's executive director. "We're trying to balance the flow of funds so they go where the need is greatest."[26]

Revenue sharing, allocations to state and local governments of federally collected taxes, is of particular importance to the Middle Atlantic states. These and other industrial states, John Shannon of the Advisory Commission on Intergovernmental Relations told Congress last year, "are carrying extraordinary welfare loads, making the greatest tax effort, and confronted with the most acute central city problems. There is no question that the withdrawal of federal revenue sharing aid to the states will be most keenly felt in this area."[27]

According to the National Governors' Association, last year 58 percent of all state revenue sharing funds were spent on education and social services for the poor, elderly and mentally ill. The rest went for capital improvement, retirement benefits for state and local government employees and other purposes. It was with dismay, then, that state officials greeted President Carter's latest series of anti-inflation measures announced March 14. Carter proposed to drop $1.7 billion of the $6.9 billion

---

[26] Quoted by Horace Sutton, in *Saturday Review,* April 15, 1978, p. 33.

[27] Statement before the House Committee on Banking, Finance and Urban Affairs' Subcommittee on the City, May 3, 1979.

in revenue-sharing funds scheduled for distribution to state and local governments in 1980.

Rep. Robert W. Edgar, D-Pa., chairman of the Northeast-Midwest Congressional Coalition, told the House Subcommittee on Intergovernmental Relations and Human Resources March 19 that Carter's proposal would have a devastating effect on states like those in the Middle Atlantic region. "Eliminating the state share of general revenue will tighten by a notch or two the fiscal straight jackets on many Northeastern and Midwestern states," Edgar said.

According to statistics compiled by the coalition, the Middle Atlantic states — especially New Jersey, Delaware, New York and Pennsylvania — tend to get far less from the federal government than they give in taxes. The ratio for a recent fiscal year, 1978, was calculated as follows:

New York	95¢	a loss of $1.9 billion
New Jersey	70¢	a loss of $5.1 billion
Pennsylvania	87¢	a loss of $2.8 billion
Delaware	69¢	a loss of $414 million
West Virginia	94¢	a loss of $175 million

The ratio for Maryland was $1.18, reflecting the large number of federal government agencies located in the Washington suburbs. Washington itself showed the biggest ratio of all, $7.48.

Officials in the Middle Atlantic states do not believe that the federal government alone can solve the region's problems. A good deal of the impetus for economic recovery, it is agreed, must come from within the region itself. "By using the resources, capabilities and ingenuity within the region — and by learning from the examples of other sections of the nation now prospering — the Northeast and Midwest can reverse many of the current economic trends which hinder the region's full recovery," the Northeast-Midwest Congressional Coalition said.[28]

---

[28] Northeast Midwest Congressional Coalition, et al., "The State of the Region," March 1979, p. 3.

Selected Bibliography

Books

Cunningham, John T., *New Jersey: America's Main Road*, Doubleday, 1966.

Ellis, David M. et al., *A History of New York State*, Cornell University Press, 1967.

Green, Constance McLaughlin, *American Cities in the Growth of the Nation*, John deGraff, 1957.

Morison, Samuel Eliot, *The Oxford History of the American People*, Oxford University Press, 1965.

Peirce, Neal R., *The Megastates of America*, Norton, 1972.

Procter, Mary and Bill Matuszeski, *Gritty Cities*, Temple University Press, 1978.

Rifkin, Jeremy and Randy Barber, *The North Will Rise Again*, Beacon, 1978.

Sale, Kirkpatrick, *Power Shift*, Random House, 1975.

Turner, Frederick Jackson, *The United States: 1830-1850*, Norton, 1965.

Articles

Fleetwood, Blake, "The New Elite and an Urban Renaissance," *The New York Times Magazine*, Jan. 14, 1979.

Ichniowski, Tom, "Letter from Delaware: A State That is Warming to Business Again," *Business Week*, Sept. 1, 1979.

Phalon, Richard, "Grim Times in Fun City," *Forbes*, March 17, 1980.

Rosen, Gerald R., "Politics: A New Ball Game in the 1980s," *Dun's Review*, January 1980.

Sutton, Horace, "Sunbelt Vs. Frostbelt: A Second Civil War?" *Saturday Review*, April 15, 1978.

Reports and Studies

Coalition of Northeastern Governors, "State Transportation Profiles," Feb. 26, 1980.

Consortium of Northeast Organizations, "Water Resource Priorities for the Northeast," Oct. 9, 1979.

Council for Northeast Economic Action, "The Regional Data Quarterly, Second Quarter 1979."

Department of Commerce, Bureau of the Census, "Population Estimates and Projections, Current Population Reports," selected issues.

Department of the Treasury, "Federal Aid to States, Fiscal Year 1979, Preliminary," Jan. 21, 1980.

General Accounting Office, "New York City's Fiscal Problems: A Long Road Still Lies Ahead," Oct. 31, 1979.

PACIFIC NORTHWEST: PARADISE LOST?

by

William V. Thomas

Apr. 18
1 9 8 0

PACIFIC NORTHWEST

T HERE was a time not long ago when the Pacific Northwest might have qualified as one of the country's best kept secrets. Life in this far corner of the United States was an unpublicized pleasure that residents jealously guarded and people elsewhere usually associated with endless rain. But the weather may be one of the few things that has stayed the same. Change is coming to the coastal states of Washington, Oregon and neighboring Idaho, and it is not entirely welcome.

Attracted by its spreading reputation for "livability," outsiders are migrating to the Northwest in growing numbers. The sharp influx of newcomers and the problems they inevitably bring with them have left many natives wondering if the region's best qualities — the unspoiled beauty of its forests and shores, the peace and quiet of its urban areas — can survive its new popularity. "We have a deep and abiding love of this land," said Washington Gov. Dixy Lee Ray. "We're all very defensive about it." Most people realize that population growth and economic development go hand-in-hand, Ray said. "But we want them to come in a way that preserves the natural flavor [of the environment]."[1]

Basic individualism and an almost religious appreciation of nature have produced a community of values and interests unique to the Northwest. Residents refer to the region as "God's country," a description which may be only a slight exaggeration. The opening stanza of "America the Beautiful" could easily have been written about this land, with its majestic mountain peaks and amber waves of grain. From the foothills of the Rockies to the Cascade and Olympic ranges, and beyond to the Pacific, it encompasses a varied geography of rain forests, fertile valleys and deserts.

The eastern sections of Washington and Oregon along with the southern part of Idaho are dry, rolling plains, while the Pacific slopes of the region are lush and green, kept that way by almost year-round rain. Here, there is "no sense of being between rains," wrote Bernard Malamud in *A New Life* (1961). Rain is "a climate and condition."[2] Forms of wildlife long since van-

---

[1] Quoted in *Time* magazine, Dec. 12, 1977.

[2] Seattle's rainfall averaged 33.99 inches in 1978, less than in New York City, which had 49.67 inches. But New York had only 115 rainy days; Seattle had 146.

ished from more densely populated states still roam protected in the snowy elevations of Washington and Oregon, while the glacier fed streams and rivers of Idaho teem with an abundance of fish.

The environment is the measure of all things in the Northwest, and even city dwellers feel close to the land. Typically, they like to boast that wilderness is never far from most towns. Cities elsewhere may be plagued by urban blight and rising crime statistics, but Portland, Seattle, Spokane and Boise are bustling, clean and, compared to many of their East Coast counterparts, safe. Because of the relatively low concentration of blacks, racial strife is at a minimum. Indians, who comprise less than one percent of the Northwestern population, are perhaps the most outspoken minority. However, they have chosen to pursue their claims to land and fishing rights in the courts rather than in the streets.

If western Washington's fortunes for better or worse are linked to the aircraft industry, other local economies are tied to renewable resources: agriculture, timber and water. It is with good reason, then, that the environment should be the object of such great concern. "Come but don't stay," Oregon's unofficial motto, has been adopted as something of a Northwest battle cry. More people only put a greater strain on the already fragile balance between the needs of man and the requirements of nature. Upset that equilibrium, the logic goes, and "God's country" would be just like any place else.

Social Change and Endangered Resources

The problems posed by increasing population and limited resources are not common to the Northwest alone. Yet it is probably true that residents there are more conscious of what they have to lose if unplanned development and wholesale exploitation of the land run rampant. These are the nerve ends of regional concern. And with the swing of the presidential race into the Northwest — for the Oregon primary on May 20 and the Idaho primary on May 27 — many voters are hoping for an opportunity to hear the candidates' views on the issues that set this area apart from the rest of the country.

But even as some people wait to hear presidential hopefuls describe how federal policies should serve local interests, a strain of anti-eastern, anti-big-government skepticism will prompt others to be wary. A curious sort of alienation from national politics seems to pervade much of western, particularly northwestern, life. Residents of the northern Mountain and Coastal states have always fancied themselves independent from remote government that until recently, they say, has

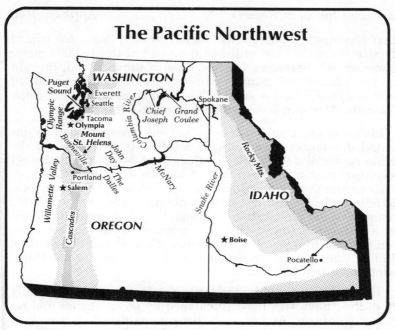

The Pacific Northwest

shown little concern for managing the timber, mineral and energy resources under its jurisdiction. On the other hand, Northwesterners have been dependent on the federal government in fundamental ways — first to protect them from Indians, then to provide them with homesteads, and later to subsidize huge dam and irrigation projects.

Politically, the Northwest ranges from the progressive populism of western Oregon to the basic conservatism of Idaho, where Mormons exercise an influence far beyond their 27 percent of the population. In Oregon, whose population rose by 18 percent during the 1960s and 21 percent from 1970 to 1979, coping with the strain of more people has become a political issue. Once thought of by many as the most liberal state in the nation — in 1971 it decriminalized marijuana and banned throw-away clear containers — Oregon may be moving gradually toward the right, as a post-Proposition 13 climate seems to be taking hold there.[3]

In Washington, less than a decade ago the main concern was jobs. The economy suffered a severe jolt in the early 1970s when the Boeing Co. began laying off aircraft workers. But the company is now back on its feet and Washingtonians are turning their attention to what some call "the hazards of good fortune" — finding work for new arrivals and supplying the state with energy enough to meet the demands of a growing population.

Idaho, principally a rural state, has escaped many of the woes

---

[3] In June 1978, California voters approved Proposition 13, a ballot initiative that effectively cut the state's property tax revenues in half.

that accompany rapid growth. Its largest city, Boise, has tripled in size since 1960 but still has not reached the 100,000 mark. However, it's beginning to show signs of urbanization, brought on by "platoons of young executives, drawn from the Stanford and Harvard business schools by [such corporations as] Boise Cascade, Morrison-Knudsen and Hewlett-Packard."[4]

Idahoans are troubled less by outside pressure than by internal differences. The state, in a sense, is split between the building social and political influence of Mormons in the agricultural southeast, the home of Idaho's much-advertised potatoes,[5] and the "live-and-let-live" outlook in the northern panhandle, where mining and lumbering are the economic mainstays and prostitution, although illegal, is openly tolerated in a number of towns. One indication of Idaho's conservative temper was passage of a Proposition 13-style tax cut in 1979. Unlike similar ballot measures elsewhere, there was no significant opposition in Idaho.

The problems faced by the three Northwest states differ only in degree. Each sees itself threatened by social change and resource shortages. And in each, the coming decade is seen as a test, one that could decide whether the region will remain livable and whether it will have enough to live on.

The Portland-Everett Population Corridor

Just as the East Coast has its megalopolis running from Boston to Washington, D.C., the Pacific Northwest has its version of a population corridor running north-south along Interstate Highway 5 from Everett, Wash., to Portland, Ore. Nearly 75 percent of the people of Washington and Oregon live in this strip, which is about 150 miles long and 50 miles wide. Industrial and manufacturing centers also have clustered there, adding not only to the overall population but contributing to undesirable side effects such as air and water pollution.

Moving northward from California and westward from New York, Illinois and other states, immigrants have come in droves to Washington and Oregon in search of an uncrowded, slower-paced life. Ironically, however, most of them tend to settle in the Puget Sound area around Seattle or in the Willamette Valley of Oregon. Seventy-five percent of the new arrivals want to live where 75 percent of the population already is. And so the density of the Everett-Portland corridor increases.

Washington, the most populous state in the region, now has almost four million people and is expected to have five million by the year 2000. State projections for King County, which in-

---

[4] Wallace and Page Stegner, "Rocky Mountain Country," *Atlantic*, April 1978, p. 88.

[5] Automobile license plates bear the slogan "Idaho — Famous Potatoes."

Northwest States' Population

State	1979 Estimates (add 000)	Population Rank Among States	Increase Since 1970*
Idaho	905	42	26.9%
Oregon	2,527	33	20.8
Washington	3,926	22	15.0

*National average 8.3%.

Source: Bureau of the Census

cludes Seattle, are that its present population of 1.2 million will increase during that time to 1.6 million.[6] The state's population has climbed steadily since 1975 and for the past three years its annual growth rate of 2 percent has been four times higher than the national average.

Oregon also has shown above-average growth patterns, moving from two million to two and a half million people during the decade. Portland, its biggest city, expanded its area-wide growth from 878,676 to slightly more than one million, according to the city's own estimates. Oregon and Washington each expects to gain an extra congressional seat on the basis of the 1980 census. Idaho reversed three decades of population decline in the 1970s. Its rate of growth (nearly 27 percent) in 1970-79, the fastest of the three states, carried the state's population above 900,000. W. LaMar Bollinger of the College of Idaho at Caldwell, who has conducted Idaho population studies, said half of the newcomers he questioned were under age 30 and a third of them held college degress. About half of these arrivals listed outdoor recreation, sparse population and low pollution as their reasons for coming. One-third were from California.

Seattle — 'America's Most Livable City'

Seattle, the Northwest's largest city, seems to have felt the changes enveloping the entire region more keenly than any place else. In 1957, the urban historian Constance McLaughlin Green wrote of Seattle life: "Living in a setting of great natural beauty with all outdoors within easy reach, people cannot bear to contemplate living [in another city]. No opportunity outside Seattle has any appeal; they have little interest in other places and the ideas of other communities."[7] If Seattlites have not changed, people elsewhere have — the city has been discovered.

From the time Seattle put itself on display by hosting the

---

[6] Prediction by the Washington State Office of Financial Management.

[7] Constance McLaughlin Green, *American Cities and the Growth of the Nation* (1957), p. 191.

1962 World's Fair, newcomers have been beating a path to its door. They are attracted in no small part by reports that what awaits them is "America's most livable city."[8] Of course, some in Seattle are proud of their spreading national reputation. Others, though, are understandably concerned about its long-term effects. "Los Angelization" is the latest buzz word for the worst that could happen. The last few years, said an apprehensive local official, "have been like culture shock and future shock all rolled into one."

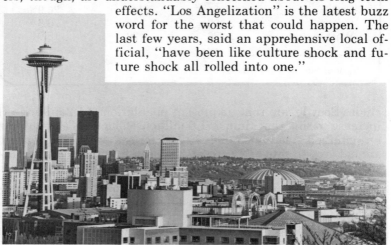

Downtown Seattle with Mt. Rainier in the background

In 1970, when Boeing, the region's chief employer, began laying off thousands of aircraft workers, Seattle's future seemed bleak. Families were abandoning their unpaid-for homes, furniture and boats and leaving the city in caravans. As they departed, many drove past a billboard that read: "Will the last person leaving please turn out the lights." The city and surrounding sections of King County lost nearly 30,000 people between 1970 and 1976, and local unemployment reached 15 percent, about three times the national average. Seattle became a prime example of what happens to a one-industry town when its one industry goes bust.

Gradually, the local economy got back on its feet. Nevertheless, the effects of the slump, some say, taught the city a lesson it will never forget. During the lean years, the area broadened its economic base by attracting a diversity of new businesses. Also, many of those who stayed behind to "tough out" the crunch opened businesses of their own. As a result, Seattle has become what one restaurant entrepreneur described as "a small business mecca."

"Seattle's a city that rewards healthy ambition," said David Brewster, publisher of *The Weekly,* a local newspaper for

---

[8] For discussions of Seattle's "livability," see *Harper's,* March 1977, and *New West,* December 1977.

"young professionals." But the city's "not for everybody," he added. "It's dangerous psychologically. The mellowness of the environment is your competition."

Oddly enough, many people now see that "mellowness" threatened by Seattle's prosperity. It is said that living in Seattle is like being on vacation. Yet there seems to be a feeling in the area that the fun could be spoiled by uncontrolled growth. A referendum to prevent that city from advertising its delights in out-of-town magazines and newspapers was defeated in last November's city election. In surrounding sections of King County, however, voters passed a measure to buy up and preserve parcels of farm land lying in the path of suburban development.

Residents say these efforts are evidence of logical civic-mindedness rather than any anti-immigrant impulse. Just the same, they admit, Seattle's secret is out. "That could be creating a lifeboat mentality," ventured a third-year transplant, *Seattle Times* editorial writer John Hamer. "Every new arrival wants to be the last one to get in, and the rest can go somewhere else."

Opening Up The Wilderness

GEOGRAPHY may be destiny, as many historians believe, but it is an idea few state boundaries observe. The borders of Washington, Oregon and Idaho seem to have been dictated more by expedience than reason. In fact, so different are the social, economic and geographical landscapes they embrace, the three Northwest states, some inhabitants say, ought to be redivided into three more. "Western state boundaries often run in straight lines, which is a very bad sign," wrote former *Life* magazine editor Thomas Griffith. "Whenever straight lines appear on a map, usually following meridians or parallels, it is easy to recognize that whoever drew [them] was not very interested in the realities of river basins and mountain ranges."[9]

John Quincy Adams, who never set foot in the Northwest, was largely responsible for its political shape, since it was Adams who, as president, decided on the two long, straight east-west lines that define the region. But long before Adams traced the northern and southern boundaries of the area, the Northwest was visited by hundreds of map-making explorers. In 1805-06, Meriwether Lewis and William Clark at the behest of Thomas Jefferson reached the northern Pacific Coast on their explora-

---

[9] Thomas Griffith, "The Pacific Northwest," *Harper's*, April 1976, p. 54.

tion of the newly acquired Louisiana Purchase. Jacob Astor's Pacific Fur Co. moved into the Oregon wilderness after the War of 1812, setting up trading posts and the first vestiges of American settlements.

Spain in 1818, and Russia in 1824, accepted border adjustments on the Pacific slope that eliminated their claims to the Columbia basin. American and British claims were settled only after years of bickering, threats of war and joint occupancy. The tide of American settlers, many of them following the famous Oregon Trail,[10] made the U.S. presence a reality that England could hardly afford to challenge. And in 1846, the British accepted Adams' old line of the 49th parallel as the far northern border of the western United States.

Indians of the Pacific Northwest initially were so peaceful that in 1831 a delegation of Flathead and Nez Perce, curious about the white man's religion, went to St. Louis, requesting that various Catholic orders send "black robes" to teach their tribes. Hordes of missionaries followed, each group claiming to represent the true faith. Eventually, the confused situation brought about tribal conflicts that culminated in 1848 in several years of Indian warfare.

By the mid-19th century, the restoration of peace led to calls for statehood in the territory. Oregon was admitted to the Union in 1859, followed by Washington in 1889 and Idaho in 1890. The completion of the Northern Pacific Railroad in 1883, after nearly 20 years of work, greatly expanded the economy of the entire region. Washington, where the rail line terminated, was the primary beneficiary of new wealth and the influx of immigrants. The population of the state rose from 75,166 in 1880 to 357,222 in 1890. Growth was spurred again in 1897 when the discovery of gold in the Klondike made Seattle the gateway to Alaska. Nearly 90 years later, with the opening of Alaska's North Slope oil fields, Seattle assumed its gateway role once again, serving first as a point of embarkation for oil pipeline workers and then as a way-station for Alaskan oil arriving in the lower 48.

Northwest Labor Unrest From the 1890s

Along with the rapid expansion of the Northwest's economy came shocking demonstrations of worker discontent. Labor wars were common in the silver mining districts of Idaho from 1892 to 1899. Local suppression of union activity in the Coeur d'Alene area produced two years of martial law. And in 1905, former Idaho Gov. Frank Steunenberg was assassinated by a disgruntled miner.

[10] The first wagon train to make this hazardous overland journey from Independence and Westport (Kansas City), Mo., reached the Pacific Northwest in 1842. Thousands of settlers followed. Their journey over this migratory route was chronicled, among others, by the historian Francis Parkman in his classic *The Oregon Trail,* first published in 1856.

The Northwest's rough and ready reputation again became the focus of national attention in the years before and shortly after World War I, when politics in Washington and Oregon briefly exploded in a series of violent acts. In both states, waves of immigrants from the Midwest and South, attracted by wartime employment, added fuel to a growing conservative mood in the region. In the late 1910s and early 1920s, a remarkably strong Ku Klux Klan in Oregon claimed 9,000 adherents in the Portland area alone. The KKK was strong enough to stage parades through the streets of Oregon cities and even got sympathizers elected to public office.

During this same period, western Washington became a center of the International Workers of the World. As the IWW, or "Wobblies," gathered strength and new members among disillusioned veterans and others after the war, local business leaders decided to take action. The result was a series of bloody clashes between workers and bands of vigilantes up and down the state.

In the summer of 1916, Wobblies went on strike in Everett, Wash., crippling for a time that town's lumber industry. Enraged Everett industrialists tried to break the strike by running the IWW out of town, but they succeeded only in raising the level of violence. Seattle Wobblies retaliated by sending 250 men to Everett where they were met by gunfire and several died. A labor journal of the day blamed the "business and professional men's army" for the strife that followed. "An intolerable situation exists in this city," the paper declared. "The beating up of men and boys by citizens clothed with temporary authority and armed with clubs, which is almost a nightly occurrence . . . is a disgrace to a civilized society."[11]

Labor trouble took place in Seattle in 1919, when a strike by shipyard workers set off a citywide strike that threw the community into chaos and threatened to become a genuine revolution. That same year, in Centralia, Wash., 100 miles south of Seattle, an Armistice Day parade turned into a riot when American Legionaires attacked an IWW headquarters. Many on both sides were killed or injured.

Despite the experience with the IWW, Washington proved hospitable to trade unions in the 1930s, and today it has one of the highest percentages of union participation in the country. Washington's union participation rate is 36.5; the national rate is 26.8. In the 1950s, however, Dave Beck of Seattle gave the Teamsters Union a bad name when, as head of its western division, he was accused of misappropriating funds and tax eva-

---

[11] Quoted by Norman H. Clark in *Mill Town: A Social History of Everett, Washington* (1970), p. 190.

sion. Beck's tumultuous career and his effort to unionize "everything on wheels" came to an end when he was sent to prison in 1962.

Postwar Upsurge in Aircraft and Timber

The Northwestern economy was enhanced during World War II when the aircraft industry began to flourish in western Washington. Boeing, which produced bombers for the war effort, is now the world's leading manufacturer of commercial airliners. According to *Fortune* magazine's latest ranking of U.S. industrial corporations, Boeing stood No. 40 in terms of sales (more than $5.4 billion in 1978).[12] A spate of new orders since then may push its standing up the scale when the next rankings are published in May. At any rate, Boeing is by far the biggest single private employer in the Northwest.

Boeing's prosperity was a prime factor in the upsurge of Washington's economy during the 1950s and 1960s. But building airplanes has proven to be anything but a steady business. Customers are limited to a few hundred buyers and sales can disappear rapidly even for an industry giant like Boeing. In fact, that is precisely what happened in 1970. In prior years, Boeing employed as many as 101,000 people in Washington — nearly 8 percent of the state's work force. In 1970, however, its employment rolls dropped to 38,000. One year later, 55,000 people left the state to search for work elsewhere. As a result, the bottom fell out of the real estate markets in Everett, Tacoma and Seattle. Washington's economy took a nose dive.

New military and civilian contracts, including work on the cruise missile, have brought Boeing's employment level back near the pre-1970 mark, and Washington's economy has improved accordingly. Once again, Boeing is the area's best provider. The company's earnings for 1979 — $505 million — more than doubled its 1977 profits.

Around the time Boeing began building World War II bombers, the Weyerhaeuser Co. started planting the first U.S. tree farm in Grays Harbor County, Wash. Like Boeing, Weyerhaeuser and other big timber companies — such as Boise Cascade, Georgia-Pacific, Crown-Zellerbach and St. Regis — flourished in the years after the war.[13] The postwar demand for housing created a boom business. Timber prices shot up, and the Northwest, where most of the nation's prime housing and construction wood grows, prospered.

---

[12] "The 500 Largest Industrial Companies," *Fortune,* May 7, 1979, p. 270.

[13] Georgia-Pacific is based in Portland, Weyerhaeuser in Tacoma and Boise Cascade in Boise, although their operations are international. In terms of *Fortune's* rankings of the top U.S. industrial companies, based on 1978 sales, Georgia-Pacific was No. 53, Weyerhaeuser No. 69 and Boise Cascade No. 111. Crown-Zellerbach is based in San Francisco and St. Regis in New York. Their *Fortune* rankings are Nos. 116 and 128, respectively.

Fishing rights have long been a bone of contention between whites and Indians in the Northwest. But in 1979, the U.S. Supreme Court upheld a 130-year-old treaty between the United States and Washington Indian tribes that, in effect, ended much of the argument. The court decided that Indians are entitled to half of all the fish harvestable in the state. The ruling, commercial fishermen say, will destroy the salmon fishing industry in Washington.

Indians, however, believe that the court's decision has implications far beyond simple fishing rights. They contend that since they are entitled to a certain percentage of fish, they have a right to make sure those fish survive until they are caught. Thus, Indians feel fish should be protected from man-caused dangers, including pollution, logging and the blocking of spawning streams by hydroelectric dams. A lawsuit aimed at protecting the fish is currently pending in U.S. District Court in Seattle.

As the lumber market expanded, Congress in 1960 enacted the Multiple Use-Sustained Yield Act, declaring that the national forests should be "utilized in the combination [of ways] that will best meet the needs of the American people." The industry in the Northwest benefited, but many environmentalists argued that the legislation was a blanket "license to log." The law, they argued, was too vague. For years, the Sierra Club and other environmental groups petitioned the federal government to tighten restrictions on the timber companies. In 1971, Congress responded by passing the National Forest Management Act. This measure directed the Forest Service to curb timber-cutting abuses on federally owned land. To make up for these curbs, however, companies stepped up harvesting by other methods.[14]

[14] See "Forest Policy," *E.R.R.,* 1975 Vol. II, pp. 865-884.

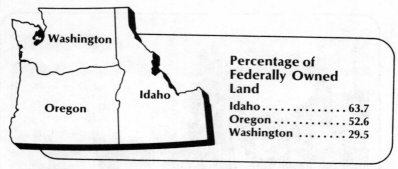

Percentage of
Federally Owned
Land

Idaho 63.7
Oregon 52.6
Washington 29.5

Generally, the states had little to complain about since they received taxes and payments for timber cut on county, state and federal land. The Washington state public school system, for example, received over $40 million by this means in 1978. But with the recent slump in the building and construction industry, Northwest communities once dependent on the lumber business face the possibility of a serious recession. Oregon officials estimate that 7,000 of the state's 76,000 lumber industry jobs have vanished since November. Authorities in Washington say that that state has lost 7 percent of the 52,000 lumber and wood products jobs it had early in 1979.

Many of those jobs may never reappear. As more northwestern forests are stripped by logging or declared off-limits by the government, lumber companies are moving their operations to the southeastern states. Even Weyerhaeuser, the Northwest's biggest private landowner, with 2.8 million acres, has built up its timber holdings in the South to 3.1 million acres. "At least you can still buy [land] down there," said John Ferry, chairman of the Boise Cascade Corp. "In the Northwest, you either already own it or rely on the government, which is releasing less. Nobody sells up there."[15]

Region's Energy Questions

WATER and the power it produces are two things Northwest residents have long taken for granted. Ever since the New Deal provided a series of massive hydroelectric generating dams on the Columbia River, the region has been a kind of energy Utopia, blessed with an abundance of low-cost electricity and was until recently exempt from the politics and economics of scarcity.

The Northwest uses a lot of electricity, largely because of the industries that its low rates have attracted over the years. Chief

[15] Quoted in The Wall Street Journal, April 10, 1980.

among these industries is aluminum smelting. The Bonneville Power Administration (BPA), the federal agency which transmits power from some 30 dams in the Northwest, supplies industrial customers and utilities in the region. On the average, Northwest electrical rates are about half what they are in other sections of the country, and Northwesterners use about twice as much electricity as people elsewhere.

Hydropower is clean, efficient and was, until recently, in ample supply. In 1979, rain and melted snow filled the Columbia and other rivers with enough water to generate 80 percent of the Northwest's electricity. But as the demand for power has increased with the growing population, output has not kept pace. There is simply not a sufficient amount of hydropower to go around. And utilities, industries, and state and local governments are fighting over who gets it.

Roll on, Columbia, roll on.
Roll on, Columbia, roll on.
Your power is turning our darkness to dawn.
So roll on, Columbia, roll on!
—Woody Guthrie

Most cities and counties in Washington operate public electric utilities, which today serve approximately two-thirds of the state's residents. In Oregon and Idaho, on the other hand, over three-fourths of all consumers are served by private power companies. Most BPA power is delivered at low rates to Washington consumers, while buyers in neighboring states served by private utilities are subject to higher costs and frequent rate increases. Herein lies the source of the current dispute.

Lawmakers in Oregon and Idaho have attempted over the years to get less costly BPA power for their states. Oregon took the boldest step in 1977 by establishing the nation's first state-run electric company to buy and distribute electricity to homes and farms. Nevertheless, basic rate discrepancies remain.

At present, there is a temporary lull in the struggle, as parties wait to see the outcome of action in Congress on the Pacific Northwest Electric Power Planning and Conservation Act (S 885). Introduced by Sen. Henry M. Jackson, D-Wash., the bill would restructure Bonneville, putting it under a single presidentially appointed administrator with broad powers to distribute electricity throughout the region. The BPA, under Jackson's proposal, would also have the authority to decide what new power sources are developed.

Many see the measure as the best solution to the cost and allocation problem. But the bill is not without its critics, some of whom say it would put too much authority in the hands of an unelected official and perhaps hasten the building of unwanted nuclear power facilities in the area. Worst of all, writes Oregon environmentalist Phillip Johnson: "Utilities wishing to bring new generating facilities on line would need the permission of the administrator: the same would hold true of conservation programs. A utility proceeding on its own could find its allocation of BPA power reduced by a corresponding amount. . . . This arrangement would actually penalize utilities for finding new sources of energy."[16]

Nation's Repository for Its Nuclear Waste

The debate between advocates and critics of nuclear power was going on in the Northwest years before it evolved into a national controversy. Two of the country's 10 nuclear waste disposal sites are located in northwestern states: the Hanford facility at Richland, Wash., and the National Reactor Testing Station near Idaho Falls, Idaho. The federal government has accumulated over 90 million gallons of highly toxic long-lasting radioactive waste from its weapons program and most of this material, some 72 percent, is stored at Hanford. Idaho Falls receives about 3 percent.

Local citizen concern about the threat posed by stored nuclear refuse has been on the rise since 1972 when the government released a report that cited 18 leaks at the Hanford storage unit, resulting in the loss of over 430,000 gallons of high-level waste into the surrounding earth. "These leaks have neither killed nor injured anyone to date," the report stated. "Nonetheless, their hazard will remain for hundreds of thousands of years."[17]

There have been other waste management problems at Hanford. From the 1950s to the early 1970s, Hanford officials dumped relatively low-level nuclear wastes into enclosed cases in the ground. These cases were open at the bottom to permit the contaminated liquid to seep down into the soil. The theory was that the soil would absorb plutonium and other radioactive matter in much the same way that a water softener traps minerals. But a government inspection discovered in 1972 that despite the precautions, too much plutonium had been allowed to accumulate in one of the cases. The plutonium contained in the soil beneath the cases could, under certain conditions, cause a nuclear chain reaction, the government concluded. Although subsequent reports tried to minimize the dangers, Congress appropriated $1.9 million to exhume the excess plutonium.

---

[16] Phillip Johnson, "Scoop Jackson: Power Broker," *The Progressive*, April 1980, p. 31.

[17] See "Radioactive Waste Management and Regulation," report to the U.S. Energy Research and Development Administration, Sept. 1, 1976.

Leakage problems also have occurred in the past at the Idaho Falls facility. In 1970, Sen. Frank Church, D-Idaho, asked the government to release a National Academy of Sciences report on waste disposal practices. The report, begun in 1955, had been suppressed since it was completed in 1966. Under pressure from Church, the academy finally released it in March 1970. The study criticized waste disposal practices at both Hanford and Idaho Falls and concluded that "considerations of long-range safety are in some instances subordinate to regard for economy of operation." The report also said that "some disposal practices are conditioned on overconfidence in the capacity of the local environment to contain vast quantities of [radioactive material] for indefinite periods without danger to the biosphere."

In a 1976 interview, Washington Gov. Dixy Lee Ray, a former chairman of the Atomic Energy Commission, said that she was "virtually certain that a suitable permanent storage site will be

Dixy Lee Ray

found for waste." The "technologies do exist for handling waste, for being able to store it safely and completely for as long as it needs to be done," she said.[18] But lately, there have been indications that Ray may be changing her mind. Last October, she temporarily shut down the Hanford works, charging that the federal government had not lived up to its promise to enforce safety regulations that apply to the packaging and shipping of radioactive materials. The moratorium lasted six weeks. It was intended, Ray said, to deliver a message to the nation's capital that her state had no intention of being a permanent nuclear waste dump for the nation.

In recent months, Ray has come out in favor of building regional "nuclear parks," to be run entirely by the federal government and located away from populated areas. These parks might generate power as well as serve as storage sites for waste. Rep. Mike McCormack, D-Wash., last November introduced a bill to require the Department of Energy to set up 14 federally run regional nuclear waste facilities. Officials in Washington and Idaho support McCormack's proposal, but at the same time admit that their states' status as waste repositories is likely to continue for the foreseeable future. The remoteness of the region in the minds of distant policy-makers, they say, unfortunately makes it the ideal place to put "problems" no one wants to face.

---

[18] Henry B. Burnett, "Interview with Dixie Lee Ray," *Skeptic* (currently *Politics Today*), July-August 1976, p. 47.

Joint Venture Into the Future

POLITICS in the Pacific Northwest is, as residents like to say, "wide open." The political process is not a "closed system" as it sometimes is in the East and Midwest where the party as a rule takes precedence over issues. In the Northwest, causes come before anything else. New people and new ideas move with relative ease in the current of local politics. Voter participation is generally high, and election campaigns are often sounding boards for notions about government.

On occasion, "political influence devolves on a set of greater or smaller political warlords and their factions, whose interests may run from patronage to extreme philosophies," Neal R. Peirce wrote in *The Pacific States*.[19] But for every Henry Jackson, whose efforts on behalf of Seattle's aircraft industry have earned him the nickname of "the senator from Boeing," there seems to be someone like Wayne Morse, the late Oregon senator whose maverick ways made him for years one of the most unpredictable lawmakers ever to serve in the Congress. During his 24-year tenure in the U.S. Senate (1945-69), Morse was a Republican, an Independent and a Democrat.

Although Washington and Oregon's ideological center is a few degrees to the left of Idaho's, all three states have adopted liberal voting reforms, such as the ballot initiative and referendum, features that frequently turn state elections into popular forums on issues ranging from school funding to nude swimming at public beaches. The power to legislate by initiative — placing issues on the ballot by petition — caught on in the Northwest shortly after the turn of the century. Oregon, where the procedure was first introduced in 1902, has always been among the national leaders in pioneering progressive voting measures, including women's suffrage, the direct primary and recall elections. In the presidential race of 1912, Washington was the only Western state carried by Theodore Roosevelt's populist Bull Moose Party. And in 1924, Wisconsin Sen. Robert LaFollette's Progressive Party received a large vote throughout the Northwest.

Given the area's political climate, it is not uncommon for voters to challenge public officials with recall when it is felt they have overstepped their authority. Former Seattle Mayor Wes Uhlman handily won such a challenge in 1975 when the city's firefighters mounted a recall drive against him for firing a popular fire department chief. Several months after the vote, Uhlman spoke to the firefighters who had tried to drive him from office. "I told them," he said, "that I didn't particularly admire what they had tried to do to me, but I had to admit they

---

[19] Neal R. Peirce, *The Pacific States* (1972), p. 239.

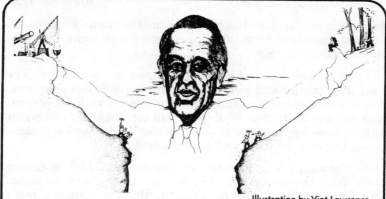

Illustration by Vint Lawrence

Sen. Henry M. Jackson's nickname, "Scoop," goes back to his boyhood occupation of delivering newspapers. He was, as the name implies, a hard worker. That same quality, at least as far as Washington voters are concerned, has stayed with Jackson through his long career in the Senate, which began in 1953 after six terms in the House.

Jackson has a national reputation for being pro-business and pro-defense. "You can't have enough security for Henry," said his former Senate colleague Eugene McCarthy. "If he had his way, the sky would be black with supersonic planes, preferably Boeings, of course." But there is also an environmentalist side to Jackson. He has steered many important conservation bills through the Senate, most notably the Natural Environmental Quality Act of 1969 and the Redwoods National Parks Act of 1968.

Jackson campaigned for the presidency in 1976, but dropped out of the race after a poor showing in the early primaries. Getting votes, however, has never been a problem in his home state where his victory margins generally run to 75 and 80 percent.

had done it all in a perfectly legal way — which was a lot better than staging illegal [work] slowdowns."[20]

Grudges, while not unheard of in local politics, are usually short-lived. "Personality conflicts don't last long here," said a Seattle activist. "The rocky road is almost always paved over quickly. . . . Everything seems to take a back seat to the greater good of moving the community forward."

Portland's Pioneering Metro Area Council

Other cities have flirted with the idea of regional government, but none has carried the concept as far as Portland. In an area where innovative government is popular, Portland prides itself in not only trying things first but making them work. In November 1978, the city and its suburbs became the first metropolitan area in the country to elect a regional governing council. The

[20] Quoted in *Harper's*, April 1976, p. 64.

Metropolitan Service District, which the new government oversees, embraces parts of three counties with more than one million people.

The Portland area, in fact, is governed on two levels. The municipal, county and local jurisdictions provide basic services, such as police protection and schools, while the regional government has authority over land use, transportation, air and water quality, sewerage and cultural activities. Voters send representatives to both the local and regional bodies.

One drawback for the Portland council is its lack of taxing power. With Oregon taxpayers in no mood to be generous, securing a financial base may be difficult. But the council's main concern, supporters say, is to bring "enlightened thinking" to metropolitan government, not pour money into it.

Enlightened thinking about government is one thing the Northwest appears to possess in abundance. While Portland's regional government may face problems, there is a feeling in the city, as there is throughout the Northwest, that difficulties can be solved if communities pull together and apply their collective intelligence to solving them.

Selected Bibliography
Books
Barone, Michael, et al., *The Almanac of American Politics, 1980,* Dutton, 1979.

Clark, Norman H., *Washington,* Norton, 1976.

Dodds, Gordon B., *Oregon,* Norton, 1976.

Hunt, William R., *Alaska,* Norton, 1976.

Kesey, Ken, *Sometimes a Great Notion,* Penguin, 1971.

Malamud, Bernard, *A New Life,* Farrar, Straus & Giroux, 1961.

Peirce, Neal R., *The Pacific States of America,* Norton, 1972.

Peterson, F. Ross, *Idaho,* Norton, 1976.

Sale, Roger, *Seattle, Past and Present,* University of Washington Press, 1976.

Articles
Argus (a weekly magazine devoted to Pacific Northwest news), selected issues.

"Dixy Rocks the Northwest," *Time,* Dec. 12, 1977.

Griffith, Thomas, "Pacific Northwest," *Harper's,* April 1976.

Johnson, Phillip, " 'Scoop' Jackson: Power Broker," *The Progressive,* April 1980.

Mungo, Raymond, "Blissed-Out in Seattle," *Mother Jones,* November 1978.

Pacific Northwest Quarterly, selected issues.

Reports and Studies
Editorial Research Reports: "Nuclear Waste Disposal," 1976 Vol. II, p. 883; "Western Land Policy," Vol. I, p. 83.

Pacific Northwest Regional Commission, "Report," Aug. 28, 1979.

U.S. Commission on Civil Rights, "American Indian Fishing Rights in the State of Washington," Vol. IV, August 1978.

C ALIFORNIA: LIVING OUT THE GOLDEN DREAM

by

Richard Kipling
and William V. Thomas

**Apr. 25
1 9 8 0**

CALIFORNIA: LIVING OUT
THE GOLDEN DREAM

FOR MORE than a century, Americans have looked at California as something different, a "new" New World at the end of the continent, the ultimate expression of manifest destiny. It is a place as distinct from the rest of the country as America was from the Old World it rejected some 200 years ago. That distinctiveness has made it the subject of much comment and criticism over the years. Short-story writer O. Henry once mused that Californians are not merely inhabitants of a geographical location but "a race of people." Other observers have been somewhat less kind, especially when talking about Southern California, which British philosopher Bertrand Russell described as "the ultimate segregation of the unfit."

It is difficult to characterize in a phrase a state that takes in over a thousand miles of coastline, a variety of landscapes and more than 22 million people. Nevertheless, it is often said that California is not just a state but a state of mind. For some, it represents the final embodiment of America's frontier spirit; for others, it is a version of El Dorado, a place to find fortunes or spend fortunes made elsewhere. California is the nation's leader in fads, fashion and self-indulgence. New religions, new living arrangements, new forms of entertainment from Disneyland to sex clubs, new attitudes towards work, family and education, all have been nurtured by California's tolerant social climate.

It may well be true that Californians are quintessential Americans. In a wealthy nation, they are wealthier than most; in a suburban society, they are more suburbanized; in a culture devoted to immediate satisfaction, they are satisfied faster; in a country where optimism reigns supreme, they are the most optimistic; and in a time of doubt and uncertainty, they have the most to be uncertain about. Californians, the saying goes, are just like the rest of us, only more so.

California stands for "absolute freedom, mobility and privacy," wrote author Joan Didion, a native of the state. It represents "the instinct which drove America to the Pacific . . . the desire . . . to live by one's own rules."[1] This sense of freedom extends beyond what has come to be known as lifestyle. It pervades the political atmosphere as well.

---

[1] Joan Didion, *Slouching Towards Bethlehem* (1968), p. 71.

While California voters do not easily fit into hard and fast ideological categories, they have consistently been in the forefront of political trend-setting. The ballot initiative, which Californians put to exhaustive use, has made state elections, in effect, public referendums on issues as diverse as tax reform and homosexuality. The power to legislate by initiative is a cherished tradition in a state where traditions are usually short-lived. And like so many other things that occur in California, the results of voter preference frequently provide an idea where the rest of the nation is headed.

Leading State in Innovative Legislation

California leads the way in defining and acting on issues of nationwide concern. In 1976, for example, it became the first state in the nation to enact a "right-to-die" law, which allowed terminally ill patients under certain conditions to refuse the aid of artificial life-assisting devices. California was also among the first states to remove criminal penalties for the possession of small amounts of marijuana for personal use.[2] On Aug. 30, 1976, California's Indoor Clean Air Act went into effect, requiring that at least half of the space in public meeting rooms be set aside for non-smokers. The same year, the state legislature enacted a comprehensive bill to protect California's 1,072-mile coastline by regulating local government use of land next to the water.

California has been a leading state in the debate over nuclear energy since 1976, when Californians were first in the nation to vote on the question of nuclear energy development. By a 2-1 margin, voters in the state defeated an initiative that would have imposed a virtual moratorium on reactor construction and an eventual shutdown of existing plants. But 10 days before the June 8, 1976, election on the ballot initiative, the California legislature passed three compromise nuclear safety laws.[3]

In June 1978, California voters approved Proposition 13 to reduce local property taxes by nearly 60 percent. Passage of the measure sent shock waves across the nation, as Proposition 13 spawned similar tax-limitation movements in other states. California voters will have another opportunity to trim taxes on June 3 when they vote on Proposition 9, a constitutional amend-

---

[2] California's decriminalization law went into effect on Jan. 1, 1976. Similar laws have been enacted in 10 other states: Oregon, Alaska, Maine, Colorado, Ohio, Minnesota, Mississippi, North Carolina, New York and Nebraska.

[3] One of the laws provided that no permits would be granted for new atomic plants until the state Energy Commission determined that the federal government had approved a technology for reprocessing spent fuel. A second called for a study of the feasibility of requiring nuclear reactors to be built underground, in view of the state's earthquake activity. The third law — which required the state Energy Commission to refuse to authorize construction of a nuclear facility until it was satisfied that safe means exist for disposing of nuclear wastes — was overturned on March 6, 1979, by Judge Willian Enright of the U.S. District Court in San Diego. Enright ruled that the statute, which had the effect of halting reactor construction in the state, was pre-empted by federal nuclear regulatory law, which clearly allows nuclear plants to be built.

California

Redwood National Park
Eureka
Coast
Sacramento River
Sierra
Sacramento River
Lake Tahoe
Sacramento
San Francisco
San Joaquin River
Yosemite
Nevadas
Pacific Ocean
Monterey
Fresno
Mt. Whitney 14,495
Death Valley
Ranges
Santa Barbara
Mojave Desert
Los Angeles
San Diego

ment that would cut the state income tax in half. Also on the June 3 ballot is an initiative — Proposition 11 — that would levy a 10 percent surtax, in addition to the current 9.6 percent state corporation tax, on the California profits of oil and gas companies. The initiative would prohibit companies from passing the extra tax on to consumers.[4]

Political Scene; Govs. Brown and Reagan

California has supplied the nation with a president (Richard M. Nixon), a Supreme Court chief justice (Earl Warren), and

[4] See Maureen Fitzgerald, "Oil-Tax Initiative Campaign: Most Expensive in State's History?" *California Journal*, April 1980, pp. 167-168.

one of the most curious collections of politicians imaginable.
The state is a breeding ground
not only for new ideas about
government but for new political types as well. "Its politics
. . . is fluid," wrote author
Garry Wills. "There is no stable
party system. Cross-filing, a
huge swing vote, and a changing
electorate make it possible for
leaders to tumble instantly
down trapdoors . . . or pop out
of nowhere. . . . There is no
latticework of party structure to
catch men's fall or slow their
climb."

Reagan

In the absence of any established tradition of party loyalty,
the important things in California politics are style and image.
Of course, these are primary ingredients in politics nationwide.
But in California, with fashion and ideology in constant flux,
they seem to count for more. "Where so many people have come
to the state as a way of protesting conditions in the place they
left," Wills concluded, "there must be a readiness to change and
seek the new."[5]

If California lifestyles tend to run to extremes, so do the
philosophies espoused by its politicians. This presidential election year, the current governor of the state, Edmund G. (Jerry)
Brown Jr., and a former governor, Ronald Reagan, both entered
the race for the White House. Brown, a Democrat, dropped out
of the running in early April. However, Reagan remains the
Republican leader in convention delegates, a position likely to
be enhanced by the results of the June 3 California presidential
primary. From the outset of the campaign, despite their differing approaches to the issues, the two stressed the same basic
theme: that serving as chief executive of the nation's biggest and
perhaps most unpredictable state is the best qualification available for being president of the United States.

Gov. Brown has piqued more curiosity and caused more consternation than almost any other political personality in recent
years. Like his native California, he is a mixture of the tried and
the unorthodox, the contemplative and the restless. And also
like California, that sometimes makes him hard for the rest of
the country to understand.

Brown's questioning of traditional politics is what distin-

---

[5] Gary Wills, *Nixon Agonistes: The Crisis of the Self-Made Man* (1970), pp. 75-76.

California's Super Primary

Hubert H. Humphrey called it the "Super Bowl of primaries." Indeed, the California presidential primary often has been the pot of gold at the end of the rainbow. California sends the most delegates to the nominating conventions, Democratic and Republican, and traditionally it is the last big-state primary. This year the California primary will be June 3.

For Republicans, the California primary is important in still another way. The winner captures all of the delegates, 168 this year, 17 percent of the number that will cast votes at the Detroit convention in July. Until 1976, the Democrats also awarded all of their California delegates to the winner. That system of bloc voting occasioned Humphrey's remark in 1972, when he opposed George McGovern for the nomination. Humphrey lost California and failed to sidetrack McGovern's presidential bid.

guished him from other presidential aspirants and what sets him apart from most other politicians in general. His sometimes startling notions about government have brought the 42-year-old Brown both praise and scorn. Detractors claim he flits from one new idea to another. They also charge that he challenges institutions for the sake of the challenge and is frequently arrogant and insensitive in the process.

Winning the governor's office in 1974, Brown probed the complexities of the state's bureaucracy, delighting people by such actions as wondering aloud why educational administrators

Brown

were paid more than teachers when teachers were carrying out the basic task of education. Reelected by a landslide margin in 1978 to a second term, Brown saw his name immediately enter speculation for the 1980 presidential race. His advocacy of a national constitutional convention to propose a federal balanced budget amendment and later his ideas on post-Proposition 13 belt-tightening captured national attention and were major issues in his second presidential campaign.

But the distance between Brown's style of fiscal conservatism and his closeness to left-wing activists such as Tom Hayden and actress Jane Fonda may have been too great a leap for most voters. Unable to draw support in the primaries, Brown gave up his campaign and returned to the task of running California, a job his father held for eight years until he was defeated by Ronald Reagan in 1966.

Like the younger Brown, Reagan took office in California promising to reduce the size of government. But where Brown often couches his efforts at reform in philosophical jargon that flies over the heads of average voters, Reagan, a one-time screen actor, has always taken the down-to-earth approach in getting his ideas across. As governor, Reagan became famous for railing against "welfare cheats" and campus radicals. He also mounted a much-publicized campaign to win voter approval for a state constitutional amendment placing a ceiling on California taxation and expenditures. The measure was soundly defeated at the polls, yet the principle behind it has been a key element of Reagan's two presidential campaign platforms.

A Midwesterner who came to the West Coast to seek his fortune in the 1930s, Reagan, 69, epitomizes "the other" California, the opposite of the mellow "laid-back" outlook commonly associated with the state. Reagan supporters in California and elsewhere tend by and large to be fundamental conservatives who embrace the traditional values of work, home and religion. Reagan's audiences cheer in agreement with his calls for a stronger defense and less government interference with private enterprise.

In 1980, Reagan has adopted the conservative anti-Washington, anti-big government theme that Jimmy Carter used successfully in 1976. But to it he has added a distinctive pro-business refrain. Behind nearly all of Reagan's pronouncements there is a kind of subdued evangelism, the same missionary appeal that urged people of other generations to see California as the last and best hope. "It may well be," Sen. Jesse Helms, R-N.C., said in introducing Reagan at a recent campaign rally, "that God is giving us one more chance to save America."

Catalysts for Development

F ROM the beginning, California promised much," historian Kevin Starr wrote. "While yet barely a name on the map, it entered American awareness as a symbol of renewal. It was the final frontier: of geography and of expectation."[6] The California promise attracted people of all classes and professions, from explorers and trappers to gold miners, farmers and intellectuals. Richard Henry Dana, Robert Louis Stevenson, Mark Twain, Horace Greeley, Henry David Thoreau and Henry James were among those who went west to see if the California dream had substance.

[6] Kevin Starr, *Americans and the California Dream, 1850-1915* (1973), p. viii.

California Population by Decades

| | Population | | Percent Increase | |
Year	California	United States	California	United States
1860	379,994	31,443,321	—	—
1870	560,247	38,558,371	47.4	22.6
1880	864,694	50,155,783	54.3	30.1
1890	1,213,398	62,947,714	40.3	25.5
1900	1,485,053	75,994,575	22.4	20.7
1910	2,377,549	91,972,266	60.1	21.0
1920	3,426,861	105,710,620	44.1	14.9
1930	5,677,251	122,775,046	65.7	16.1
1940	6,907,387	131,669,275	21.7	7.2
1950	10,586,223	151,325,798	53.3	14.9
1960	15,717,204	179,323,175	48.5	18.5
1970	19,968,004	203,235,298	27.0	13.3
1978	22,294,000	218,059,000	11.6	7.3

Source: *California Journal Almanac of State Government and Politics*, 1977, and U.S. Department of Commerce, Bureau of the Census.

Of course, the dream preceded their visits. The Spanish explorers who discovered America's west coast in the 16th century dreamed of finding gold and other precious metals. Hernando Cortez, the Spanish conqueror of Mexico, explored the peninsula of lower California in 1535 and, according to some accounts, gave the region its name.[7] On Sept. 28, 1542, Juan Rodriquez Cabrillo, a Portuguese navigator in the Spanish service, sailed into what is now San Diego harbor. By the end of the year, Cabrillo had explored some 800 miles of California's coastline.

The new province was not actually colonized until 1769, when Franciscan Father Junipero Serra built a mission at San Diego. During the next half century, 21 Franciscan missions were built about a day's journey apart along what came to be known as El Camino Real, or the King's Highway, extending from San Diego north to Sonoma. The missions, although designed primarily to convert the Indians to the Christian faith, soon became the cultural and agricultural centers of the region. Civilian towns were established at San Jose (1777), Los Angeles (1781) and Santa Cruz (1798). Presidios, or military garrisons, were located at San Diego, Santa Barbara, Monterey and San Francisco. But as late as 1812, there were only 372 Spanish soldiers in the entire province.[8]

Although California took virtually no part in Mexico's strug-

[7] California was the name of an imaginary island, an earthly paradise, in *Las Sergas de Espladián*, a book written by Garcia Ordonez de Montalvo in 1510.

[8] See Warren A. Beck and David A. Williams, *California: A History of the Golden State* (1972).

gle for independence from Spain in 1821, early the next year Californians declared their allegiance to Mexico. And though many of the institutions set up by the Spanish continued to operate, the mission system, the backbone of Spanish influence, was broken up. The land holdings of the Franciscans were reduced to only a few acres and former mission lands granted to private citizens.

Statehood; Gold Discovery Near Sacramento

Almost 700 Americans were living in California in 1846 when war broke out between the United States and Mexico. U.S. forces occupied California early in the war and two years later, at the war's end, the territory was ceded to the United States by the Treaty of Guadalupe Hidalgo. On Sept. 9, 1850, California was admitted to the union as the 31st state.

While the United States and Mexico were engaged in treaty negotiations, an event of equal magnitude for California's future unfolded at John Sutter's sawmill on the American River near present-day Sacramento when one of Sutter's co-workers looked into the water near the mill and noticed the glint of gold. By the end of 1848, the word had spread around the world: The gold the Spanish had searched for in vain 300 years before had finally been discovered — by Americans.

The Gold Rush had a profound influence on the development of California. Enormous fortunes were amassed almost overnight. One year after the discovery at Sutter's mill, more than 40,000 men were in the California hills and on the rivers trying to strike it rich. The Gold Rush mentality soon became incorporated in the California dream. "The California ideal . . . partly because of the discovery of gold . . . included not only the notion of a new start, but also the notion of new money," Michael Davie wrote in 1972. ". . .California has allowed the get-rich-quick instinct to flourish openly, undisguised and unrestrained."[9]

Many of the "Forty-niners" who came to California during the Gold Rush decided to stay. Between 1846 and 1850, the year California became a state, the number of Americans living there increased from less than 1,000 to more than 100,000. By the time of the 1860 census, there were nearly 400,000 Californians. This pattern of rapid growth continued well into the 20th century *(see chart, p. 313)*.

The Gold Rush did more than bring people to California; it also supplied a certain spirit. "The energy of the Gold Rush, the thirst for excitement, and the habit of speculation remained

---

[9] Michael Davie, *California: The Vanishing Dream* (1972), p. 5.

part of the Californian temperament," Kevin Starr observed.[10] It took a certain spirit to make the trek across the country. By ship it took as long as eight months to travel around the Horn from the East Coast to San Francisco. By land, it often took even longer. "The men who packed themselves overland direct across plains and mountains were a minority of those who reached the California gold fields," wrote Constance McLaughlin Green. "In that difficult journey by horse, mule or ox-train, men had to guard against Indian attack, thirst and hunger. . . . The hardships of traveling the overland route discouraged all who could choose any other way."[11]

Impact of the Transcontinental Railroads

In 1862, Congress, after a decade of surveys and debates, chartered the Union Pacific Railroad to build across the continent westward from Omaha, Neb. At the same time, permission to build eastward from Sacramento was given to the Central Pacific Railroad, a company formed by a group of Californians widely known as "The Big Four" — Charles Crocker, Leland Stanford, Collis P. Huntington and Mark Hopkins. On May 10, 1869, the two rail lines were joined by golden spikes at Promontory Point, Utah, and a new era in California's history was begun.

Even before the first transcontinental railroad was completed, the four owners of the Central Pacific began taking steps to secure a monopoly of railroad traffic in and from California. In 1868, they acquired the Southern Pacific Railroad, which had been chartered in 1865 to connect San Francisco and San Diego. By 1882 they had pushed the Southern Pacific eastward to El Paso, Texas, where it joined the Texas Pacific, which was soon absorbed.

Another transcontinental railroad, the Santa Fe, finally reached San Diego in 1883. For a time, the Santa Fe and the Southern Pacific competed for passengers from the Midwest. A rate war began that brought fares down from $125 to $5 and one time to $1. The period of competition was short-lived. In 1886, the charter for the Santa Fe fell to Collis P. Huntington and Jay Gould, who controlled the Union Pacific.

"Huntington, Stanford, Hopkins and Crocker now had a monopoly on land transportation in a vast region," historians Lembert W. Patrick, Frank L. Owsley, Oliver P. Chitwood and H. C. Nixon observed. "In order to eliminate competition by sea they brought a fleet of steamships whose rates were kept high, and reached satisfactory arrangements — by the payment of

---

[10] Starr, *op. cit.,* p. 67.
[11] Constance McLaughlin Green, *American Cities in the Growth of the Nation* (1957), pp. 131-132.

large fees — with rival steamship companies. . . . With a virtual monopoly throughout the Southwest, the California 'quartet' . . . held the population of that part of the country at their mercy. The freight rates were ruinous to the farmers and merchants and the rebates and special rates granted the Standard Oil Company and other favored groups helped eliminate smaller rivals."[12]

The man credited with ending California's economic and political domination by the Southern Pacific and its owners was Hiram W. Johnson, who served as governor from 1910 to 1917, when he became a U.S. senator. During his first year in office, Johnson pushed through a number of bills intended to blunt the power of special interests. Among them were the initiative, referendum and recall, non-partisan election of judges and a civil service merit system. Despite its obvious excesses, it is important to remember the great contribution the Southern Pacific made to California's growth in the late 19th century. Between 1880 and 1890, the population of southern California increased by almost 300 percent, sparking a real estate boom that reached its peak in 1887.[13]

During the first half of the 20th century, the history of California largely paralleled that of the rest of the nation. Perhaps the biggest event of the early part of the century was the giant earthquake and fire that almost destroyed the city of San Francisco in 1906. During the prosperous years of the 1920s a tide of people flooded southern California from the Midwest, a phenomenon Carey McWilliams called "the first great migration of the automobile age." The economic depression of the 1930s generally was less pronounced in California than in other states. It did bring in thousands of "Okies" and other refugees from the Dust Bowl area of the Southwest, a trek chronicled by John Steinbeck in his novel *The Grapes of Wrath* (1939).

World War II accelerated changes already under way — the shift from an agricultural to an industrial economy and the movement of wealth and population from northern to southern California. Thousands of military personnel, defense workers and their families moved to the state, producing a tremendous housing boom. "The influx of war workers from 1940 to 1945. . . ," John Gunther wrote, "was nothing more or less than the Gold Rush all over again in a different dimension, a gold rush in aviation, the result of which was to make Los Angeles the 'Detroit of airplanes.' "[14]

---

[12] Lembert W. Patrick, Frank L. Owsley, Oliver P. Chitwood and H. C. Nixon, *The American People,* Vol. II (1962), pp. 27-28.

[13] See Carey McWilliams, *Southern California: An Island on the Land* (1973), p. 123.

[14] John Gunther, *Inside U.S.A.* (1947), p. 8.

Continued North-South Rivalry

CALIFORNIA is a land of extremes — in geography as well as living patterns. Within its more than 158,000 square miles are snowcapped mountains, dense redwood forests, fruitful valleys and scorching deserts. The highest peak in the continental states, Mt. Whitney at the eastern edge of the Sequoia National Park, is located about 60 miles from Death Valley, at 282 feet below sea level, the lowest point in the nation. Some areas near the coast of northern California receive almost 100 inches of rain a year, while certain desert regions in the southwestern part of the state receive little or no measurable rainfall.

California's major physiographic regions are the narrow coastal area between mountains and the sea; the Central Valley walled by the coastal ranges on the west and the Sierra Nevada Mountains on the east; the desert basins of the southern interior; and the rugged mountainous regions of the north. The Tehachapi Range — a short connecting link between the coastal ranges and the Sierra Nevada situated approximately 335 miles south of San Francisco and 115 miles north of Los Angeles — is the unofficial dividing line between northern and southern California.

The contrasts between northern and southern California go beyond geographic differences. The Gold Rush, so important to early California history, hardly touched the southern part of the state. It was not until the 1880s that the first significant migration to the southland occurred. As late as 1906, more than a third of the state's population lived within 75 miles of San Francisco. Today more than 60 percent of California's residents live in the southern third of the state. As the south's population grew, so did its political power. "It is becoming increasingly difficult for anyone outside Los Angeles to win a statewide race," California political analyst Ed Salzman wrote recently.[15]

Although the population shift was the primary reason for the growing rivalry between northern and southern California, the disputes were long-standing. In 1859, the California legislature actually voted to split into north and south states, "a proposal frustrated only by the failure of Congress to approve it."[16] State-splitting ideas are not likely to come to fruition, but the north-

[15] Ed Salzman, "Must a Candidate Move to Los Angeles to Find Political Happiness?" *California Journal,* November 1979, p. 388.
[16] Neal R. Peirce, *The Pacific States of America* (1972), p. 21.

south rivalry will continue to color the texture of California politics. As a result of reapportionment after the 1980 census, California expects to add two additional seats in the U.S. Congress. With 45 seats, California will hold more than 10 percent in the House of Representatives.

San Francisco, Central Valley and Environs

San Francisco frequently is called America's most European city. Famed for its natural beauty, mild climate, restaurants and cable cars, its liberalism and tolerance, it is still small enough, with a population of about 660,000, to escape the big-city frustrations and anomie that characterize New York, Los Angeles and Chicago. In recent decades, San Francisco has undergone a series of traumatic changes. In the 1950s, there was the beatnik movement. In the 1960s, the topless-bottomless craze was accompanied by an influx of "hippies," drugs and disillusion. The 1970s brought crippling strikes, soaring taxes and declining population. In November 1978, San Francisco Mayor George Moscone and city supervisor Harvey Milk, a popular member of San Francisco's "gay" community, estimated at one-sixth of the city's population, were shot to death by a former supervisor, Dan White.

Despite its problems, there still is an elusive magic about "the city by the bay" that keeps its national reputation high. "The culture of civility" sets San Francisco apart from other American cities, Howard Becker and Irving Horowitz suggested in a 1970 article. "Because its politicians and police allow and can live with activities that would freak their opposite numbers elsewhere, San Francisco is a natural experiment in the consequences of tolerating deviance," they wrote. ". . .Like ethnic minorities, deviant minorities create enclaves whose differences add to the pleasure of city life. . . . Deviance, like difference, is a civic resource, enjoyed by tourist and residents alike."[17]

North across the Golden Gate Bridge from San Francisco is Marin County. Its group-therapy, hot-tub lifestyle was humorously portrayed by Cyra McFadden in her book *Serial: A Year in the Life of Marin County* (1977). The rugged coastline north of Marin County "is a land of rolling fog, breakers smashing against high bluffs and of moist, deep forests." Most of the towns in this area are small fishing or lumbering villages. The two counties of "the Peninsula," directly south of San Francisco, are San Mateo and Santa Clara, known principally for their prestigious universities, think tanks, research centers, and electronics and aerospace industries.

---

[17] Howard Becker and Irving Horowitz, "The Culture of Civility," reprinted in *Culture and Civility in San Francisco* (1971), edited by Howard S. Becker, pp. 5-6.

California: An Economic Giant

If California was an independent country, its gross national product — estimated at close to $300 billion — would be greater than those of all nations save six — the United States, the Soviet Union, West Germany, Japan, France and China. Agriculturally it would be among the leading nations; it already ranks first in the United States. California farm goods brought more than $12 billion into the state's economy in 1979. California ranks behind Alaska and Texas as the third largest oil-producing state. Its 40,000 wells produce approximately 918,000 barrels of oil a day.

East of San Francisco is the great Central Valley, which covers about a sixth of the state's land area. Here is the heart of California's agribusiness *(see p. 146)*, its wine industry and its capital, Sacramento. "It is when you remember the Valley's wealth that the monochromatic flatness of its towns takes on a curious meaning, suggests a habit of mind some would consider perverse," wrote author Joan Didion, a native of Sacramento. "There is something in the valley mind that reflects a real indifference to the stranger. . . . An implacable insularity is the seal of these towns."[18]

Southern California's Diversified Economy

Southern California, the third of the state below the Tehachapi Range, has a character and a mood quite different from the north. "This is the California of petroleum, crazy religious cults, the citrus industry, towns based on rich *rentiers* like Santa Barbara and Pasadena, the movies, the weirdest architecture in the United States, refugees from Iowa, a steeply growing Negro population, and devotees of funny money," John Gunther wrote. "It is, above all, the world where climate is worshipped as a god."[19] Gunther made his observations in 1947, but, for the most part, they still hold true today.

The sprawling south, centered in the 6,600-square-mile Los Angeles Basin, is the economic center of the state. The tax revenues from its citizens and companies provide California with much of its income. The Los Angeles area ranks behind New York as the second largest commercial center in the United States. Southern California's economy is diversified, but four areas dominate: the entertainment business, including films, television and recording studios; aerospace and defense industries; the oil industry, including both production and refining; and real estate development and sales.

At first, Angelenos, as citizens of Los Angeles are called, showed a pronounced dislike for members of "the movie colony"

---

[18] Joan Didion, "Notes From A Native Daughter," in *Slouching Towards Bethlehem* (1968), pp. 181-182.

[19] Gunther, *op. cit.*, p. 4.

— signs on apartment buildings often read "No Dogs or Actors Allowed." But by 1915 the residents had undergone a change of heart. The movie industry brought with it not only kooks and deadbeats, but money and prosperity. In 1911, Hollywood, "the most beautiful suburb in America," had only 4,000 residents; by 1920, more than 36,000 people lived there. Within a decade Hollywood's population had jumped to almost 250,000.

People made a lot of money from the movies, and Hollywood and Los Angeles reaped the benefits. Real estate values soared as actors, producers, and movie moguls built residential monuments to their success. Businesses grew up around the industry — fine restaurants, hotels and shops. And there was all that free publicity. Because its name was linked to the world's most publicized industry, Hollywood became one of the best-known cities in the world.

Despite the growing popularity of location shooting, Southern California still retains much of the glitter if not all the gold of the movies. Almost 150 films a year are made in the Hollywood-Los Angeles area. Though 60 percent of the 20,000 members of the Screen Actors Guild are unemployed at any given time, the entertainment industry — films, television, and records — brought in $13 billion in 1979.

Southern California's aerospace-defense industry dates from World War II, when massive government involvement in the aircraft industry brought thousands of workers and jobs to the southland. Today the list of leading aerospace and defense industries headquartered in Southern California includes General Dynamics, Hughes Aircraft, Lockheed Missiles and Space Company, McDonnell Douglas, and Rockwell International.

In 1892, Edward Doheny, a metals' prospector, discovered oil in the form of tar inside the city limits of Los Angeles. Three years later, according to a contemporary account, oil wells in Los Angeles were "as thick as the holes in a pepper box." The new fuel was substituted for coal, and California suddenly found itself with an enviable supply of energy. In the 1920s, huge deposits of oil were discovered in Huntington Beach, Long Beach and Whittier. Los Angeles became the oil capital of the world. The dollar value of oil produced in California in the 1920s exceeded the value of gold mined in the state.

One of the byproducts of the oil boom became more associated with Southern California than did the huge deposits themselves. Gasoline, initially an unwanted byproduct of petroleum, was found to be the perfect fuel for the horseless carriage. As early as 1925, Los Angeles was heralded as the unabashed leader of the car culture, with one automobile for every three residents.

One outgrowth of Los Angeles' car mania is that it has one of the lowest population densities of any major American city. The scores of small towns that developed because of the presence of highways and access to the city have led to the characterization of Los Angeles as "one hundred suburbs in search of a metropolis." Today, with one of the best intra- and inter-city road systems in the country, the Los Angeles area remains built around the car. It is one of the few major cities in the world without an extensive mass transit system.

The Los Angeles love affair with the automobile has its underside: pollution. The word "smog" was coined in the city, and for good reason. According to the Environmental Protection Agency, Los Angeles ranks as the most air-polluted city in the country, and experts have laid the blame squarely on the automobile. Recent developments affecting the price and availability of gasoline have curtailed southland driving to some extent. Last November, after Iran halted oil imports to the United States, Gov. Brown signed an order making mandatory the odd-even day restriction on gasoline sales California had first adopted in May 1979. Most of the state's counties had discontinued the plan before Brown's order.

Soaring Housing Costs, Rental Shortages

Los Angeles began the century as a paradise for promotion and speculation, and there are indications that it will end the century the same way. The price of an average home in Los Angeles, according to a recent report by the Los Angeles Task Force on Housing Production, is now $115,000, almost three times what it was in 1973. Among major U.S. cities, only Boston and Washington have more expensive housing. All of California suffers from high housing costs. According to the National Association of Home Builders, the median price of a new home in the U.S. today is $65,000. In California it is almost $94,000.

Housing has become so expensive in Los Angeles that many prospective home buyers have turned to the rental market, producing a supply crunch.[20] Vacancies consistently run at less than 2 percent in many Southern California communities; less than 5 percent is considered critical. Almost half of California's 22 million residents live in rental accommodations and, if projections are correct, the majority will be renters sometime in the early 1980s.

To conteract the shortages, renters have organized in a number of communities around the state in an attempt to enact rent control legislation. Santa Monica, adjacent to Los Angeles, approved one of the nation's strictest rent control ordinances last year and Los Angeles has given thought to similar legislation.

[20] See "Rental Housing Shortage," *E.R.R.*, 1979 Vol. II, pp. 921-940.

The specter of rent control has caused a number of California builders to get out of the rental market and has mobilized real estate interests to sponsor an initiative to forestall it. On the June 3 ballot is a measure — Proposition 10 — that would abolish existing rent controls on the local level and allow only the voters — not city councils — to institute controls, and then only for a period of four years.

Prospects for the Eighties

SOUTHERN California's success story was due, to a great extent, to large-scale water-transfer projects. After exhausting its local supply, Los Angeles reached out for water from California's mountainous regions. The 233-mile-long Los Angeles acqueduct was completed in 1913 to bring water from Owens Valley on the eastern slopes of the Sierra Nevada. Charges were made at the time that Owens Valley landowners had been duped by Los Angeles officials and that certain leading citizens of Los Angeles had acquired extensive land holdings in the San Fernando Valley, which, with the addition of water, would soon become very valuable. The accusations were never proven, however.

Today California finds itself at the center of a bitter struggle over who should receive federally subsidized irrigation water in the West.[21] The U.S. Senate voted on Sept. 14, 1979, to increase fourfold the amount of federally irrigated land a small farmer can own, but exempted from the acreage limits several of the largest agribusiness operations in California. The bill faces tough going in the House, however, where Rep. George Miller, D-Calif., called it "socialism for the rich" and "the biggest Western stage coach robbery of the public since Jesse James."

The Senate bill, sponsored by Sen. Frank Church, D-Idaho, represented the first time in more than 50 years that Congress had tried to update the Reclamation Act of 1902. The original act, which authorized massive irrigation programs in order to develop and settle the arid West, was designed to promote family homesteads. To do this, it limited to 160 acres — or 320 per man and wife — the amount of land a farmer could own and irrigate with water from federal water projects. There were no limits on leasing additional irrigated land, but the law specified that the farmer had to live on the land in order to receive rec-

---

[21] Information for this section provided by Kathy Koch, *Congressional Quarterly's* environmental writer. See "Senate Water-Use Bill Pits Big Firms Against Small Farms," *Congressional Quarterly Weekly Report*, Sept. 29, 1979, pp. 2121-2133. See also "Western Water: Coming Crisis," 1977 Vol. I, pp. 21-40.

lamation water.[22]

However, decades of non-enforcement of the acreage and residency requirements by the Interior Department enabled landowners to acquire more and more irrigated land, developing huge agricultural conglomerates — most of them in California. With the department's blessing, the agricultural giants literally turned the desert into the nation's hothouse, using cheap, federally-subsidized water from billion-dollar dams hundreds of miles away. In many cases the landowners were merely "paper farmers" — absentee real estate investors and railroad and oil companies.

In 1976, the department was sued by a small farmers' group, National Land for People, for not enforcing the law. A federal district court that year ordered the department to draw up a set of regulations to enforce the act. When the regulations were issued in 1977, the large landowners were infuriated. The department intended to enforce the acreage limitation, forcing the companies to divest themselves of huge chunks of farmland. The large landowners promptly sued, claiming the department had not submitted an environmental impact statement before issuing the regulations. While the impact statement was being completed, the department was prohibited from enforcing the new regulations. Meanwhile, the landowners formed the Farm/Water Alliance, a well-financed lobby group made up of landowners, farmers, water districts and banking and real estate associations, that lobbied heavily to get the act amended in Congress.

One provision in the Senate-passed bill allows individuals and small corporations (defined as those with fewer than 25 stockholders) to own or lease up to 1,280 acres of federally irrigated land. Large corporations would be allowed to own 160 acres, but would not be allowed to lease reclamation land; under existing law there are no limits on leasing. However, the bill exempted

---

[22] Farmers could own more than 160 acres of federally irrigated land and continue receiving water as long as the owner signed a "recordable contract" with the Interior Department, promising to sell the excess land within a specified period, usually 10 years. The farmer also had to agree to sell the excess land at a "dry land" price that excluded the value added to the land because of the irrigation water it received.

from the acreage limits growers in the 530,000-acre Imperial Valley. The provision is a controversial one because the area, on the California-Mexican border, has been the target of boycotts and intensive unionization attempts by Cesar Chavez's United Farm Workers Union *(see below),* and because large chunks of the lands are owned by subsidiaries of agribusinesses. Also exempted from the Reclamation Act's acreage limitations were landowners in the Kings River and Kern River areas, two of the four U.S. Army Corps of Engineers' flood control and irrigation projects in central California.

The question of unlimited leasing is especially critical to the Westlands water district of California's San Joaquin Valley, which has the largest concentration of land — 309,345 acres — that would have to be sold under current law. The favorite targets of reclamation reformers in the Westlands area are the Southern Pacific Railroad, which owns through two subsidiaries over 200,000 irrigated acres, and J. G. Boswell Co., which owns 23,980 acres through its subsidiary, Boston Ranch. Boswell, the world's largest cotton grower, also owns 109,000 acres in the Kings and Kern river areas.

The wealthy Westlands farmers, who provide most of the financial backing for the Farm/Water Alliance, oppose the bill as it was passed by the Senate. Many of them grow specialty crops such as lettuce and melons. In order to have those products available throughout the year, the farmers lease land in several states with different growing seasons so the crops mature at different times. Gordon Nelson, executive director of the alliance, predicted that if the bill passes the House in its present form, much of the lettuce and melon production will shift to Mexico which has no acreage limits.[23]

United Farm Workers and Chicano Politics

Among the other problems confronting California agribusiness, labor unrest tops the list. The farm labor problem is hardly new. When the demands of World War II left hardly anyone to bring in the harvest, the U.S. government made a series of agreements with Mexico for large numbers of workers to be transported north to replace the Americans in uniform. This was the origin of the "bracero" program, which continued until 1964, when Congress refused to renew it.[24]

---

[23] The U.S. Supreme Court agreed Dec. 3, 1979, to hear arguments in a California case that could determine the validity of the 1902 reclamation law. The court said that it would hear an appeal from a 1977 ruling by the Ninth Circuit U.S. Court of Appeals that upheld the acreage limitation in the 530,000-acre Imperial Valley irrigation district. The court's eventual decision is expected to affect how Congress deals with the question whether it should legislatively exempt the Imperial Valley from the acreage limit.

[24] "Bracero" is Spanish for "strong-armed one."

Since that time, farmworkers and growers have been locked in battle over the unionization of field workers. The effort toward unionization has been led for 15 years by Cesar Chavez of the United Farm Workers. His fledgling union gained its first victory in 1966 when a big grape grower agreed to recognize it as sole bargainer for the company's field hands. Over the years, Chavez has initiated strike after strike — the most recent in the California lettuce fields last year — in a continuing effort to organize and improve the pay and working conditions of Southwestern farm workers, who tend to be of Mexican ancestry. By March 1977, his union had made peace with the rival Brotherhood of Teamsters, and it became the sole bona fide labor representative of America's farm workers.

"California is a place in which a boom mentality and a sense of Chekhovian loss meet in uneasy suspension; in which the mind is troubled by some buried but ineradicable suspicion that things had better work here, because here, beneath that immense bleached sky, is where we run out of continent."

Slouching Towards Bethlehem
Joan Didion (1968)

The union is a powerful ally of Gov. Brown. In 1975, Brown led and won the fight for California's farm labor law, which gave workers the right to organize unions of their choice. Since then, he and Chavez have been politically close, to the chagrin of agribusiness interests. Brown's alliance with Chavez, his appointment of numerous Latinos to positions in his administration, and his many proposals for closer U.S. and California cooperation with Mexico have made him attractive to the Mexican-American community. Nearly 80 percent of Spanish-surnamed voters cast their ballots for Brown in the 1978 gubernatorial election, according to some political analyses.

The Chicano population constitutes the largest minority in California — almost four million, twice the size of the black population in the state — and is the fastest-growing population as well. Well over two million Latinos live in Los Angeles, giving it the largest Mexican urban population outside of Mexico City. But, it is often noted, there is no representative with a Spanish surname on the City Council.

It is not known with any certainty how many Mexican nationals are in this country illegally. The Census Bureau believes the number is below three million and possibly is between 1.5 and 2.5 million, although estimates from other sources tend to run higher. A Census Bureau official notes that most Mexican nationals who enter the country illegally tend to return to Mexico for at least part of the year, and thus are less likely than others to take up permanent residence in the United States. Separate studies indicate that about half of the Mexicans in this country — illegally and legally — are in California.

Whether Chicanos become a potent political force in California politics in the 1980s depends not on their numbers, which they have, but on their organization, which they do not have yet. Though they are beginning to be heard on issues like "undocumented workers" — illegal aliens — and appointments to government positions, their mobilization as a bloc vote is still a dream.[25]

Future of Gov. Brown and California Linked

Brown's political fortunes are equally up in the air, and will likely remain there for another two years. From 1975 to 1977, Brown appeared to be a staunch supporter of the conservationist cause. He advocated and signed into law measures providing land-use planning, limitations on nuclear power development, strict pollution and other environmental laws. In 1977, however, there was a business backlash against his politics. Numerous reports and press accounts painted a dismal picture of the business climate in California under Brown's regime.[26]

The Fantus Co., a large industrial location consulting firm, released a report that ranked California's business climate 47th among the 48 continental states (New York was 48th). During the first half of that year, two events further clouded California's business future. After two years and a $4 million investment, the Dow Chemical Co. announced that it was abandoning plans to build a $500 million petrochemical plant in the Bay Area because of environmental regulations, bureaucratic red tape and California business taxes. A few months later, SOHIO (Standard Oil of Ohio) dropped its plans for converting a natural gas pipeline to oil so it could send Alaskan crude from California to the Midwest.

Brown defended his policies, but then quickly indicated he was more receptive to business. He set up a business-development office, introduced legislation to cut permit-granting time,

---

[25] See "Chicano Power," *New West,* Sept. 11, 1978, pp. 35-40.
[26] See, for example, "California's Paradise Lost," *Forbes,* Jan. 15, 1977, and "California: Heading for Trouble?" *U.S. News & World Report,* July 11, 1977.

and made a trip east to drum up business for the state. Whether it was circumstances, good government or the results of Proposition 13, which Brown originally opposed, California's economy zoomed upward during the next two and a half years. Whatever the cause, Brown took the credit.

Aside from an approaching national recession, it is uncertain whether California can maintain its boom. The problem of access to water is real and growing. With its high cost of living, particularly housing, plus the shortage of places to buy or rent, California could be headed for a severe housing crunch. Already, many management executives and other professionals are refusing to move there because of housing costs and scarcity. Businesses, too, are looking elsewhere because of the difficulty of attracting personnel, the high cost of doing business, and the vulnerability of California to energy shortages.

Still, tens of thousands of immigrants, legal and illegal, stream into the state every year pursuing their version of the California Dream. Despite its problems, California remains a Mecca for the dispossessed and the adventuresome. Both in the character of its problems and its possibilities, it is still the final frontier.

Selected Bibliography

Books

Bean, Walton, *California: An Interpretive History*, McGraw Hill, 1978.
Beck, Warren A., and David A. Williams, *California: A History of the Golden State*, Doubleday, 1972.
Davie, Michael, *California: The Vanishing Dream*, Dodd, Mead & Co., 1972.
Didion, Joan, *Slouching Towards Bethlehem*, Delta, 1968.
Gunther, John, *Inside U.S.A.*, Harper & Brothers, 1947.
McWilliams, Carey, *Southern California: An Island on the Land*, Peregrine Smith, Inc., 1973.
——ed., *The California Revolution*, Grossman Publishers, 1968.
Peirce, Neal R., *The Pacific States of America*, Norton, 1972.
Roberts, Steven V., *Eureka!* Quadrange-The New York Times Book Co., 1974.
Seidenbaum, Art, *This is California: Please Keep Out!* Peter H. Wyden, 1975.
Starr, Kevin, *Americans and the California Dream, 1850-1915*, Oxford University Press, 1973.

Articles

Blaustein, Arthur I., "California Still Dreaming," *Harper's*, June 1977.
California Journal, selected issues.
"California's Paradise Lost," *Forbes*, Jan. 15, 1977.
Lapham, Lewis H., "Lost Horizon: Imitations of Immortality in California," *Harper's*, February 1979.
New West, selected issues.
Politics Today, special California issue, July-August 1979.
Reeves, Richard, "Boom," *The New Yorker*, Dec. 24, 1979.
——"California vs. the U.S.," *Esquire*, February 1978.
Torres, Juan de, "The West Coast: Economics and Geography," *Across the Board* (Conference Board publication), July 1977.

Reports and Studies

"California Journal Almanac of State Government and Politics," 1977.
"California Statistical Abstract: 1979."
Editorial Research Reports: "Western Water: Coming Crisis," 1977 Vol. I, p. 21; "Western Land Policy," 1978 Vol. I, p. 81.

THE PLAINS STATES: WORLD'S BREADBASKET

by

William Sweet

**May 23
1 9 8 0**

THE PLAINS STATES

T HE PIONEERS who first settled the western plains confronted conditions quite unlike those their ancestors had contended with in the East. When the first colonists came to North America from England and central Europe, they found a wilderness which, if not inviting, was in some respects familiar. Aside from New England winters, the climate was temperate. The native tribes cultivated the soil, and wildlife was abundant. The lush forests, which the settlers cleared as they pushed methodically inland, provided building material and fuel, and the stockade afforded protection against Indian attack.

But when the settlers began to cross the Mississippi River in the early 19th century, they found vast, flat grasslands, resistant to the plow, barren to the eye, and above all else exposed to marauding Indian horsemen and ferocious weather. On the prairie, the pioneers confronted the raw elements at their rawest: earth, wind and sky, seldom relieved by hill, meadow or tree.

Many of the traits that historians have come to think of as characteristic of the American pioneer appeared at their starkest in the settlers of this section of the country. The people who fashioned hard sod into productive farms had to be resourceful, hard-working, tolerant of loneliness but willing to help in times of adversity. They had to be stubborn in their dedication to the practical needs of the day. And as for romance, that was provided by the struggle with the Indian, the soil and the weather. In marriage and family life, there was little room for soft-heartedness or flights of fancy.

When Antonia, the protagonist of Willa Cather's novel, had to work the fields to help her struggling 19th century Nebraska family, some people worried that she'd "lose all her nice ways and get rough ones." But not grandfather, the man who had made a go of it in the plains and who was listened to with respect, because his words were "not worn dull from constant use." When the young man complained of Antonia's bulging muscles and noisy yawns, he just smiled and said, "She will help some fellow get ahead in the world." The woman's role was to tend the kitchen, the vegetables and the chickens, and to see to it that male offspring arrived.

Even today, the people who write sensitively about farm life in the upper Midwest regularly stress the stolid purposefulness of the men and the rigors of the woman's life. In a recent novel, *An American Romance,* John Casey tells of a young man named Mac who moves with his talented girlfriend to Iowa, and apprentices himself to a successful Scandinavian farmer, Sigurd. About the time Mac has learned to cope with farming, Sigurd discovers he has cancer, an affront to a lifetime of careful management and hard work. He is sorely troubled that his wife has borne him a daughter but no sons. Unmoved by sentimental concern for his daughter's feelings, Sigurd offers her to Mac together with his farm as a package deal. The younger folk are a bit embarrassed but not particularly surprised.

Geographic Heartland as Middle America

If we think of the plains states today as Middle America, this is not merely because this is the heart of the country, and certainly not because the people are "ordinary" or "average." On the contrary, they are from that breed of people who conquered the country's last and most forbidding frontier and made it feed the world. They have emerged from the struggle with what we imagine to be America's unique qualities etched in their faces. Like the landscape around them, in their utter lack of complicating features, they sometimes achieve a certain grandeur.

In a country that is predominantly Caucasian, the plains states are whiter than average. As recorded by the 1970 census, about 5 percent of their population is black, less than half the national average. Only New England (3.6 percent) and the Rocky Mountain states (2.3 percent) have proportionally fewer blacks. In a country that is predominantly Protestant, the plains states are more Protestant, less Catholic and much less Jewish than average.[1] And in a country which still likes to think of itself as based on the ideal of the yeoman farmer, this is the one region in which a fairly sizable part of the population still is on the farm *(see box, p. 162).* While the farm population has declined here since World War I, just as it has elsewhere, it has dropped at a somewhat lower rate. Today in the Dakotas about a quarter of the people still live on the land, far more than in other states.[2]

Just as many Americans imagine, residents of the agrarian heartland seem to be more rugged and wholesome than average. Of the eight states examined in this Report, five — Minnesota, North Dakota, Nebraska, Kansas and Iowa — rank among the 10 states with the highest life expectancy rates in the country.

---

[1] The Bureau of the Census does not compile comprehensive statistics on religious affiliation, but it would appear from numbers collected by various religious organizations that the proportion of Jews in the plains states is about one-third the national average, while the proportion of Catholics is several percentage points below the national average.

[2] In 1920, almost two-thirds of the people were living on the farm not only in the Dakotas but also in Alabama, the Carolinas, Georgia, Mississippi and several of the border states.

The Plains States

As a geographic expression, the term "western plains" means different things to different people. Generally, though, the section between the Rocky Mountains and the 100th meridian is referred

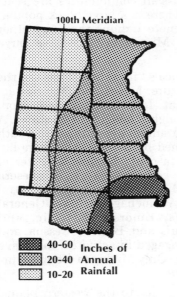

100th Meridian

40-60 Inches of
20-40 Annual
10-20 Rainfall

to as the Great Plains. Sometimes it is also called the High Plains, but usually the term High Plains refers only to that part of the Great Plains from Nebraska southward.

The area stretching east from the 100th meridian to the Mississippi River often is called the Prairie Plains. This region was once covered by tall grass, and it receives an annual rainfall of 20 to 40 inches, enough for grain crops to thrive. On the Great Plains, rainfall diminishes to 20 inches or below — indeed, the 100th meridian is sometimes called the 20-inch rainfall line. On the dry Great Plains, farming — other than irrigated farming — gives way to ranching.

The region profiled in this Report embraces most of the Prairie Plains and some of the Great Plains. It includes Oklahoma plus the states that the U.S. Census Bureau calls the "West North Central" region: Iowa, Kansas, Minnesota, Missouri, Nebraska and the Dakotas. All of Oklahoma but the easternmost section and the Panhandle are part of the Prairie Plains.

Since state lines rarely conform precisely to contours of topography, parts of other states also blur into neighboring geographic areas. Northeastern Minnesota and southeastern Missouri are heavily forested and, in the case of Missouri, quite mountainous.

South Dakota has the 11th highest rate, Oklahoma 19th and Missouri 26th. Crime statistics suggest that this region is more law-abiding. Burglary, larceny, robbery and aggravated assault rates, as compiled by the Federal Bureau of Investigation, are lower in the plains states than in any other census region, and only New England records proportionately fewer murders and rapes. The divorce rate is below the national average and the abortion rate less than half of the national average.

Farm Belt's Urban Majority and Problems

People of this region have a tendency to see themselves as the champions of American virtue, and to look askance at the forces corrupting other sections of the country. Isolationism, nativism and the temperance movements all found strong support in the

agricultural Midwest, and in recent years the right-to-life movement has had a strong impact on several elections here.[3] But of
course not everybody in the plains region is an America-firster or
white. Eastern European and Russian communities are scattered about much of the region. There is a large black population in Missouri; Oklahoma has more Indians than any other
state, while South Dakota and Minnesota also have large
numbers.[4]

Though these states lie in America's "farm belt," most of the
people are not engaged in agriculture. Mines and factories account for much of the employment. In petroleum production,
Oklahoma ranks fifth and Kansas eighth among the 50 states. A
large part of the country's known uranium deposits are in South
Dakota, much of it on lands claimed by Indians, and huge lig-
nite coal deposits in North Dakota could become a center of
synfuels production.[5] Numerous corporations — Minnesota
Mining and Manufacturing ("3M"), Honeywell, and Control
Data in Minnesota, Maytag and Winnebago in Iowa, General
Dynamics, McDonnell Douglas, Emerson Electric, and
Chromalloy American in Missouri, and Boeing, Cessna and
Beech aircraft in Kansas — are engaged in activities that have
little or nothing to do with farming. Only Michigan manufactur-
ers more automobiles than Missouri.

St. Louis, historically a gateway city to the western plains,
suffers many of the same problems that afflict most large cities:
surburban migration, shrinking tax revenues, a stagnant inner-
city economy, and — in recent months — loss of automobile industry jobs.[6] From 1970 to 1977, the inner-city population
dropped nearly 17 percent, and St. Louis now has the highest
murder rate of any major city in the United States — more than
double New York's. Wichita, Kan., on the other hand, resembles
a southwestern boom town. It is the nation's leading producer of
small aircraft; Boeing, Beech and Cessna aircraft companies all
have installations there. According to a journalist who recently
visited the city, the aircraft manufacturers "can't begin to fill
the positions they have available."[7]

For every St. Louis or Wichita, however, there are five or ten
medium-sized cities, prosperous but unspectacular, that function as banking, insurance, food processing and farm machinery

[3] Pro-abortion stands are believed to have contributed to the defeats in 1978 of Sen. Dick
Clark, D-Iowa, and Rep. Donald M. Fraser, D-Minn., who sought the Senate seat vacated
by the death of Hubert H. Humphrey.
[4] In Oklahoma, 98,468 persons identified themselves as American Indians in the 1970 census. Arizona (95,812) and California (91,018) ranked second and third. South Dakota
(32,365) and Minnesota (23,128) were seventh and ninth.
[5] See Bruce Johansen, "Uranium Rush in Black Hills, S.D.," *The Nation*, April 4, 1979,
pp. 393-396, and "Synthetic Fuels," *E.R.R.*, 1979 Vol. II, pp. 631-650.
[6] See "A Resurging City Suffers a Setback," *Business Week*, April 7, 1980, pp. 24A-24E,
and "St. Louis: A Dying City Bounces Back," *U.S. News & World Report*, July 23, 1979, pp.
62-63.
[7] Richard Kipling, on special assignment for Editorial Research Reports.

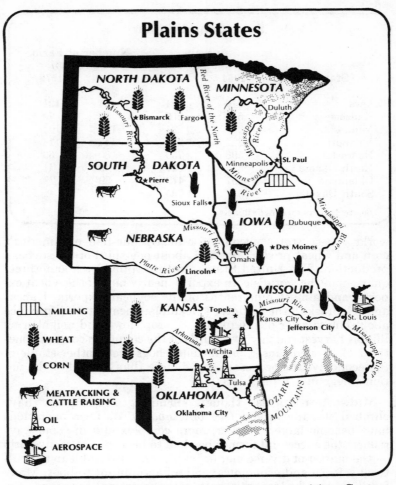

Plains States

NORTH DAKOTA
Bismarck★ Fargo●
Red River of the North
MINNESOTA
Duluth
Missouri River
Mississippi River

SOUTH DAKOTA
Pierre★
Minneapolis● ★St. Paul
Minnesota River
Sioux Falls●

NEBRASKA
Missouri River
IOWA
Dubuque●
★Des Moines
Omaha●
Platte River
Lincoln★

MILLING
WHEAT
CORN
MEATPACKING &
CATTLE RAISING
OIL
AEROSPACE

KANSAS
Topeka
★
Arkansas River
Wichita●

OKLAHOMA
★
Oklahoma City
Tulsa

MISSOURI
Missouri River
Kansas City● Jefferson City★
St. Louis●
Mississippi River
OZARK MOUNTAINS

centers for the surrounding agricultural communities. Companies like John Deere have manufacturing plants and retail outlets throughout the region. And in the larger cities too, big industries depend heavily on the agrarian hinterland. Kansas City, its downtown rejuvenated by the Hallmark Center and convention site, today presents to the world a more cosmopolitan air than in years past when its vast (and now vanished) stockyards filled the nostrils. But agriculture still accounts for much of the city's prosperity. It ranks first in farm equipment and frozen food distribution, and second in grain elevator capacity and wheat flour production. In Minneapolis, General Mills and Pillsbury vie for leadership in commercial bakery products.

Agribusiness With Wheat, Corn and Hogs

The economy of the plains states thus continues to depend heavily on agriculture, and the monetary value of farm products hardly captures their importance to the country and indeed the

159

Farm Consolidation

State	Average Acreage per Farm		Number of Farms (add 000)	
	1964	1979	1964	1979
Iowa	219	281	154	121
Kansas	544	669	92	72
Minnesota	235	291	131	104
Missouri	222	274	147	118
Nebraska	596	759	80	63
North Dakota	875	1,017	49	41
Oklahoma	407	479	89	73
South Dakota	917	1,095	50	42

Source: Department of Agriculture.

world. These states account for nearly one-half of America's corn and wheat production, and about one-third of the soybean production. The United States, in turn, provides about three-quarters of the world's corn exports, nearly half of the wheat exports, and almost nine-tenths of the soybean exports. Kansas and Nebraska, the country's leading wheat states, produce about one-quarter of the total U.S. crop. Iowa and neighboring Illinois harvest roughly two-thirds of the country's corn and one-third of its soybeans. Corn-fattened hogs are another staple of the economy; the two states raise more than a third of the nation's hogs in a typical year.

Midwestern farms, though shrinking in number, have climbed steadily in size *(see box, above)*. As farm operations have become larger, costlier, more complex and in some ways riskier, the successful farmer has had to be a man of many parts — the master of diverse manual skills, knowledgeable in agricultural science and economics, and an accountant to boot. Many families now hedge their bets with "marginal farming," the standard term for an arrangement in which one or more members of the family work at paying jobs away from the farm.

As farming has come to resemble other business operations, standard forms of business ownership have become prevalent. Many farms are organized as partnerships, and a partnership can be a stepping stone toward a corporate structure. The Bureau of the Census found in its 1974 survey of agriculture that the "1,421 farm partnerships which plan to incorporate had average sales of $172,347, or more than two times the average sales for all partnerships reporting. . . ."[8] Incorporation may lead in turn to a takeover by an absentee agribusiness company; in many cases the original farm family stays on the property to act as employee-overseer for the company.

[8] U.S. Department of Commerce, *Partnerships in Agricultural Production,* 1974 Census of Agriculture, Vol. IV, Part 6, p. 9.

Closely related to anxiety about the family farm is concern about loss of cropland to urban and industrial development, foreign purchases of U.S. farmland and the agribusiness shipping scandals that have afflicted the Mississippi River transportation system in recent years.[9]

When Sigurd — the dying Iowa farmer portrayed by novelist John Casey — offers Mac his property, the old man stresses its viability as a family venture: "This is a big enough farm to be one of the farms in the county that will keep on. That's not true of most family farms. . . . [T]here's land over there as good as any of them experimental farms near Cedar Rapids. And they push theirs all the way." And when Sigurd offers Mac his daughter as part of the package deal, Sigurd makes it plain what her main asset is, and what's of secondary importance: "Just take a look. She's a smart girl. She's not just a secretary for that company, she's an assistant vice president. She'll be twenty-eight this June. That's a little old, but she's Swedish on both sides — her looks won't change till she's fifty. And you wouldn't get any foolishness."

Pushing Land's Productivity to Its Limits

A farmer does well to marry the assistant vice president of a company, provided he can persuade her to keep the books, follow commodity, fertilizer and energy prices, keep up with government policy, and act as a trusted adviser on investment decisions. This, after all, is the kind of work that Rosalynn Carter was able to do for her husband at the Carter Warehouse, and this is what gave him the time and money to forge a successful political career. Last January in Iowa, participants in the nation's first election-year caucuses left no doubt in interviews that they understood the Carter marriage.

Even with a Rosalynn at his side, however, an Iowa farmer has a big job ahead. Many, like the farmers trained at the experimental farms near Cedar Rapids, manage to get by only by pushing their land "all the way." In a system increasingly devoted to cultivation of just a few crops, with intensive application of water, fertilizers and pesticides, there is concern about how the modern agricultural technology is affecting both farmland and farmer.

One important source of concern is the falling level of water in the Ogallala Formation, a vast underground reserve which stretches from South Dakota to Texas. Farmers in the western parts of Kansas and Nebraska, southwestern South Dakota and

---

[9] For background, see Lester R. Brown, *The Worldwide Loss of Cropland* (1978); National Agricultural Lands Study, *Where Have the Farm Lands Gone?* (1979); "Foreign Investments in the United States," *E.R.R.*, 1979 Vol. II, pp. 725-754; and Dan Morgan, *Merchants of Grain* (1979).

Plains States Population

State	1979 estimates (add 000)	Increase since 1970*	Pop. per sq. mi.	Farm Pop. 1970**
Iowa	2,903	2.7%	52.3	19.2%
Kansas	2,369	5.3	29.0	11.2
Minnesota	4,060	6.7	51.2	12.7
Missouri	4,868	4.1	70.6	8.6
Nebraska	1,574	6.0	20.6	17.1
N. Dakota	657	6.3	9.5	24.9
Oklahoma	2,892	13.0	42.0	8.2
S. Dakota	689	3.4	9.1	25.8

* National average 8.3%
** National average 4.0%

Source: Bureau of the Census

the Oklahoma Panhandle, along with the Texas Panhandle, depend heavily on this geologic formation for water. It is brought to the surface by heavy pumps fueled with natural gas. With water supplies dropping and natural gas prices rising, more and more farmers are shutting off their wells and putting fields back into dryland cultivation.

Like water, the number of plant varieties also has been decreasing, and this too worries some environmentalists. Farmers naturally have concentrated production in the crop varieties that give the highest yields, but if blight were to hit, uniform varieties might mean uniform disaster.[10] With the country and much of the world dependent on midwestern agriculture, a crop failure would be very disastrous indeed.

People naturally are reluctant to criticize a system that has turned an unproductive area into the world's granary, but even in Iowa researchers are beginning to worry about some of the effects of current agricultural technology. A recent study done at Iowa State University in Ames found that male farmers in Iowa are much more susceptible than men living in cities to six forms of cancer. The people responsible for the study do not know what accounts for this unexpected result, and they believe a variety of unrelated factors may be at work — excessive exposure to the sun, viruses found in dairy products, or other things. One contributing factor, the researchers surmise, might be the extensive use of organo-phosphate and carbonate insecticides. These are dangerous substances which often cause occupational poisonings and occasionally contaminate livestock feed.[11]

[10] See Carey Fowler, *Reaping What We Sow: Seeds and the Crisis in Agriculture* (1979). Fowler contends that the monopolization of the seed business by a few corporations, some of which have an interest in promoting fertilizer- and pesticide-intensive crops, has contributed to the loss of genetic heritage. See also Judith Miller, "Genetic Erosion," *Science*, Dec. 21, 1979, pp. 1231-1233. On "plans to ban certain plants or promote corporate takeovers of the seed industry," see Congressional Quarterly's *Weekly Report*, April 19, 1980, pp. 1031-1032.

[11] Interview with Dr. Dan Morgan, principal investigator with the Iowa Community Pesticide Study, Ames, Iowa, April 17, 1980.

Region's Ecology and Economy

FEW REGIONS of the world have experienced such drastic ecological modifications in the modern era. First the Indians and then the white settlers transformed the western plains in far-reaching ways. Of the original tall and short grasses, wild buffaloes and antelopes, prairie dogs and coyotes, and indeed the indigenous Indian cultures, only traces remain today.

The grasslands that once covered the Plains may to some extent have been the deliberate creation of the Indians, originally primitive nomads who wandered about on foot, and who are said to have burned extensive areas to drive and trap game.[12] During the centuries following the arrival of the first Europeans in North America, the native American cultures of the plains went through a revolutionary change. Of course, contact with the Europeans had modified Indian tribal cultures in the eastern and Great Lakes regions as well. "Every river valley and Indian trail became a fissure in Indian society," the historian Frederick Jackson Turner noted. "Long before the pioneer farmer appeared on the scene, primitive Indian life had passed away. The farmer met Indians armed with guns."[13]

Horses stolen or captured from Spanish settlements in Mexico and the Southwest provided the nomadic Indians with rapid mobility. They became the world's most accomplished mounted fighters. Their valor in combat, and their lack of any concept of surrender, made them formidable adversaries. The white man, armed with the clumsy rifles of the day and far less skilled on horseback, was often at a disadvantage.

Two developments accounted in large part for the white man's final victory. One was the invention and refinement, between 1838 and 1842, of the six-shooter. The revolver was the product of a curious collaboration between Samuel Colt, its inventor, Eli Whitney, one of the first persons to perfect mass-production techniques, and Capt. Samuel H. Walker of the Texas Rangers, who was one of the first to appreciate the new weapon's possibilities. With the six-shooter, in effect the first machine gun, the white man was able to match the Indian's firepower.[14]

Still more devastating than the six-shooter, however, was the virtual extermination of the buffalo, the Indian's lifeblood. This

---

[12] See Carl Sagan, et al., "Anthropogenic Albedo Changes and the Earth's Climate," *Science*, Dec. 21, 1979, pp. 1363-68.

[13] Frederick Jackson Turner, "The Significance of the Frontier in American History" (1893), in *The Frontier in American History* (1976 edition), p. 13.

[14] As Walter Prescott Webb points out, the collaboration between Colt and Whitney is especially striking in the context of a regional analysis of the United States. "Whitney's invention [the cotton gin] made the cotton kingdom possible, and Colt's invention became the characteristic bit of machinery of the early Westerners. These were the first great evidences of the Industrial Revolution in the two sections" — Walter Prescott Webb, *The Great Plains* (1931), p. 178n.

took place between the 1850s and the 1880s. Gradually the Indians were pushed to the periphery of the plains, culminating in Geronimo's capture in 1886 and the defeat of Sitting Bull's confederation during the same decade. By the end of that decade the humiliated Indians of the northern Plains turned *en masse* to the Ghost Dance religion, which promised them a return to the old life and reunion with dead kinfolk. Alarmed by what they saw as a subversive movement, government agents began to take leaders into captivity, and on Dec. 15, 1890, Sitting Bull was killed — allegedly for resisting arrest.

On Dec. 29, 1890, at Wounded Knee, S.D., the U.S. 7th Cavalry shot down more than 200 men, women and children who already had agreed to return peaceably to their homes. While there is no agreement as to who fired the first shot — a trigger-happy soldier or one of the Indians — Wounded Knee became a symbol to Indian militants in the 1960s and 1970s.[15] It was the last sizable military action of the western Indian wars, and significantly it occurred the same year the Census Bureau declared that the frontier had ceased to exist.

Homesteading the Plains; Busting the Sod

By the time of the Indians' final defeat, much of the plains had been transformed from grassland to cropland, and a boom-bust cycle that was to afflict the region for decades to come already was manifesting itself. Oklahoma, which had been reserved as an Indian Territory for the tribes that were removed from the East after an act of Congress in 1830, was opened to homesteaders at noon on April 22, 1889 — the day of the famous land rush.[16] The Dakotas became states that same year. The eastern territories had achieved statehood well before the Civil War: Missouri in 1821, Iowa in 1846 and Minnesota in 1858. As for the Kansas-Nebraska Territory, it was there — in "bleeding Kansas" — that settlers from the South and the North fought the first battles over slavery during the 1850s. Statehood came to Kansas in 1861 and to Nebraska in 1867.

The Kansas-Nebraska Act of 1854, which left the question of whether the territory would become a slave or free state to popular sovereignty, was widely regarded among northern abolitionists as a conspiracy to extend the peculiar institution into the West. Advocates of compromise, on the other hand, argued during the 1850s that a plantation economy would not be viable anyway in the far western and southern parts of the plains. It was, in fact, a prevalent view at the time that no farm economy would be viable in these seemingly desolate areas. Atlases published between 1820 and 1850 showed the whole region between the Missouri and the Rockies as "The Great American Desert."

---

[15] See "Indian Rights," *E.R.R.*, 1977 Vol. I, pp. 265-288.

[16] Oklahoma became a state in 1907, following the discovery of oil in 1905.

Kansas prairie photo by Wes Lyle, courtesy of Save the Tallgrass Prairie Inc.

Attitudes toward the "Great Desert" changed drastically in the following decades. The new transcontinental railroad companies, land speculators and civic boosters placed extravagant advertisements in the East describing the plains as heaven on earth. This new mythology about the West, historian Daniel Boorstin has written, "testified to man's indomitable will to believe. Now the settlers who moved up the valleys of the Platte and the Kansas rivers . . . replaced the myth of the Desert by the myth of the Garden."[17] Promotion of the West's wonders, together with the prospect of free land provided by the Homestead Act of 1862, soon lured thousands of pioneers to the western plains.[18] The migration westward continued for decades, cresting with a massive wave of Germans, Scandinavians and Russians in the 1880s. There was an especially large influx of Russian Mennonites, who pioneered in large-scale farming and introduced the Turkey Red winter wheat into the upper Midwest.

Unlike the Mennonites, who knew prairie country from the Russian steppe, many of the migrants to the West had no idea how to deal with the new environment, and many were bitterly disappointed with what they found. Harsh winters spent in tiny sod huts, and the lingering threat of Indian raids, were not what some settlers had bargained for. Though the range wars between cowboys and homesteaders contributed much to American mythology, at the time they made many a pioneer less than bullish about America.

[17] Daniel J. Boorstin, *The Americans: The National Experience* (1965), p. 231.
[18] The Homestead Act gave any citizen over 21, or the head of a family, the right to 160 acres (80 in especially favorable areas), provided the settler was on his claim and making improvements within six months of filing application.

165

The sheer numbers of homesteaders and the industrial technology which they were rapidly acquiring made their ultimate victory over the cowboys a foregone conclusion. John Deere had set up a shop to manufacture farm implements in Grand Detour, Ill., in 1837, and two years later he manufactured the world's first steel plow, just what was needed to break the hard prairie sod. By the late 1870s, his disc gang plows — manufactured in Moline, Ill. — were in wide use. So were the McCormick harvesters and binders, which Chicago plants had been producing in ever-improving versions for several decades. Barbed wire was manufactured in De Kalb, Ill., and windmills in Batavia, Ill.

Exceptionally harsh winters in 1880-81, 1885-86 and 1886-87 hurt the cowboys worse than the farmers; according to one authority, the blizzards of 1880-81 killed thousands of cattle and marked "the beginning of the final triumph of the homesteader."[19] But then it was the homesteader's turn to suffer. A 10-year cycle of blizzard and drought began in 1887, and by the early 1890s large areas of Kansas and Nebraska were virtually depopulated.

Despite the havoc wrought by the weather, the agrarian crisis of the late 1880s and early 1890s did not find the farmer wholly unprepared. As early as the Civil War, farmers had begun to organize, and by the end of the 19th century farmers in all sections of the country had learned to work together for economic, social and political objectives. The Grange, founded in 1862 by a U.S. agriculture official, spread through the plains during the 1870s. The Grange encouraged farmers to educate themselves in agronomy, to deal collectively with the large institutions that were increasingly seen as the farmer's enemy — the railroad companies and the banks — and to form cooperative selling and purchasing arrangements. (Montgomery Ward and Co. of Chicago was established in 1872 as a wholesale supply house for grangers.) The Grange also encouraged farmers just to get together and have some fun, something that was especially appealing to the women during the lonely winters.

As the farmer's situation became increasingly difficult, the Grange struck many as too limited in its objectives, and farmers began to form so-called alliances throughout the South and West. After the Civil War, the Republican Party had become identified with the great banks and corporations of the Northeast, which were determined to keep a tight rein on the nation's money supply. This "sound money" policy came to recognize only gold — not silver or the "greenback" that had been introduced during the Civil War — as legal tender. It assured that creditors would be paid back in increasingly valuable dollars,

---

[19] Everett Dick, *The Sod-House Frontier* (1937), p. 153.

while debtors — notably farmers — would find it ever harder to raise money to pay off loans.

Populism's Appeal on the Western Prairie

As farmers became more and more dependent on suppliers of credit and essential goods, the alliances gathered strength. In the South, their main target was the "furnishing merchant" — the town store owner who typically monopolized the local supply of goods and credit — while in the West the railroads, the banks and the middlemen were seen as the main villains. Out of the farmer alliances grew the so-called populist revolt.

As explained editorially by the *Omaha World-Herald,* a newspaper published in the heartland of 19th century populism: ". . . [It] was essentially a rural-vs.-urban feeling, inspired mostly by the suspicion among small farmers and others that they were being had by big-city interests, such as bankers and railroad magnates."[20] To the wheat growers of Kansas, Nebraska and the Dakotas, railroad rates seemed patently discriminatory. The rates on wheat shipped from Fargo to Duluth in 1890 were nearly double those from Minneapolis to Chicago — a distance twice as great. It was, in fact, possible to ship wheat from Chicago to Liverpool for less than from certain points in the Dakotas to the Twin Cities.

There was obviously more to populism than resentment of railroads and Wall Street. But reputable scholars differ over what all it embraced and sought. Historians have been unable to agree even about who and where the "real" populists were. Early accounts stress the role of the northern plains states. Some see the culmination of the movement in William Jennings Bryan's presidential campaign of 1896.[21] Bryan, a son of the Nebraska prairie, championed the free coinage of silver and three times won the Democratic Party's nomination (in 1896, 1900 and 1908) but never the White House.

Recent revisionist historians have placed the movement's core in Texas, and they treat Bryan's silver crusade as a perversion of populism's serious objective, namely the enactment of Charles W. Macune's "subtreasury" plan.[22] Under this plan for a flexible currency, warehouses would have been erected for farmers to store their crops and await favorable prices before selling. They would have been permitted to borrow money on the stored crops and sell "subtreasury" certificates of deposit at prevailing market prices.

---

[20] Editorial published April 21, 1972, at a time when populism had re-entered the political vocabulary. It was sometimes applied to the presidential campaign that Sen. George McGovern, D-S.D., was waging that year. See "The New Populism," *E.R.R.,* Vol. I, 1972, pp. 335-354.

[21] See John D. Hicks, *The Populist Revolt* (1931).

[22] See Lawrence Goodwyn, *The Populist Movement* (1979).

As an attempt to take over the reins of national government, populism failed — not only with Bryan but with the People's Party. The newly founded party, meeting in Omaha in 1892, nominated Gen. James B. Weaver for president. He polled more than 8 percent of the popular vote and carried five states with 22 electoral votes — Colorado, Idaho, Kansas, Nevada and North Dakota. With the exception of the Republicans in 1856, no third party had done so well. The populists' best showing that year was in Kansas where they elected their entire state ticket and five members of Congress.

But victory was short-lived. Bryan's defeat in 1896, even with the People's Party endorsement, and the return of prosperity that year doomed populism's electoral appeal. But its ideas lived on in the Democratic Party as late as the New Deal — some say in 1972 during Sen. George McGovern's campaign for president — and they infused the Progressive wing of the Republican Party for several decades. Sen. Robert M. LaFollette's breakaway Progressive Party in Wisconsin and the upper Midwest drew liberally on populism. But the farm country of the Midwest retains a basic conservatism. And in politics that conservatism usually translates as mainland Republicanism.

Nature is seldom kind to the plains' farmers for long. That was true during the time of the populist revolt. The period from 1879 to 1886 had been one of unusually ample rainfall in the newly settled portions of western Kansas, Nebraska and the Dakotas. Then, in 1887, disaster struck. For the next decade there were only two years in which the central and western portions of the wheat belt had enough rain to raise a full crop, and for five seasons out of ten they had practically no crops at all.

Dust Bowl and New Deal Farm Programs

Drought again beset the plains states during the second decade of the 20th century, in a 20-year cycle that has afflicted the region from the time the homesteaders arrived. Drought-induced scarcities, together with the food demands of World War I, drove farm prices up. In 1920, however, prices began to drop sharply, signaling the onset of a farm depression that would remain until the coming of World War II. It preceded the Great Depression by nearly a decade. On top of that, starting in the early 1930s, dust storms began to sweep the plains, carrying away its precious top-soil. In his book *Dust Bowl,* Donald Worster wrote:

> Weather Bureau stations on the Plains reported a few small dust storms throughout 1932, as many as 179 in April 1933, and in November of that year a large one that carried all the way to Georgia and New York. But it was the May 1934 blow that swept in a new dark age. On 9 May, brown earth from Montana and Wyoming swirled up from the ground, was captured by extremely

high-level winds, and was blown eastward toward the Dakotas. More dirt was sucked into the airstream, until 350 million tons were riding toward urban America. . . .[23]

The most severe erosion occurred in southeastern Kansas, Oklahoma and the Texas Pan-handle, but most of the plains states were affected in some degree. Analysts attributed the disaster to poor land management and various other factors. Whatever the other causes may have been, it was obvious that the sod grasses had been torn up all over the Plains, and it was these grasses that held the topsoil in place.

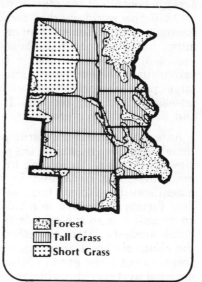

Forest
Tall Grass
Short Grass

Franklin D. Roosevelt, upon assuming the presidency in 1933, moved energetically to help the troubled farmer. He put the Department of Agriculture under the direction of Henry A. Wallace, the son of another agriculture secretary and the former founder and editor of *Wallaces Farmer,* a farm magazine published in Iowa. Wallace brought many of the New Deal's most idealistic and energetic people into his department, and during Roosevelt's first two terms these people forged the farm policies that have been used — with only some variation — to manage U.S. agriculture ever since.

Today's Mixed Political Outlook

SINCE World War II, Democratic presidents have tended to employ the price support and crop limitation system established in the New Deal, while Republican presidents have tried — with various success — to dismantle it. Eisenhower's agriculture secretary, Ezra Taft Benson, wanted to restore a free market system in agriculture, but he was unable to go far, as the late Fifties were a time of huge farm surpluses. Nixon's agriculture secretary, Earl L. Butz, was able to go further, but largely because of a new policy of selling grain in massive quantities to the Soviet Union.

---

[23] Worster, *Dust Bowl* (1979), pp. 13-14.

The Agricultural and Consumer Protection Act of 1973 eliminated the goal of assuring farmers a real income roughly equivalent to what they got around the time of World War I ("parity"), and it gave the secretary of agriculture the authority to lift acreage controls if the market warranted that action. From 1973 to 1976 the world market for U.S. agricultural products was strong, and government support programs were kept to a minimum, but then conditions began to deteriorate once more, and President Carter took office with a commitment to do more for agriculture. The Food and Agriculture Act of 1977 provided for a target price support system, a commodity loan program, acreage set-asides, and crop reserves. It also extended the Food Stamp and Food for Peace programs.[24]

America's fluctuating farm policies reflect the lack of a national consensus regarding the overall merits and demerits of the New Deal legacy. According to one school of thought, the farm programs have succeeded in maintaining a prosperous and magnificently efficient farm sector, have enabled the independent farmer to survive in a volatile world, and have done so at an overall cost to the consumer that is not overly burdensome. Some analysts detect the effects of a well-regulated market in the relatively great economic stability of the plains states. Unemployment rates, even in Missouri, are regularly well below the national average, and when recession hits, it hits this region less hard than most of the country.[25]

According to an opposing school of thought, the farm programs have been self-contradictory, inasmuch as they have simultaneously encouraged and discouraged production; they have failed to protect the consumer and the small-farm owner; and they have created a massive fiefdom — the Department of Agriculture.[26] From the political left to the political right, many Americans believe the typical farmer has come to resemble the alfalfa farmer portrayed by Joseph Heller in *Catch-22*:

> [He] was a sober God-fearing man whose idea of a good joke was to lie about his age. He was a long-limbed farmer, a God-fearing, freedom-loving, law-abiding rugged individualist who held that federal aid to anyone but farmers was creeping socialism. He advocated thrift and hard work and disapproved of loose women who turned him down. His specialty was alfalfa, and he made a good thing out of not growing any. The government paid him well for every bushel of alfalfa he did not grow. The more alfalfa he did not grow, the more money the government gave him, and he spent every penny he didn't earn on new land to increase the amount of alfalfa he did not produce.

---

[24] See "Farm Policy and Food Needs," *E.R.R.*, 1977 Vol. II, pp. 807-810.

[25] See Robert B. Bretzfelder, "Sensitivity of State and Regional Income to National Business Cycles," *Survey of Current Business*, April 1973, pp. 2-27.

[26] See Grant McConnell, *Private Power and American Democracy* (1966), pp. 70-79, and Theodore J. Lowi, *The End of Liberalism* (1969), pp. 102-115.

Whether farmers work hard at growing or not growing alfalfa, they do tend to think of themselves as hard workers, and they often have nothing but contempt for those who appear to be languishing on the public dole. Traditionally, midwestern farmers have also held military spending in low esteem. Except in Missouri and Kansas, military installations and businesses doing work for the Pentagon are relatively few, and this may flavor the region's attitude toward military expenditures.

Soviet Grain Embargo; Post-Isolationism

U.S. military commitments abroad traditionally have fared poorly among the people of the plains, not only because of attitudes toward the Pentagon and arms spending, but also because isolationists, populists and Progressives all tended to share a distrust of the East, of Wall Street, and of England. While some of these attitudes did not survive World War II and the Cold War, the tradition did not disappear. Henry Wallace from Iowa, George McGovern from South Dakota and Eugene McCarthy from Minnesota became notable critics of America's global intervention in the postwar years. They follow in the line of Bryan, heir to the populist legacy who resigned as Woodrow Wilson's secretary of state in opposition to the president's pro-British policies prior to World War I, and Robert La Follette who was censured by the Senate for opposing U.S. entry into that war.

Because of this dissenting tradition, many analysts expected the plains states to react with hostility to the embargo on grain sales to Russia, which President Carter imposed on Jan. 8 after the Soviet Union invaded Afghanistan. After all, the embargo directly threatened the farmer's wallet, and involved the threat of military confrontation. But the embargo did not appear to have hurt Carter in the Midwestern primaries and caucuses. Indeed, the region's attitude toward national and global affairs may be far different from what it was once perceived. Donald M. Fraser, the mayor of Minneapolis, speaks of "a maturing of perspective toward international relations as a result of the last two decades. People realize you can't isolate yourself from the world and you can't dominate it either."[27]

What could hurt Carter in the plains states is the deteriorating economic position of the farmer. Immediately after he imposed the embargo on grain sales, government intervention in the commodity markets kept prices stable. But they have begun to drop, while at the same time interest rates reached record heights before they recently began to ease slightly. With fertilizer and pesticide and energy prices also climbing, and credit tight, many farmers are hard-pressed.

---

[27] Interview, Jan. 23, 1980.

It will be interesting to see whether high interest rates reawaken the traditional antipathies toward banks and the East. But the farm country may recall that the tight money policies were implemented under a farmer-president.

Selected Bibliography

Books

Boorstin, Daniel, *The Americans: the National Experience,* Random House, 1965.

Dick, Everett, *The Sod-House Frontier,* D. Appleton-Century Co., 1937.

Duncan, Patricia D., *Tallgrass Prairies: The Inland Sea,* The Lowell Press, 1978.

Goodwyn, Lawrence, *The Populist Movement: A Short History of the Agrarian Revolt in America,* Oxford University Press, 1978.

Hicks, John D., *The Populist Revolt,* University of Minnesota Press, 1931.

Morgan, Dan, *Merchants of Grain,* The Viking Press, 1979.

Webb, Walter Prescott, *The Great Plains,* Ginn and Co., 1931.

Worster, Donald, *Dust Bowl,* Oxford University Press, 1979.

Articles

Agricultural Outlook, U.S. Department of Agriculture, selected issues.

Miller, Judith, "Genetic Erosion: Crop Plants Threatened by Government Neglect," *Science,* Dec. 21, 1973.

Sagan, Carl, et al., "Anthropogenic Albedo Changes and the Earth's Climate," *Science,* Dec. 21, 1979.

Wallaces Farmer, selected issues.

Reports and Studies

Brown, Lester R., *The Worldwide Loss of Cropland,* Worldwatch Paper No. 24, 1978.

U.S. Department of Commerce, Bureau of the Census, *Corporations in Agricultural Production* and *Partnerships in Agricultural Production,* 1974 Census of Agriculture, Vol. IV, Parts 5 and 6, 1974.

Editorial Research Reports: "Foreign Investments in the United States," 1979 Vol. II, p. 745; "Farm Policy and Food Needs," 1977 Vol. II, p. 805; "Rural Migration," 1975 Vol. II, p. 581.

Fowler Carey, *Reaping What We Sow: Seeds and the Crisis in Agriculture,* Seed Directory, The Frank Porter Graham Center (Wadesboro, N.C.), 1979.

National Agricultural Lands Study, *Where Have the Farm Lands Gone?,* 1979.

WASHINGTON, D.C. VOTING REPRESENTATION

by

William V. Thomas

Jan. 5
1979

Editor's Note: Since this report was originally published, six additional states have approved the proposed constitutional amendment to give Washington, D.C., full voting representation in Congress. They are Connecticut, Hawaii, Maryland, Massachusetts, Minnesota and Wisconsin. This brought the total to nine. Michigan, New Jersey and Ohio had previously approved.

WASHINGTON, D.C.
VOTING REPRESENTATION

ALL 50 state legislatures[1] convene this year — 47 this month —and one question most are likely to consider is the political destiny of the District of Columbia. Specifically, state lawmakers will decide whether to accept or reject a proposed constitutional amendment to grant Washington, D.C., full voting representation in Congress. Approval by at least 38 states in the next seven years is required for the measure to take effect. The proposed amendment would give the District representation in the House based on population; give it Senate representation "as though it were a state"; grant participation in the electoral college; and grant participation in the process whereby the Constitution is amended.

The amendment proposes that the city be treated as a state only for the purposes of congressional representation. Its close relationship to the federal government, including its economic ties, would not be affected. Of course, passage of the proposal would not rule out statehood for the District at some future date.

Under a federal law enacted in 1973, Washingtonians gained a form of limited "home rule" which, for the first time in this century, permitted them to elect their own mayor and city council. However, Congress reserved the right to "exercise exclusive Legislation in all cases whatsoever" over the District.[2] Last year, though, both the House and the Senate voted to surrender that prerogative. By large voting majorities, the House (289-127) in March and the Senate (67-32) in August passed a resolution placing before the states the proposed constitutional amendment to give the District full political autonomy. Many supporters assumed that the states would be eager to ratify the measure. But so far, Pennsylvania and Delaware have rejected ratification, and California, after a protracted debate, delayed action. Only New Jersey, Michigan and Ohio have given it their approval.

Sentiment against full voting rights for the District of Colum-

---

[1] Kentucky, the only state without a regularly scheduled legislative session in 1979, will hold a special session beginning Jan. 8.

[2] Article I, Section 8.

175

bia seems to spring from the basic apprehensions that any senators or representatives elected by District residents would be liberal, black, urban-oriented and Democratic. If the Senate vote is any guide, opposition may be strongest in states west of the Mississippi and south of the Potomac. Both senators from each of 11 states — eight western and three southern — voted against the amendment.[3] Residents in many sparsely populated states tend to look askance at any challenge to their collective influence in the Senate, where each state, regardless of its size or population, has two votes. "If you start giving representation to the District, you water down the representation of people in other areas," said Meldrim Thomson Jr., New Hampshire's lame-duck Republican governor.[4]

Washington's biggest problem in gaining the states' approval for full representation may be its image. The public perception of the city as the home of federal regulations, profligate spending and "high living" bureaucrats has been abroad for years. Watergate furthered the notion of corruption in the nation's capital and a number of national political figures, including presidential candidate Jimmy Carter, chose to "run against Washington" in the 1976 elections. Many state legislators no doubt regard a vote against the amendment as a chance to get revenge on the city.

While the amendment's backers are busy formulating a national strategy for ratification, opponents are mounting a campaign to block the effort. Both groups claim to have "right" on their side. But the outcome could depend more on organization and money than anything else. Proponents of the amendment admit to having little of either. "There is a great deal of feeling that this thing is not organized right," said Joseph Rauh, the civil liberties lawyer who is treasurer of Self-Determination for D.C., the coalition directing the push for ratification. This year, the coalition estimated, some $750,000 will be needed to support a nationwide drive. However, under current leadership, Rauh said, the fund-raising effort has fallen far short of the mark.

Advocates' Emphasis on Civil Rights Issue

The District of Columbia, covering 69 square miles on the Maryland side of the Potomac River, is a city of 690,000 people, according to 1976 Census Bureau estimates, of which blacks number 511,400 and account for 74 percent of the population. No major American city is populated by such a small percentage of whites. No world capital matches Washington's racial incongruity — a city three-quarters black in a country that is 85 percent white. "This racial paradox would be comparable to

---

[3] The states are New Mexico, North Dakota, Nevada, Wyoming, Montana, Nebraska, Oklahoma, Utah, Louisiana, Virginia and North Carolina.

[4] Interview, WDVM-TV (Washington), Nov. 22, 1978.

Text of Proposed D.C. Amendment

SECTION 1. For purposes of representation in the Congress, election of the President and Vice President, and article V of this Constitution, the District constituting the seat of government of the United States shall be treated as though it were a State.

SEC. 2. The exercise of the rights and powers conferred under this article shall be by the people of the District constituting the seat of government, and as shall be provided by the Congress.

SEC 3. The twenty-third article of amendment to the Constitution of the United States is hereby repealed.

SEC 4. This article shall be inoperative, unless it shall have been ratified as an amendment to the Constitution by the legislatures of three-fourths of the several States within seven years from the date of its submission.

Protestants controlling Rome, Arabs running Jerusalem or French-Canadians ruling Ottawa," wrote Chuck Stone, a black newspaper columnist.[5] Of the 115 countries of the world that have elected legislatures, only two, the United States and Brazil, deny full representation to the people who live in their national capitals. Although Washington residents lack voting representation in Congress, they have been able to vote in presidential elections since ratification of the Twenty-third Amendment in 1961.

Washington's racial make-up was a critical factor in getting the amendment resolution through Congress. It would not have passed, many observers believe, if it had not been portrayed as a question of civil rights for blacks. "The civil rights orientation helped the D.C. amendment get visibility," wrote Rebecca Leet of the Joint Center for Political Studies. "It provided the pressure needed to get attention and action in Congress."[6]

Supporters of the amendment concede the same approach may not work with state legislators, since black political influence is stronger in Congress than with many state legislative delegations. "A successful ratification effort will hinge on the same overall strategy that worked in Congress," Leet wrote. But in addition, the national drive should concentrate on bringing together "a bipartisan group of lawmakers with diverse political philosophies and outlooks."

For the most part, the ratification movement has been led by Walter E. Fauntroy, the District's non-voting congressional delegate. "The linchpin of our plan was not to try to conceal the social, political or economic nature of the District's population," Fauntroy has said. "Instead we appealed directly to the conscience of the Congress in the hope that they would [see] the

[5] Writing in *The Washingtonian* magazine, April 1978, p. 123.

[6] Rebecca Leet, "D.C. Representation," *Focus,* October 1978, p. 4. *Focus* is a monthly publication of the Joint Center for Political Studies, a Washington-based research organization that studies black political issues.

amendment as a matter of equity and fairness."[7] Fauntroy is aware, however, of opposition from regional interests. "We have to figure out how to neutralize as many of these as possible," he said. "We can't do that from Washington, or by sending Washingtonians to testify directly before the legislatures. We have to do the kind of research that shows us which are the principal elements of opposition, then select people who have relevance to the local situation."[8]

Opposition to the amendment has centered on a provision in Article V of the Constitution stipulating that "no State, without its Consent, shall be deprived of its equal Suffrage in the Senate." But during Senate Judiciary Committee hearings last April, several noted constitutional scholars agreed that this clause presented no legal barrier to D.C. representation. Charles Alan Wright of the University of Texas had sent the committee a statement saying: "It seems to me that the clear purpose [of Article V] was to ensure that . . . representation in the Senate would not be put on the basis of population." That purpose, he stated, "is not compromised by allowing the District to have two senators any more than it is when a new state is admitted."

Similarly, Stephen A. Saltzburg of the University of Virginia testified: "[I] find . . . nothing in the language of this Article that states that the Constitution cannot be amended to give entities other than states voting power in the Senate. All that is required is that a state have an equal vote. If the District is given two senators, no state is in an unequal position when compared to any other state or to the District."

Conservative Groups' Organized Opposition

Vowing not to make "the same mistakes" they made with the Equal Rights Amendment, many conservative political groups are uniting in a well-financed campaign against the proposed D.C. amendment. Formal opposition to the measure has been taken up by such organizations as the American Conservative Union, the Conservative Caucus, the Citizen's Committee for the Right to Keep and Bear Arms and the Young Americans for Freedom, as well as individuals with concerns as diverse as right-to-life, prayer in the schools and states' rights. Only 13 "no" votes by state legislatures are necessary to defeat the measure, and with two states already having voted against it, opponents are confident they can obtain 11 more rejections.

Groups opposed to ratification have lined up behind the leadership of the American Legislative Exchange Council (ALEC), a national organization of conservative state legislators, whose

---

[7] Walter E. Fauntroy, writing in *The Washington Star*, Dec. 10, 1978.

[8] Quoted in *The Washington Post*, Nov. 29, 1978.

Amendments That Failed

Congress has submitted only 33 amendments to the states for ratification; only five (excluding the Equal Rights Amendment and the District of Columbia Voting Representation Amendment) were not ratified. Two of the five were proposed in 1789, along with the Bill of Rights. One concerning the apportionment of representatives was ratified by 10 states — one less than the required number. The other, providing that no law changing congressional pay should be effective until after the next national election, was ratified by six states and rejected by five; three states took no action.

In 1810, an amendment providing for revocation of the citizenship of any American accepting a gift or title of nobility from any foreign power, without the consent of Congress, was submitted to the state for ratification. The amendment was ratified by 12 states and by the Senate of the South Carolina legislature; had it been approved by that legislature's lower house, it would have become part of the Constitution. The impression prevailed for nearly a generation that the amendment had been adopted.

A proposed amendment to prohibit interference by Congress with the institution of slavery in the states, offered in 1861 as a last effort to ward off the impending conflict between North and South, was ratified by the legislatures of only two states — Ohio and Maryland. A convention called in Illinois in 1862 to revise the state constitution also ratified the amendment, but since Congress had designated state legislatures as the ratifying bodies, this ratification was invalid.

A more recent amendment proposed by Congress but not ratified by the states was the Child Labor Amendment. It would have empowered Congress to "limit, regulate, and prohibit the labor of persons under 18 years of age." The amendment sought to reverse rulings by the Supreme Court in 1918 *(Hammer v. Dagenhartj)* and 1922 *(Bailey v. Drexel Furniture Co.)* which had struck down child labor laws enacted by Congress.

Submitted to the states June 4, 1924, the Child Labor Amendment had been ratified by 28 of the 48 states by 1938. In that year Congress again enacted a child labor law. In 1941 the Supreme Court, in *U.S. v. Darby Lumber Co.,* upheld the law, specifically reversing its 1918 decision. Since then, there have been no further ratifications of the proposed amendment.

membership numbers around 7,000. At a conference sponsored by ALEC in Arlington, Va., on Dec. 2, delegates heard speeches on strategies for blocking the ratification effort. "The reason why the amendment passed through Congress was that it was being called the Civil Rights Act of 1978," said James Hinish, counsel to the Senate Republican Policy Committee. "If you were against this you were against blacks. It passed because [this tactic] was used very effectively by the proponents." But this "is not a civil rights issue," Hinish added, advising legislators to turn their arguments away from the racial question and toward the legal and constitutional soundness of the measure.

Another speaker, Jules B. Gerard, professor of law at Washington University in St. Louis, told conference delegates that "debating [the merits of the issue] is a no-win proposition." Gerard cautioned legislators to "debate the amendment" not "the problem" when they return to their respective states. Gerard explained that while it may be possible for supporters of D.C. voting rights to argue that they deserve some representation in Congress, it will be difficult for them to defend the "all or nothing" amendment passed by Congress. As a solution to the problem, it was suggested that the District be allowed voting representation in the House only. Another possibility raised by anti-amendment forces was returning the residential portions of the District back to Maryland.

Few opponents of full representation attempt to disguise their political bias on the question. Two senators from the nation's capital, they say, would probably be ultra-liberal Democrats. "That would mean two more sure votes for federally financed abortions, for labor law 'reform' and all other bills pushed by the [Democratic] chieftains," wrote conservative columnist Frank van der Linden.[9] Republican Party Chairman William Brock has come out in favor of the amendment as a way to open up the GOP to blacks. However, according to James Hinish, "there is very little likelihood the Republican Party will benefit [if the amendment is ratified]."

Meanwhile, opposition to the amendment is mounting in Washington's own "backyard." Maryland, once considered a state where passage could be counted on, is now beginning to waver. Many Maryland legislators, especially those representing constituents who live in nearby Prince George's and Montgomery counties and work in the District, are apprehensive that if the District ever became independent of Congress, local officials would impose taxes on commuters. Acting Gov. Blair Lee of Maryland recently predicted the measure will "not have an easy time of it" when the state legislature considers it during the new session.[10] Virginia's conservative state legislature seems certain to reject the amendment.

Question of City Revenues, Financial Needs

The principal argument for full representation and home rule, proponents say, is the same one expressed in the battle cry of the Revolutionary War: "Taxation without representation is tyranny!" Washingtonians pay more federal taxes than the

---

[9] Writing in the *Nashville Banner*, Oct. 7, 1978.
[10] Quoted in *The Washington Post*, Dec. 10, 1978.

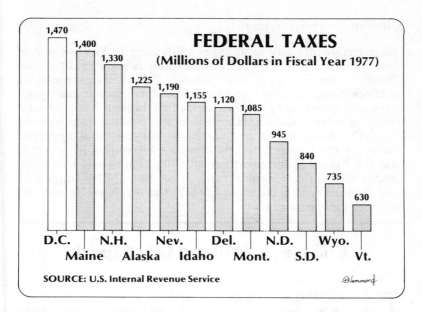

FEDERAL TAXES
(Millions of Dollars in Fiscal Year 1977)

1,470 — D.C.
1,400 — Maine
1,330 — N.H.
1,225 — Alaska
1,190 — Nev.
1,155 — Idaho
1,120 — Del.
1,085 — Mont.
945 — N.D.
840 — S.D.
735 — Wyo.
630 — Vt.

SOURCE: U.S. Internal Revenue Service

residents of 11 states *(see above)*. And that fact alone, it is maintained, entitles the city to equal political recognition.

The District has always had a special financial relationship with the federal government. In 1878, when Congress took over control of the city, it was agreed that congressional appropriations would finance 50 percent of the city's operating budget. This practice was followed until 1921, when the federal contribution was cut to 40 percent. The percentage fell slowly and irregularly thereafter, reaching a low of 8.5 percent in 1954. In fiscal year 1978, Washington received $276 million (20 percent) in payments.

It is believed in some quarters that the federal contribution would cease if home rule were ever granted. But advocates of autonomy see no contradiction between self-government and a measure of federal support. They point out that the federal presence imposes unusual economic burdens on the city and at the same time cuts into usual sources of revenue. The federal government currently owns about one-third of the land in the District — land that is exempt from the local tax rolls. Even as it supports the District, Congress, in the view of many, prevents Washington from supporting itself. It has not permitted the city to:

1. Enact a commuter tax, even though such taxes exist in some places.

2. Issue tax-free bonds as states and other cities do.

3. Allow buildings to exceed a certain approved height, thus restricting business development and tax revenue.

181

District residents pay local taxes equivalent to 11.7 percent of their incomes, a higher percentage than is paid in 23 states. Clearly, federal payment is not a device that allows people living in Washington to avoid their share of local taxes. Last year, taxes and other city revenues topped $1 billion. That amount would have been much greater if Congress had not restricted the District's taxing power and increased congressional appropriations for the District. Nearly everyone recognizes in principle that the federal government has an obligation to assist in maintaining the nation's capital, and in all probability support in lieu of taxes would continue even if the city were to gain its political independence.

Changes in Status of U.S. Capital

THE DECISION to locate the nation's capital on the Potomac was reached in July 1790 only after considerable debate and after Maryland and Virginia had consented to cede any territory required. The original ten-mile-square site, including the settlements of Georgetown in Maryland and Alexandria in Virginia, was marked out by President Washington. Although there were persistent complaints that the swampy region was unfit for habitation, Congress and the outgoing President John Adams took up residence in the new city in November 1800.

The framers of the Constitution, while not of one mind on where to place the capital, were in general agreement that it should be under complete federal control. The intent of the founding fathers concerning the political status of the future federal district was reasonably clear. Article I, Section 8 of the Constitution provided: "The Congress shall have power . . . to exercise legislation in all cases whatsoever over such District . . . as may, by cession of particular states and the acceptance of Congress, become the seat of the government of the United States."

Notwithstanding the comprehensiveness of this grant of power to Congress, self-government in local affairs was not precluded; rather, it seems to have been taken as a matter of course. James Madison indicated in *The Federalist Papers* (No. 43) what was in the minds of the drafters of the Constitution:

> The indispensable necessity of complete authority at the seat of government carries its own evidence with it. It is a power exercised by every legislature of the Union, I might say of the world, by virtue of its general supremacy. Without it . . . the public authority might be insulted and its proceedings interrupted with impunity. . . .

First published plan for Washington, D.C., drawn up by Pierre L'Enfant and published by Thackara and Vallance of Philadelphia.

Courtesy of the Library of Congress

As the inhabitants will find sufficient inducements of interest to become willing parties to the cession; as they will have had a voice in the election of the government which is to exercise authority over them; as a municipal legislature for local purposes, derived from their own suffrages, will of course be allowed them, and as the inhabitants of the ceded part of it, to concur in the cession, will be derived from the whole people of the state, in their adoption of the Constitution, every imaginable objection seems to be obviated.[11]

Local Autonomy in Pre-Civil War Period

Events preceding and following adoption of the Constitution suggest that the object of setting apart a federal district was to forestall conflicts between state and federal interests. There was no plan to deny residents the right to manage their own affairs. In fact, the implicit promise of self-government for the District

[11] Quoted from *The Federalist Papers*, No. 43 (American Classics Edition, 1964), p. 186. *The Federalist Papers* were a series of articles published anonymously in New York City newspapers after the 1787 constitutional convention to explain and defend the newly drafted Constitution during ratification debates in the various states. The authors were James Madison, John Jay and Alexander Hamilton.

of Columbia was fulfilled with little delay. A charter adopted May 3, 1802, established an elective city council and provided for the president to appoint a mayor. (Jurisdiction of the new local government did not extend to Alexandria or Georgetown, which continued to be governed as they were before they became part of the District of Columbia.) Beginning in 1812 the mayor was named by the council, and from 1820 until 1871 mayors were chosen by popular vote.

The eclipse of self-government in the District resulted largely from partisan conflict immediately after the Civil War between local residents and the "radical" wing of the dominant Republican Party in Congress which pushed Reconstruction in the South. However, there had been earlier quarrels. When the city elected a Whig mayor in 1840 and flaunted the victory by erecting a log cabin, the campaign symbol for President-elect William Henry Harrison, in the center of town, the still-dominant Van Buren forces in Congress suspended the corporate privileges of District banks. A bill to abolish the city charter, moreover, got as far as a third reading in the Senate.

A continuation of this infighting led in 1846 to the retrocession of Alexandria to Virginia. By this time, John Tyler had come and gone as president, and the Democrats were again in control. Unable to get funds from Congress for needed improvements and still rankled by the bank action, both Georgetown and Alexandria sought to be ceded back to their respective states. The Maryland legislature, not wanting to assume added financial burdens, refused Georgetown's overtures, but Virginia was willing. When Alexandria voters approved the transfer, by a margin of 7 to 2, Congress passed a bill restoring to Virginia the part of the District south of the Potomac.

Conflict With Congress; Loss of Home Rule

Throughout the pre-Civil War period, relations between the District of Columbia and Congress were complicated by the slavery question and by the city's predominantly southern attitudes. A move in Congress to abolish slavery in the District almost carried in 1840. The slave trade, though not slavery, was forbidden in the city as a part of the Compromise of 1850. Washington was early a gathering place for freed slaves. When slavery in the District was finally abolished in April 1862, the influx of blacks began in earnest. By 1866, some 30,000 ex-slaves had made their way to the city. Racial enmity gradually engulfed the town, wrote historian Constance M. Green. "Whites appeared increasingly prone to make no distinction between educated, responsible colored people and the mass of ignorant, often shiftless freedmen flooding in from the South."[12]

[12] Constance M. Green, *The Secret City: A History of Race Relations in the Nation's Capital* (1967), p. 65.

The District quickly became a testing ground in the drive of radical Republicans to establish black suffrage. It was likewise a focal point in the struggle for power between Reconstruction forces in Congress and President Andrew Johnson. An act passed over Johnson's veto on Jan. 7, 1867, conferred the elective franchise on citizens over 21 years old without distinction of race or color who had resided in the District one year preceding the election.

When the first city election under the new suffrage law was held in June 1867, many whites refrained from voting. Blacks, however, trooped to the polls to back the party which had given them freedom. The resulting near-sweep put the Republicans in control of both chambers of the council and set the stage for contention with a carryover Democrat left in the mayor's office.[13] The situation was reversed when the white voters streamed back to the polls at the election of 1868. The Republican candidate for mayor, Sayles J. Bowen, won a narrow victory but one chamber of the council went Democratic and the other was evenly divided. Racial violence and charges of illegal voting by blacks followed.

Projects started by Mayor Bowen to open up new areas of the city promptly put it in financial trouble. A Republican landslide in the local election of 1869 did not help matters. The new council took up integration problems to the neglect of financial problems. Meanwhile, as ward leaders were jostling one another for places at the pork barrel, the Republican ranks were divided by factionalism.

Alexander Shepherd, a prominent local businessman, stepped into the breach with a proposal for a modified territorial form of government. The Bowen forces were overwhelmed in the next election, and in February 1871 Congress passed a territorial bill after only brief debate. The act abolished the separate status of Georgetown, provided for an appointed District of Columbia governor, an elected non-voting delegate in the House of Representatives, and a territorial assembly with one elected and one appointed member. It also established a five-member Board of Public Works. Shepherd, a favorite of President Grant, was named to the board and quickly became its moving force.

Shift to a Federally Appointed Commission

Shepherd's leadership proved arbitrary and costly. Determined to modernize the city in one stroke, he and his colleagues tinkered with the debt limit and the valuation rolls to finance

---

[13] All candidates for office were white. Blacks ran for the first time in 1868, when a black was elected to each chamber of the council. Seven blacks were among 21 Republicans elected to the lower chamber, and a second black was elected to the upper chamber in 1869. Five blacks were elected to the upper chamber in 1870.

their special projects. Charges of corruption made against Shepherd were never proved, and later judgment was that they were substantially groundless. But there can be no doubt that he treated his office as an autarchy and took little care to assume maximum return for each dollar spent. "Taxpayers' dismay at the workings of the spoils system and at the legislature's extravagance . . . became secondary to their consternation over the untrammeled power of a body of men responsible neither to the local public, nor, save indirectly, to Congress," wrote Constance M. Green in her history of Washington.[14]

Matters were aggravated when Grant in September 1873 named Shepherd to succeed Henry D. Cooke as governor. A petition from aggrieved taxpayers resulted in the appointment of a joint congressional committee to investigate District affairs. The committee, known by the name of its second chairman, Sen. William B. Allison, R-Iowa, turned up a tale of financial mismanagement and maladministration. The upshot was a report issued in June 1874 blaming the Board of Public Works for the situation, although the fault was held to be an excess of zeal rather than corrupt intent. In any case, the city was in debt $11 million above its regular funded debt of nearly $10 million. Civic improvements for which nearly $19 million had been laid out were said to be far in excess of their estimated costs.

The failure of the existing government was regarded as absolute. The Allison Committee recommended that the District be placed temporarily under three commissioners appointed by the president, with an Army engineer in charge of public works. The territorial assembly and the post of delegate to the House of Representatives were abolished. Congress promptly enacted these recommendations into law in June 1878, establishing the kind of government the District of Columbia would have for nearly a century.

Limited City Self-Government Since 1967

Under President Lyndon B. Johnson's plan for local reorganization, which Congress approved in 1967, the three-commissioner arrangement was replaced by a single commissioner, afterward called "Mayor," a deputy commissioner and a nine-member city council. The new officials were all appointed by the president, but the added number made the government more representative of a greater part of the city. Johnson subsequently named a black man — Walter E. Washington — as the new "mayor" and appointed five black persons — a majority — to the city council.

Full self-government for the District of Columbia continued to

---

[14] Constance M. Green, *Washington: A History of the Capital 1800-1950* (1962), p. 344.

be blocked during Presient Nixon's first term (1969-72). The House District Committee relented somewhat in 1970 when it reported out a bill calling for the election of three members of the nine-member city council; however, the full House took no further action. In 1971, the Senate again passed a home-rule bill expanding the size of the city council and providing for the election of council members and the mayor. Nevertheless, supporters on the House District Committee failed repeatedly the following year to obtain a quorum to consider the home rule proposals before it, including the Senate-approved measure which died at the end of the 92nd Congress.[15]

In December 1973, the 93rd Congress provided for partial self-government in passing a bill that: (1) permitted the partisan election of a mayor and a 13-member city council; (2) exempted federal employees who were candidates for local office from compliance with the Hatch Act, which prohibited government workers from participating in partisan politics; and (3) allowed Congress to continue to make annual appropriations for the District, including a federal payment in lieu of taxes on tax-exempt federal property. But Congress retained control over the District's purse strings. It also required that any act passed by the city council and approved by the mayor lie before Congress for 30 legislative days before taking effect. In that time Congress, if it chose to, could pass a resolution nullifying the measure.

America's Perception of Washington

POLITICAL LEADERS of the country have done what they could to sustain the character of the nation's chosen metropolis," visiting British novelist Anthony Trollope wrote of Washington in 1862. "There has been no rival in soliciting favor. . . . And yet of all the places I know it is the most unsatisfactory — I fear I must also say the most presumptuous in its pretentions."[16] Many people today would agree with Trollope's assessment. Across the country, Washington is often seen as an ornate symbol of well-insulated prosperity, a "company town" basking in tax-supported luxury.

The principal reason for local good fortune lies in the fact that the city's economy depends largely on the federal government, which employs some 400,000 of the three million residents of the

---

[15] See Congressional Quarterly, *Congress and the Nation*, Vol. IV, pp. 797-799.

[16] Anthony Trollope, *North America* (1862), from *Trans-Atlantic Crossing: American Visitors to Britain and British Visitors to America in the Nineteenth Century* (1971), Walter Allen, ed., pp. 287-288.

Washington metropolitan area. Layoffs, factory closings and similar economic uncertainties common in other parts of the country are not felt to the same degree in Washington. Even during the depression of the 1930s, Washington's economic base remained strong as the size of the federal work force increased to keep pace with the number of government agencies.

There is "a fundamental conflict of interest between Washington and the fifty states," wrote Sen. S. I. Hayakawa, R-Calif. "Washington is a city that thrives on crisis, real or imaginary. It is fat with bureaucrats, lawyers and lobbyists. Unlike the states, Washington produces no wealth; its primary function as the seat of government is to spend money," Hayakawa continued. "What is good for Washington is therefore not good for the states. If, say, the Congress should propose to shut down a huge agency of government, the people of the states would probably cheer; but a shudder would run through Washington. . . . [Any legislators representing the District] would be duty-bound to want more bureaucrats here. The people in Washington would want their representatives to vote against any shrinkage of the federal government because it would be contrary to the well-being of the city."[17]

Advocates of the voting representation amendment acknowledge that Washington's image as the capital of the bureaucracy is a hindrance in the ratification drive. Many people see Washington existing in a parasitical relationship to the rest of the country. But Meg Greenfield, deputy editor of *The Washington Post* editorial page, contends that many national politicians have used Washington as a scapegoat for their own mistakes and shortcomings. District residents, she wrote in a *Newsweek* column, have been stereotyped by a "misleading shorthand" into "some kind of single-minded creature called 'Washington.' " The population of the District is as deserving of political rights as any other American citizens. "That is what the amendment fight is about," she wrote. Or at least "that's what it would be about, if [anti-Washington] mythology were not so powerful."[18]

City's Portrayal: High Pay, Affluent Living

It is undoubtedly true that many residents of other parts of the country who oppose political autonomy for Washington do so on constitutional grounds, but it is equally possible that some are motivated by jealousy. In the last decade, affluent Washingtonians have evolved an enviable lifestyle, and in the process the metropolitan area has become the wealthiest in the nation.

Washington is first in per capita income among the nation's 20 largest metropolitan areas, according to the most recent

---

[17] Sen. S.I. Hayakawa, writing in *The Sun* (Baltimore), Oct. 29, 1978.

[18] Meg Greenfield, writing in *Newsweek*, Oct. 9, 1978.

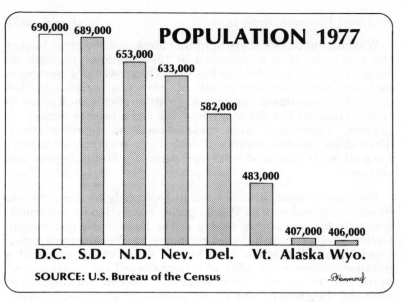

POPULATION 1977

690,000 689,000 653,000 633,000 582,000 483,000 407,000 406,000

D.C. S.D. N.D. Nev. Del. Vt. Alaska Wyo.

SOURCE: U.S. Bureau of the Census

Census Bureau figures. At $21,282, its median family income for 1976 was 42 percent higher than that of the Los Angeles metropolitan area ($14,961) and 40 percent higher than that of the New York City area ($15,166). Moreover, Washington has sharply increased its lead over most other areas through the years. In 1960, local income was only 7 percent higher than in Los Angeles and 15 percent higher than in New York.

Increasingly, Washington has become a city of two-income families. Couples who hold mid- to upper-level jobs in the federal bureaucracy may earn over $80,000 annually in combined salaries. In a two-lawyer family, joint incomes may reach as high as $200,000 a year. Families with two salaries in the $60,000 range are common in many neighborhoods of the city. Washington's federal workers are well paid. In 1962 Congress passed a law under which federal white-collar pay must be comparable to that in private industry, and in 1970 assured automatic raises for government workers.

One effect of the local income boom is reflected in Washington's housing market, which some observers have compared to a middle-class "gold rush." Housing prices are rising all over the country. But only in San Francisco and Los Angeles do new home costs exceed those in Washington. As of last October, a new house in Washington sold for an average of $62,400. Given the city's limited building space, older homes have become desirable both as investments and places to live. Used homes in Washington sell for an average of $87,400, the highest price in the nation.[19]

---

[19] See "Housing Restoration and Displacement," *E.R.R.*, 1978 Vol. II, pp. 861-880.

Washington has its share of millionaires, but the great bulk of the area's wealth is represented by the well-do-do professional class. A main reason for this has been the growth of government and the accompanying growth of private organizations that serve the government. As federal programs have multiplied in recent years, so has the number of the city's private workers — lawyers, consultants and trade association representatives. Their high salaries combined with high government salaries have added to the inflationary pressures for homes, offices and services.

President Carter came to town in 1976 pledging to reform the bureaucracy and change Washington's reputation for self-indulgence. In his acceptance speech at the Democratic convention, Carter said in unmistakable reference to Washington's privileged class: "Too many have had to suffer at the hands of a political and economic elite who have shaped the decisions and never had to account for mistakes. . . . When unemployment prevails, they never stand in line looking for a job. When deprivation results from a confused welfare system, they never do without food or clothing or a place to sleep. When the public schools are inferior or torn by strife, their children go to exclusive private shools. And when the bureaucracy is bloated and confused, the powerful always manage to discover and occupy niches of special privilege."

Many outsiders see Washington as dominated by a "pleasure dome" mentality, a condition that seems to reinforce the sense that the District is populated by a governing elite that is more privileged than the people they are governing. Emphasizing thrift and hard work, President Carter seemed determined to commit his administration to a sterner regimen. As if to set an example, Carter sent his daughter, Amy, to a public school, barred hard liquor at White House social functions and eliminated limousine service for his top assistants. However, when Carter later raised presidential staff salaries — some as high as $48,500 a year — it was charged that he too was helping to encourage the same mandarin lifestyle he had once railed against.

Effect of Amendment's Outcome on Blacks

For decades, the District has been an economically divided city of "haves" and "have-nots." The resulting racial tensions and animosities are a basic local reality. The city's public schools — among the worst in the nation — its crime problems, even its embarrassing tardiness in counting election ballots are viewed by most white Washingtonians as black problems. "Let's not kid ourselves," said Sterling Tucker, a black former chairman of the city council. "Many whites in this city and throughout the country nurture the unshakable belief that whenever blacks are in authority chaos is inevitable."[20]

With the media less restrained in its coverage of incidents of mismanagement in City Hall, some blacks have suggested that Washington's wealthy white minority is gearing up to regain control of the District. The trend of white families moving back into town, often displacing blacks in redeveloped neighborhoods, has also contributed to the belief that whites are conspiring to take over the city.

Most of the District's black residents tend to regard full congressional representation — and the hope of complete freedom from congressional oversight — as a protection against the possibility of a white political offensive. Anxiety over home rule has long had a deterrent effect on white immigration into Washington. But recently, for the first time in 25 years, the city's white popultion has shown an upturn. The number of whites in predominantly black Washington, according to city government estimates, increased in 1976 by about 7,000, from 162,000 to 169,000. The black population has declined since 1973 — down to about 511,400 at the time of the latest estimates, in 1976. If the percentage of District whites continues to grow, some observers believe the prospects of gaining the states' approval for autonomy would also increase. But many local black officials feel by that time their political power will be diminished.

Black leaders equate the District's present status with the political position of blacks in the country as a whole. If the voting representation amendment were to be ratified in a few years, the city's congressional delegation would probably be made up entirely of blacks. However, if the measure is rejected or is rewritten to permit representation in the House only, the political influence of blacks — both locally and nationally — would suffer accordingly.

Most supporters of the amendment see it as a civil rights issue and look forward to passage as a way of increasing the participation of blacks in the political process. Opponents, on the other hand, regard the matter in an entirely different light. To many, Washington is synonymous with the federal bureaucracy, special privilege and free-spending liberal politics. "Individually the residents of Washington may deserve representation," wrote Walter Berns of the American Enterprise Institute. "Collectively, however, they constitute an interest that should be checked, even discouraged, and above all, not represented."[21] It remains for the individual states to decide which view to uphold.

---

[20] Quoted in *The Sun* (Baltimore), Oct. 29, 1978.

[21] Walter Berns, "Rome on the Potomac," *Harper's*, January 1979, p. 33.

Selected Bibliography

Books

Collier, Barney, *Hope and Fear in Washington: The Story of the Washington Press Corps,* Dial, 1975.

Gorey, Hays, *Nader and the Power of Everyman,* Grosset & Dunlap, 1975.

Green, Constance McLaughlin, *The Secret City: A History of Race Relations in the Nation's Capital,* Princeton University Press, 1967.

——*Washington: A History of the Capital, 1800-1950,* Princeton University Press, 1962.

Green, Mark J., *The Other Government: The Unseen Power of Washington Lawyers,* Grossman, 1975.

Mencken, H. L., *A Gang of Pecksniffs: And Other Comments on Newspaper Publishers, Editors & Reporters,* ed. Theo Lippman, Arlington House, 1975.

Seidman, Harold, *Politics, Position and Power,* Oxford University Press, 1975.

Smith, Sam, *The Captive Capital, Colonial Life in Modern Washington,* Indiana University Press, 1974.

Vaughn, Robert, *The Spoiled System: A Call for Civil Service Reform,* Charterhouse, 1975.

Whyte, James H., *The Uncivil War: Washington During Reconstruction, 1865-1878,* Twayne Publishers, 1958.

Wright, William, *The Washington Game,* Saturday Review Press, 1974.

Articles

"A City that Came a Long Way Despite Problems," *U.S. News & World Report,* Jan. 24, 1977.

Bethell, Tom, "Washington's World of Style," *Harper's,* January 1978.

Blum, David, "Barry, Barry, Not Contrary," *The New Republic,* Dec. 2, 1978.

Jordan, Robert "Growing Up White in D.C. Schools, *Education Digest,* November 1977.

Leet, Rebecca, "D.C. Representation," *Focus,* October 1978.

"The Good Life in Washington Is Bad For America," *The New Republic,* July 9, 1977.

Washington Monthly, selected issues.

Studies and Reports

Editorial Research Reports, "Self-Government for City of Washington," 1959 Vol. II, p. 513.

"People of the District of Columbia: A Demographic, Social & Physical Profile of the District of Columbia," Office of Planning and Management, Washington, D.C., 1973.

"Report on Civil Disturbances in Washington, D.C., April 1968," Office of the Mayor, 1968.

Index

A

G

H

I

J

K

L

P

Pacific Northwest
Agriculture - 112
Bibliography - 128
Economic conditions - 113, 116, 120-122
Energy - 122-125
Federal lands - 121-122
Geographic, cultural identity - 111-112, 117
History - 117-120
Indians - 112, 118, 121
Industry - 112, 116, 120-123
Labor unions - 118-120
Map - 113
Natural resources - 111-114, 122-123
Nuclear wastes - 124-125
Politics - 112-114, 119, 126-128
Population patterns - 113-115
Population statistics (chart) - 115
Race relations - 112, 119
Pennsylvania - 94, 96-97, 99
Philadelphia - 94, 98, 100-101, 106
Phoenix - 58, 59, 67
Pittsburgh - 94-95
Plains states
Agriculture
Agribusiness - 159-161
Current political issues - 169-172
Dust Bowl - 168-169
Farm consolidation (chart) - 160
Homesteading - 164-167
Resources and technology - 161-162
Bibliography - 172
Economic conditions - 158-159, 167-172
Energy - 158, 162
Geographic, cultural identity - 155-157
History - 163-169
Indians - 158, 163-164
Industry - 158-159
Map - 159
Politics - 161, 167-172, 176
Population patterns, urbanization - 156-159
Population statistics (chart) - 162
States included (box) - 157
Politics and elections
Blacks - 42-46, 177, 185-186, 190-191
California - 131-136, 142, 148-151
District of Columbia rights - 175-192
Ethnic groups - 10, 15-16, 21-22, 74, 76-78, 87
Great Lakes states - 74-81, 87-88
Importance of regionalism - 3-4
Middle Atlantic states - 94, 95
New England - 4, 9-10, 16, 21-24
Pacific Northwest - 112-114, 119, 126-128
Plains states - 161, 167-168, 169-172
Rocky Mountain West - 52, 54, 56-65
South - 42-46

Population patterns. (*See also* Population statistics.)
California - 141-142
District of Columbia - 176-177, 184, 191
Pacific Northwest - 113-115
Plains states - 156-159
Rocky Mountain West - 56-59, 62-63, 65-68
South - 28, 31 (box), 37-39
Population statistics (charts)
California - 137
District of Columbia - 189
Great Lakes states - 75, 87
Middle Atlantic states - 95, 103
New England - 9
Pacific Northwest - 115
Plains states - 162
Rocky Mountain West - 57
South - 37, 40
Portland, Ore. - 114, 115, 127-128
Proxmire, William (D Wis.) - 77
Public lands. See Federal lands.
Puritanism - 4, 10-11, 14

Q

Quakers - 99

R

Race relations
District of Columbia - 184, 185, 190-191
Great Lakes states - 72, 77-78
Middle Atlantic states - 104
Pacific Northwest - 112, 119
South - 28, 30-33, 42-44
Ranching - 54-55, 60-61, 165-166
Ray, Dixy Lee - 111, 125
Reagan, Ronald
California governorship - 133-136
Presidential campaign, 1980 - 23, 88, 134, 136
Religious groups
California missions - 137
Calvinists - 13, 14
Catholics - 10, 16, 77, 99
Jews - 16, 77, 102
Mennonites - 165
Mormons - 63, 113, 114
New England history - 10-15
Plains states composition - 156
Puritans - 4, 10-11, 14
Quakers - 99
Transcendentalists - 13-15
Unitarians - 13-15
Reuss, Henry S. (D Wis.) - 77
Reuther, Victor - 81
Reuther, Walter - 81
Rhode Island - 9, 11, 16, 17